THE
CREATION
& FALL OF THE
FAMILY

STUDIES ON THE FAMILY FROM GENESIS 1-5

STEVE PIXLER

THE
CREATION
& FALL OF THE
FAMILY

STUDIES ON THE FAMILY FROM GENESIS 1-5

STEVE PIXLER

PUBLISHED BY
CONTINUUM MINISTRY RESOURCES
5200 DAVID STRICKLAND RD. FORT WORTH, TX 76119

ISBN13: 978-0-9796261-1-1
ISBN10: 0-9796261-2-0
US $19.95

Library of Congress Control Number:
2007936959

Table of Contents

Preface

This book is a collection of studies on the family from Genesis 1-5. It is adapted and expanded from a series of lessons that I taught in our church over a period of about two years. The basic structure of the material is largely as I first presented it with some expansion and development. The original series was prepared and presented as a response to very real family issues that we were facing within our local congregation. As a pastor, I was deeply troubled by the high incidence of divorcing couples and deviating children. The "present distress" (as Paul would describe it) of family disintegration drove me to desperate prayer and study for answers from the Lord for the problems we faced. We needed answers that would work for a lifetime—indeed, for eternity.

Our crisis demanded much more than hacking and chopping at the stem of the problem. It was time to lay the ax at the root of the tree. It became clear to me that the breakdown of the family is a systemic and fundamental problem. In order to correct this problem, we needed to get to the heart of our assumptions concerning the family, its form and function. For many of the assumptions governing our ideas on the family were clearly false. This root of deceit was producing an awful harvest of error. Therefore, I felt compelled to trace the problem back to its origins, back to the Book of Genesis where the deep-rooted problems of the family first began.

We set out to consider the story of the first family, their creation and fall. We looked to see what the family was like when God first formed it and what it became through sin. We sought lessons that could be applied to current concerns. We found just what we were looking for. The story of Adam and Eve offers tremendous parallels to the present circumstances of the Christian family. Just below the surface of the Genesis text lay wonderful treasures of wisdom. The Word of God began speaking to our "present distress" and amazing transformations began in our homes. Those who were reared with a godly heritage discovered a biblical basis for the truths they once had taken for granted, while those who were converted from pagan homes learned entirely new ways of thinking about the family.

As a Bible-believing church, we firmly presuppose the sufficiency of Scripture. There is no situation that the Word of God does not address either explicitly or implicitly. God's truth is revealed in His Word both as precept and principle. As Paul said, "All scripture is given by inspiration of God, and is profitable for doctrine, for reproof, for correction, for instruction in righteousness: That the man of God may be perfect, throughly furnished unto all good works" (II Timothy 3:16-17). Therefore, the method of our studies is deliberately biblical and expository. The Word of God (including the Old Testament) never ceases to be current and practical. We simply must extrapolate its truth and draw out its lessons properly. Consequently, we have self-consciously ignored the modern psychological approach to human improvement and deliberately inquired of Scripture concerning the mind of God. There is no psychology here. Our studies are focused on the Word of God revealed in Scripture.

This means, then, that this book is not a casual read. It is not written to appeal to the popular, quick-fix mentality. It is intended to be studied and considered carefully. Moreover, these lessons were prepared as a family-focused exposition of Genesis 1-5 and presented publicly with a great deal of additional comment and explanation. Thus, this book serves only as an introduction to further studies pursued by the reader. We have only begun here to mine out the wealth of insight latent within the opening chapters of Genesis. Truly, "whatsoever things were written aforetime were written for our learning, that we through patience and comfort of the Scriptures might have hope" (Romans 15:4). My goal is to produce a work that appeals to those who are passionate about substantive family renewal. I do not relate to those who are merely grubbing about for the latest self-help manual. Those interested in a "how-to" handbook for convenient daily reference will be sorely disappointed here. There are no shortcuts. Faithful family renewal requires an expansive renewing of our mind.

The insights gained from our studies here are more general and conceptual than detailed and prescriptive. I do not spend a great deal of time giving "1-2-3" instructions. The larger concepts basic to family renewal are in view. As a result, this leaves many specific issues barely introduced and crying out for further elaboration. Hopefully, future studies can provide more detail on the general ideas presented here. However, in my view, this initial focus on Genesis 1-5 provides a necessary primer for later discussions. First, we need a reformation of our basic assumptions on the family. Then, we can move toward more specific and practical applications. Also, there are several sections where I may appear to wander from the point a bit and spend a great deal of time discussing seemingly unrelated issues. However, the occasional departure from the immediate subject at hand to discuss larger biblical themes is fundamental to my approach. It is my steadfast conviction that our oversight of these fundamental themes is the cause of spiritual breakdown in the family. So, the time and effort is not wasted.

As I noted, the studies here are biblical and expository. And yet, they are so in a unique way. This work is a sort of commentary, but with a narrow focus. I set out to read Genesis 1-5 with a view to applying its story to the present concerns of the family. Thus, my applications go far beyond the general details of the narrative. You might say my method is *application from implication*. However, I seek to be faithful to the overall witness of Scripture. Therefore, I spend considerable effort comparing and submitting my study of Genesis 1-5 to the rest of Scripture. Hopefully, I have formed a comprehensive result that faithfully applies the Word of God as a whole to our current crisis.

You may notice that much of the material is somewhat circular. It is repeated and re-stated. However, this is not mere redundancy. The repetition flows out of the text. Repetition is God's way of driving truths deep down into our heart. As Scripture says, "stir up your pure minds by way of remembrance" (II Peter 3:1). The Lord speaks in Isaiah of this repetitive manner of teaching: "For precept must be upon precept, precept upon precept; line upon line, line upon line; here a little, and there a little" (Isaiah 28:10). Though my presentation may be somewhat circular, hopefully, it goes around like a spiral until it reaches the apex of its intended conclusion. Otherwise, I have done nothing but make us all dizzy.

I offer thanks first of all to the Lord Jesus Christ Who purchased every Christian family with His blood and graciously extends mercy and restoration to us all. He alone can bring about the family renewal that we so desperately need. It is my firm conviction that the Lord has promised this renewal, and He is bringing it to pass even now. His promise of salvation is to us, to our children and to all others whom He shall choose to call (Acts 2:39).

Next, I am deeply grateful to the congregation of Cornerstone Apostolic Church for spending nearly two years patiently hearing and receiving these lessons on the family. Their passion for righteousness and hunger for the Word of God is remarkable. I consider it a great privilege to serve them as pastor.

I also wish to express my deepest love and gratitude to my lovely wife, Jeana, and children, Alaina, Natalie and Nicolas. Their continual encouragement and support has made this effort possible. To my parents-in-law, Rev. Forrest and Judy Smith, thanks so much for your decision to serve the Lord when your family was young and for the deep consecration that you passed on to my wife. I am the beneficiary of your faith and commitment to the Lord.

Finally, this book is dedicated to my parents, Rev. James and Linda Pixler, for the wonderful Christian heritage they preserved and passed on to me and my siblings. I first learned the lessons of building a godly family by watching my parents live those lessons before me every day. Much of this book flows out of their insight. They have continually provided a truly great example of a Christian family. For that, I am forever grateful.

Steve Pixler
Fort Worth, TX
June 2007

Introduction

We shall begin our study on the family by going back to the beginning. We shall consider the creation and fall of the family from Genesis 1-5. Both Jesus and Paul referred to the story of Adam and Eve when teaching on the family (Matthew 19:3-12; I Corinthians 6:16; 11:7-10; 14:34,35; Ephesians 5:30,31; I Timothy 2:13-15). In the New Testament, the story of creation serves as a sort of original ideal, a model that Christians should measure their lives against. This series of lessons follows that approach. We shall look to the story of Adam and Eve as a model of both the creation and the fall of the family. In our discussion of Adam and Eve we shall sketch a general outline of the family in a preliminary way. We shall color in the specifics in future studies, God willing.

There are at least two things we must remember as we begin. First, we cannot build our families with human wisdom or strength. As the Psalmist says, "Except the Lord build the house, they labor in vain that build it" (Psalm 127:1). The Lord must build our house. Man was created dependent upon the Spirit of God from the start. Adam became a living soul when God breathed into his lifeless form. Just so, the family is but a corpse upon the ground until the Spirit of God breathes life into it. What was begun in the Spirit cannot be made perfect in the flesh (Galatians 3:1). The family, just like the individual Christian, is saved by grace through faith. We need the Spirit of God to build up our family.

Second, we must count the cost before we build. "For which of you, intending to build a tower, sitteth not down first, and counteth the cost, whether he have sufficient to finish it? Lest haply, after he hath laid the foundation, and is not able to finish it, all that behold it begin to mock him, Saying, This man began to build, and was not able to finish" (Luke 14:28-30). In setting out to build a godly house, we are taking to ourselves a tremendous task. This work cannot be completed by those who are unprepared.

We acknowledge that the work of family-building is done by the power of the Holy Spirit within us, and we trust the grace of God to see us through. However, this does not mean that we can take the grace of God for granted. Rather, we must consider fully the tremendous commitment that we are called to make. Building a family is not child's play. It is the work of full-grown, mature adults who have the capacity to understand fully what is involved.

Every wise builder counts the cost before he begins building. We must do likewise. We must take inventory of our resources and ensure that we are prepared to finish the building. We must turn to the Giver of all good things and receive the gift of wisdom He has offered (James 1:5). We must draw out the riches of practical wisdom contained in the Word of God. Then, we shall be fully equipped to finish the task. There is no reason to be caught unprepared. God will finish in us what He has started (Philippians 1:6). By the grace of God we shall complete the building.

PART I

The Creation of the Family

1

Creation and the Image of God

Genesis 1:26, 27. "And God said, Let us make man in our image, after our likeness: and let them have dominion over the fish of the sea, and over the fowl of the air, and over the cattle, and over all the earth, and over every creeping thing that creepeth upon the earth. So God created man in his own image, in the image of God created he him; male and female created he them."

Our study on the family from the Genesis account begins with the formation of man and woman on the sixth day of creation. In fact, the story opens with the Lord announcing, presumably to the angels, that He *intends* to form man in His image and likeness (v. 26). The actual formation of man comes a bit later in the story (v. 27). This highlights God's fundamental approach to formation. He always makes plans first. He declares what He intends to do long before He actually does it. Then, the plan of God is revealed in God's proclamation. In other words, God spells out what He plans to do in His Word. The Word of God, whether spoken, written or living, always has priority.

The plan of God is revealed by His Word, and all creation is formed according to the plan. As John's Gospel says, "In the beginning was the Word, and the Word was with God, and the Word was God...And the Word was made flesh, and dwelt among us" (John 1:1, 14). John declares that all creation flows out of the Word of God: "All things were made by him; and without him was not any thing made that was made" (1:3). The Word of God is the wisdom of God spoken into existence. So in a sense we could say, "In the beginning was the *wisdom* of God...and the *wisdom* of God became flesh." Paul confirms this idea when he speaks of Christ as "the wisdom of God" (I Corinthians 1:24). And Christ, as the wisdom of God, is the pattern and plan of all creation (I Corinthians 8:6; Ephesians 3:9; Colossians 1:16; Hebrews 1:2,10-12). All things were made by Christ, the wisdom of God. Thus, wisdom is primary (Proverbs 8:22-31). God does not create by trial and error. He plans perfectly and then performs perfectly.

God's creation is divine wisdom displayed in manifest reality (Romans 1:20). Our world is wisdom perfectly expressed. Indeed, God's Word/Wisdom is the very "DNA" of the universe. The essence of all things is intelligence, information, data. Of course, this should not be understood in a pantheistic, "cosmic mind" sort of way. Rather, the mind of God, the thoughts of God, the intelligence of God, is the essence of all things. "For in him we live, and move, and have our being" (Acts 17:28). God thinks, speaks and forms. Thus, creation begins with God's plan. As the Lord spoke to Israel, "For I know the plans I have for you, declares the LORD, plans for wholeness and not for evil, to give you a future and a hope" (Jeremiah 29:11 ESV). The plan of God, the mind of God, is expressed in all material things. Christ is "upholding all things by the word of his power" (Hebrews 1:3). This is the right sort of "mind over matter"!

So, God created Adam according to His plan. God did not form man *ad hoc* out of dust. He *declared* man's creation first. He wrote man's creation into His plan and purpose. Adam was made as an expression of God's eternal wisdom. Adam's creation was not aimless and without purpose. Adam was a planned man, a man with a plan. Therefore, man is a "Word-creature," created by the Word of God for the purpose and plan of God. And because he is a "Word-creature," man cannot fulfill his purpose apart from the Word of God.

If Adam was a "Word-creature," then it follows that the family must be a "Word-family." Every Christian family must be established upon the Word and wisdom of God. The family cannot be established in its true purpose if it is not in harmony with the creative Word of God. This is how a godly family is built. God speaks His Word into our lives, and the Christian family becomes an "incarnational" expression of the Word of God. This fact is fundamental to everything we shall consider below about the family. If we do not accept at the outset the absolute priority and necessity of the Word of God, then we shall struggle with every concept presented here. Everything we believe about the family must be formed, informed and reformed by the Word of God. The Word of God is the original and final authority on man and man's relations, for the Word of God defined man's creation from the beginning.

The Bible speaks of two "wisdoms" that compete for our attention: the wisdom from above and the wisdom from beneath (James 3:15-18). The wisdom from above is God's wisdom, but the wisdom from below is the wisdom of the world. The Christian family must be built according to the wisdom from above. We cannot create through earthly wisdom what God created by heavenly wisdom at the first.

Many of our families today are like Israel in the days of Josiah the king (II Kings 22). The people of God had turned to idols because they had lost the written Word of God. The law was missing. Sadly, this is the same condition of many Christian families. The Word may not be lost *actually*, but it is lost *practically*. By looking to every authority other than the Word of God for direction on family life, we have turned unwittingly to disobedience and idolatry. The only remedy is to rediscover the Word of God and turn back to the laws of God for the family.

We often seem to think that the Word of God speaks only to our religious life, and that our "secular" life—such as education, economics, occupation, parenting, and so on—is governed by the practice of the world. If we are not careful we shall divide life into sacred/secular categories and allow the Word to govern our religious practice while everything else is governed by the humanistic philosophies of men. This sort of dichotomy produces confusion in the home. We become double-minded men building double-minded families (James 1:8). We must see that man was formed as a Word-creature, and that his family cannot be formed otherwise.

Image and Dominion

After the Lord God declared that He would create man, He described the sort of man He would create: "And God said, Let us make man in our image, after our likeness." God also defined

17

the authority and responsibility that this man would be given: "And let them have dominion...." When Adam was formed, he was created in the image and likeness of God and was given, as God's regent ruler, total dominion over all earthly creation. These two concepts, *image* and *dominion*, have a direct bearing on the form and function of the family. Image and dominion have to do with man's initial and essential role and responsibility in the home. The man of the house is God's image in the house. In other words, he represents God to the family. Furthermore, the man was made from the first to have dominion in the earth. Therefore, the man of the house is called to exercise dominion in the house. This dominion begins in his heart and extends into every room of the home. The man's role in the family cannot be fully appreciated without recognizing that he is the image of God with dominion over all.

The family that fails to understand image and dominion will inevitably distort the role and responsibility of the man. This sort of misunderstanding leads the family into sin and disobedience. This shall become much clearer further along in our study. But for now, bear this point in mind: the family must recognize that the man—her husband, their father—was created from the first in the image and likeness of God and given dominion over all. Their recognition of this fact affects how they relate and respond to dad's position in the home.

We shall consider dominion below, but first, look at several aspects of image.

The Man is "Like" God

First, Adam was created like God, yet he was not God. This obvious fact outlines a subtle distinction that must be observed by godly fathers. They are *like* God but they are *not* God. This limits the authority of the man within the home. The stream of his authority flows within the levees of God's law. No man is a law unto himself. Everything man is and has is derived from God and is contingent upon God's grace. This recognition helps prevent the abuse of masculine authority.

This means, then, that because the man of the house is only *like* God in the home, he cannot feel and act as if he is autonomous and sovereign. He cannot represent himself. As a faithful father and husband, the man represents God to the family. He is God's agent in the home. Jesus said, "My judgment is just; because I seek not mine own will" (John 5:30). The man must reflect this conviction. He cannot enshrine his own will as divine and force his family to bow before it. The will of the man must be an expression of the will of God.

Man shares the attributes of God because he is formed in the image of God, and yet, he shares in the divine attributes in a limited sense. For example, Adam was created with sovereignty and free-will, yet both were limited within the confines of man's responsibility and obedience to his Creator. Certainly God created Adam with an amazing degree of knowledge, presence and power. Yet Adam was not given *all* knowledge, presence and power. It is good for every man to remember this simple fact. Those who forget this tend to impose their own will upon the family as if they were lord of all.

And so, the man that remembers these things stands in the home as the visible image of the invisible God. He reveals the likeness of God to his family. By doing the will of God he looks like God and acts like God before the family. If he lives any other way he becomes a lying image of God and his family's service to his will becomes idolatry. The Christian man must truthfully portray the similitude of God in the home.

The Man Must Grow In Likeness

Second, when Adam was created, he was mature physically in every way. And yet, he was immature spiritually and emotionally. The first man was innocent and unschooled. Adam was created with the ability and necessity to grow in knowledge, presence and power. Adam was full grown with a lot of growing to do. Adam was created in the image and likeness of God, and yet he had to grow into that likeness. We see this sort of thing in a sense in young children. A son may be "the spirit and image" (not spitting image!) of his father, but he must grow into his father's likeness. Adam was created in the image and likeness of God, but he was expected to grow into God's likeness through continued, daily fellowship.

The same is true of the man of the house. The man stands upright in the home as the image and likeness of God. And yet,

19

no husband and father perfectly mirrors the image of God at first. The man must grow into divine likeness. Though much growth and development occurs long before a man is married, no man enters a marriage perfectly prepared for the challenges he will face. Every man must enter the marriage prepared to grow. He must recognize his innocence and ignorance. He must be aware of his need to grow in the image and likeness of God.

And yet—and this is the salient point—the man is the image of God to the family *from the start*. This means that he must be respected *from the start* by the family as the man of God in the home. Even though he may not be perfectly all he should be, or even will be, he must be respected as the image of God as he grows in maturity before God.

This exposes the lie that a man is not qualified to lead if he is not a perfect example from the start. If only perfect examples can lead, then we shall have no leaders. And that, of course, is Satan's objective. Satan too often has paralyzed the leadership of husbands and fathers because they were not altogether the man they needed to be. Too many wives have been duped into believing that they need not respect a man who is less than perfect. So there is no man they will respect.

Disrespectful wives communicate this idea to their children both verbally and non-verbally, and the entire family learns from mom to dishonor dad. Many justify their disrespect on the grounds that they are not expected to honor a flawed man. However, if this is the case then no family can honor any man, for "all have sinned and come short of the glory of God" (Romans 3:23).

Of course, this sort of confusion is Satan's strategy. It is a trick of the devil. He leads many to believe that the man cannot lead his family unless he is perfect, and that paternal lapses of judgment mean that the family is free to mock the man and refuse to follow his direction. This is dangerous nonsense.

Jesus declares that the only effective way to spoil a house is to bind the strong man (Matthew 12:29). Of course, Jesus uses this idea to describe how Satan is defeated. But we can be sure that Satan has studied the strategy, for this perfectly describes his method of attack on the home.

Satan knows he cannot spoil the family of its spiritual treasures if a vigilant father is standing watch with mom and kids trusting in his faithful, if flawed, leadership. Satan must first neutralize dad's influence in the home so he can have his way with the woman and children. So, the devil is out to bind the strongman, the head of the house.

The man is *the* man regardless of his failures. And while this does not excuse the man's failures, it does rebuke those who would justify their own disrespect and disobedience because dad is not all the man he should be. The man is raised up as in the image and likeness of God from the first moment the family is formed in holy matrimony. He may not be perfect—indeed, he *shall* not be perfect—but he is the man, and he must be respected as such.

The man of the house stands as the image of God from the start, and yet, he must grow into that image. This, then, says two things. The man must be prepared to grow, and the family must be prepared to let him grow. Both the man and his family should recognize the fact that the man is both mature and immature at the same time. He is mature in position and prestige, but he is immature in procedure and practice.

This recognition would prevent so much unnecessary division in the home. Men could then stand with boldness before the family as God's agent acknowledging that, while he may not be all he should be, he *is* the image of God and shall be respected as such. This would allow the wife and children to respect the man as the full-grown image of God while recognizing that dad is growing into God's likeness.

The best way to grasp this idea is to understand that the man occupies an office, the office of husband and father. This is an idea that recurs often in our study, and this idea will help the woman and children learn how to respect the man even when his behavior is less than respectable. The man must be respected for the office he holds.

As noted above, the man is mature in position and prestige: he occupies a fully vested office. He must grow into that office, but the office comes with immediate powers that must be exercised at once. The man will make mistakes while in office, but he must simply correct the mistakes and keep performing his role in office. For no one else can occupy his office, and no one else can play his part. Anyone else who attempts to fill his office is a usurper. God has authorized the man alone to occupy his office as the image and likeness of God.

Origin and Destiny

The third aspect of image is this: man was created with an *origin* and a *destiny*. Adam's origin was creation in the image of God. His destiny was to behold and manifest the glory of God forever. Indeed, Paul speaks of man as "the image and glory of God" (I Corinthians 11:7). Man's origin is image and his destiny is glory.

When Adam stood upright, he stood squarely between his past and his future, between his origin and his destiny. Ever since creation, all men remain in this "present" stance. We are creatures of the here and now. However, we cannot allow our existence to be reduced to *only* the present. Our present is determined by our past and our future. A man that does not understand his origin and destiny will never understand his present existence. The man who cannot tell where he is coming from and where he is going will be unable to tell where he stands.

Man's origin and destiny give meaning to his present. Moreover, both man's origin and his destiny are rooted in relationship with God. Man is directly related to God both in image and glory. God created man in the first place so that he could finally be taken up into the life and love of God and share in the ineffable glory of the divine through resurrection.

Man is made in the image of God to share the glory of God. This is *essential* to man's existence. Man cannot escape the fact of his creation. Thus, when unbelievers lie about man's origin, they strip his present existence of all meaning. And when man's created origin is denied, his destiny is distorted. In fact, they end up denying his destiny altogether. This renders life totally meaningless. Unbelievers seek to exalt man by denying God and end up debasing man below the level of beasts. Man's existence has no meaning apart from divine origin and destiny. Deny God, and you deny man.

Unbelievers believe the lie that man is fulfilled in the present alone by serving immediate demands and desires. They seek existential meaning in instant self-gratification. Sinful man seeks to find fulfillment within himself all by himself. Even his relationships with others are cultivated to serve his own selfish interests. There is no higher meaning for the unbeliever than to serve self here and now. When God is thrust from the center of a man's world, it collapses inward, and he becomes the lone center of his own self-created universe. When man is all there is, man is all there is to live for. This kind of shrunken world becomes a very lonely place. Indeed, it becomes hell on earth.

However, this problem is not unique to unbelievers. Christians are often mired in the present with no meaning beyond the here and now. We sometimes lose sight of our origin and destiny and seek meaning only in the gratification of self. This sort of self-worship is particularly tragic for the man who has been called to "deny himself, and take up his cross, and follow [Jesus]" (Matthew 16:24). As it is said, the only prerequisite for selfishness is to have a self. It seems that we all qualify.

Atheists deny that God exists. And while Christians hotly contest such blatant unbelief, they often make an ironically similar statement by living a life devoid of any real sense of God's presence. Christians often live as *practical* atheists by failing to acknowledge their Creator every day. They do just fine without God's help, thank you very much. As Paul said, they "profess that they know God; but in works they deny Him" (Titus 1:16). Many of us are far guiltier of this sort of denial than we wish to admit.

So fallen man descends below the level of a beast and lives only for momentary, personal satisfaction. This self-absorption occurs when a man forgets that he was formed for a purpose higher than himself, for a purpose before and beyond himself. He loses sight of his origin and destiny.

The Christian man, however, must pause where he stands and turn his eyes back toward creation, toward that defining moment when God formed man in His image and likeness. Then he must turn his eyes toward the glorious future that God promised to those whom He has chosen. The Christian must lift his eyes up toward heaven and behold the outer limits of God's predestined purpose. Only when a man has truly contemplated the implications of his origin and destiny, of image and glory, can he really break free of this slavery to self. We were created for a purpose larger than a moment. We were created for eternity.

Christians must not permit the world to define the meaning of life. If we believe in God, then we must live as we believe. The

Lord Jesus Christ must be the center of our life. We must remember where we came from and where we are going. Our origin and destiny must define our daily life.

The family shares in the origin and destiny of man. The family was created in the first place to be the on-going extension of man and his purpose in the earth. Man was created in the image of God to share in the glory of God, and the family propagates this purpose. This means, then, that the family must be built around the purpose that God invested in man. The family must manifest the image and glory of God.

Christian fathers must cultivate a sense of purpose beyond selfish, present gratification. The man must bring home more than the bacon. He must bring home a sense of eternal purpose that defines his family and finances, his work and worship. The family inherits the man's perspective on life whether good or bad. His perspective becomes an enduring legacy for future generations.

The man who fails to live up to God's purpose inevitably distorts the fundamental purpose of his home. And the family that fails to live for the larger purpose of God will inescapably sink down into the abyss of self-centered existence that swallows up the man. The entire family is damned to the hell that dad has enlarged. When we understand the importance of origin and destiny, then we shall entreat God to recreate our family in His image. We shall see the home as the canvas upon which the Master paints His own portrait. We no longer see the family as the center of selfish existence. We shall begin to see the family as the center of divine purpose. We shall begin to build our family in light of man's created origin and eternal destiny.

Headship

The fourth fact related to image and likeness is that Adam was created first. This creates a precedence of position within the home. The office of husband is the highest office in the home because it is the first office in the home. Paul speaks of this priority of creation as the basis for the man's authority: "For the man is not of the woman; but the woman of the man. Neither was the man created for the woman; but the woman for the man. For this cause ought the woman to have power on her head because of the angels. Nevertheless neither is the man without the woman, neither the woman without the man, in the Lord. For as the woman is of the man, even so is the man also by the woman; but all things of God" (I Corinthians 11:8-12).

Paul also says, "Let the woman learn in silence with all subjection. But I suffer not a woman to teach, nor to usurp authority over the man, but to be in silence. For Adam was first formed, then Eve" (I Timothy 2:11-13). The fact that man was formed first is the basis for his leadership in the family. This leadership is called "headship."

Paul speaks explicitly of the man as head of the home in at least two passages (I Corinthians 11; Ephesians 5). There are other places where the concept is implicit (I Corinthians 14:34; Colossians 3:18; Titus 2:4, 5; I Peter 3:1-6). Headship is the concept that describes the relationship between Christ and the church (Ephesians 1:22; 4:15, 16; Colossians 2:10, 19). The man is the head of the home just as Christ is the head of the church (Ephesians 5:23). Thus, Christ's ecclesial headship is the model of man's familial headship.

It is important to define headship carefully. The word "head" does not mean "boss." This is often very conveniently misunderstood by boorish men who love to defend their overbearing rule by swinging select verses around their head like a blunt hatchet. Certainly the biblical idea of headship speaks of the man's first and final authority, but it does not imply that men are to be authoritarian autocrats. This sort of man needs a good Bible study on headship.

A much better meaning for "head" is "source" or "origin." The man is the source of authority in the home much as the spring is the source of the river. Paul states that God is the head of Christ, that Christ is the head of the man, and that the man is the head of the woman (I Corinthians 11:3). Kingdom authority flows down from God through Christ and into the family through the man.

Now, this definition of "head" changes everything. Rather than the man seeing himself as the "boss" in the home, he sees himself as the responsible leader in the home, the fount of all that occurs there—both good and bad. He sees himself as the source of the river that flows through his home. The man is the spring, and everything flows out of him.

If the household river flows with bitter water, then the man must look to himself as the bitter fountain that produced the poison (James 3:11, 12). Everything that flows into the home flows out of the man. The spiritual condition of the family is directly related to the spirit that flows out of the heart of man. The "issues of life" flow out of the man's heart (Proverbs 4:23) and affect everyone in the house.

This redefines headship. No longer is headship a matter of male privilege and prerogative, but now headship becomes a matter of male accountability and responsibility. No longer is headship a weapon that the man uses to enforce his rule and impose his will upon the family. But now, headship becomes a matter of honorable service to the family and humble submission to the Lord.

With this newfound understanding the man presents himself as nothing more or less than the agent of divine authority in the home. The man sees himself as the open channel through which the Spirit of God flows into the family. Everyone is affected by his genuine relationship with God. He becomes the gracious source of blessing and righteousness in the home. When the man sees himself as the source of the river of living water for the family, then the land downstream becomes verdant and vibrant with life as the waters of spiritual headship heal the land.

Headship is a matter of covenantal relationship, not biological superiority. Too often critics of biblical headship think that the Bible is asserting a patriarchal society where men are deemed superior to women by virtue of biological necessity. In other words, all men are superior to all women as a matter of nature. This view of male superiority holds that women are inferior creatures *per se*. However, this is not at all what the Bible teaches. There are many women who are superior to many men by every possible means of measure. Furthermore, a mistaken view of biblical patriarchy holds that *all* women are subjugated below *all* men. That is nonsense. The Bible teaches that headship is covenantal and thus relationship specific. A *particular* woman is submitted to a *particular* man (Ephesians 5:33). The *wife* is subject to the *husband*. One man's wife is not subject to all other men. She is not inferior to all men. She is subject to one man and that by her free choice. She submits willingly. Otherwise, it would not be true submission. Coerced subjection is not biblical submission.

This brings us back to the idea that the man and woman both occupy unique and distinct offices within the home. The man occupies the office of husband, and the woman occupies the office of wife. The office of husband is a superior office to that of wife. This has nothing to do with biological superiority. It is a matter of official superiority. It is the same as two men of similar merit and worth occupying the offices of president and vice-president in a corporation. Both men are equal, but their offices are not. Sometimes, the man who occupies the lesser office may even be the greater man, but he must yield to the greater office and officer.

The same is true in the home. There are many wives smarter than their husbands, more disciplined than their husbands, more well-mannered than their husbands, and so on. However, they occupy a lesser office, and they must humbly and willingly submit themselves to this reality. Of course, the man should recognize that God gave him this woman with such wonderful and superior gifts to be his ready helpmeet. If the husband is a wise man, he will allow his wife to contribute her gifts to the marriage thereby making him look much smarter than he really is.

Headship is a covenantal idea. It is a matter of covenant between man and wife before God. Covenantal headship is fundamental to properly orienting the roles of man and woman within the home. The man is the head of the home just as a captain is the head of a team. The man leads the home, but everyone must do their own individual part on the team.

The "team concept" is important here. Everyone on the team works for the good of the team. Those who lead the team understand that their leadership is for the good of the team not the good of the leader alone. There are even times when leaders step aside to allow certain members of the team to perform their specialty on behalf of the team. A captain of a football team must allow everyone on the line to do his individual part. A surgeon who heads a team of doctors must step aside to allow an anesthesiologist to do his work. A commanding officer in the military must step aside at times to allow a specialist, say, a demolitions expert, to do his job. Each leader understands that the work of the team cannot be accomplished apart from the contributions of each member.

So, the family is a team, and the man is the captain of that team. And the wise man recognizes that each member of the team contributes their part to the overall success of the family. There are times when the husband must step back and allow the wife to do her part. He must allow her great latitude in managing the household and rearing the children. This is the woman's specific task as outlined in scripture (I Timothy 5:14; Titus 2). The man must not be so insecure that he is threatened by the capable leadership of those under his authority. The man must allow authority to flow through him to the entire family. Each member of the family should be authorized by the man to play their respective parts in the home.

One final point about headship: It is interesting that Paul never speaks directly to the man with regard to his headship. The apostle always addresses his remarks on headship to the woman. This means, then, that the man should not gratuitously assert his headship. Rather, the woman should willingly recognize the headship of man. The man should not be required to run wildly about the house flexing his muscles and pounding his chest while bellowing at the top of his lungs that he, and he alone, is the head of the house. The man should simply *be* the head because he *is* the head, which is true whether or not he is so faithfully. However, the exhortation concerning headship is to the woman. She must recognize the man's leadership and submit to it cheerfully.

Confidence and Dependence

A man must recognize the importance of being created in the image and likeness of God so that he may live up to his high calling. He must learn to walk worthy of his vocation (Ephesians 4:1). A man that is aware that he was created will be aware of his Creator. The man must derive his personal image, his significance and self-worth, from the image of God within him. He must not seek fulfillment and meaning from other things. His orientation must be toward God. He must keep his eyes first on the Creator and then on His creation. Jesus must be the gravitational center of all life. Life consists (is held together) by Christ (Colossians 1:16, 17).

The man of the house must pause to consider: I *am* a man; therefore I must *be* a man. A godly man must be more than just a male. He must be a *man* with all that being a man entails. God made him a man because God determined to make a man out of him. God made him to be a man with a plan. This recognition of his origin will give him the confidence to fulfill his destiny.

When the man remembers that God—the all-wise God—made him in His image and likeness, it shall embolden him to seek after the destiny for which he was created. The man that recognizes that God created him to be a man will no longer question whether or not he can be the man he was made to be. If the man sees his masculine identity as an accident of nature with no divine purpose beyond the random selection of a mindless chromosome, then he will miss the point of his purpose altogether. He will live a lifetime wondering if he can be a man. But if the man sees himself as the product of God's sovereign providence over biological conception, if he comes to believe that God formed him in his mother's womb (Job 31:15; Psalm 22:9, 10; 139:13; Jeremiah 1:5; Galatians 1:15), then he shall be emboldened to be a man—since that is exactly what he is.

Materialists and evolutionists have nearly won the battle here. Christians who would never accept that the universe was created by a godless, meaningless "Big Bang" accept every day that babies are conceived in the womb apart from any divine oversight and intervention. We have practically lost the beautiful, biblical idea that the Creator continues to form the children of men from the womb. And this unbelief, which Paul calls "science falsely so called" (I Timothy 6:20), has robbed so many men of their sense of having been formed by God for an individual purpose. Christians still believe that God made Adam, but most believe some impersonal force called "Nature" made them. No wonder so many lead aimless lives. We must believe that once again *God made man in His image and likeness* when we were conceived. Even in this fallen world God is the only Author of life.

When a man forgets the fact of his creation and stops living like a man with a plan, then his confidence collapses into self-doubt and insecurity. This brings a myriad of problems that only get worse with time. Man's boldness before God and others flows out of his recognition that he is made in the image of God. He must realize *who* he is before he can focus on *what* he is to do. A man's identity determines his destiny.

29

The recognition of image and likeness should also humble the man. When he considers his creation by the hand of God, it should remind the man of his total dependence upon God. Adam was a lifeless lump of clay until the Master Potter formed him and breathed the breath of life into his lungs. Therefore, a man's awareness of his creation should do two things: It should embolden the man to *confidence* in his calling, and it should humble the man to *dependence* on God. We must have this balance of *confidence* and *dependence*.

The man must stand before his family with this blend of confidence and dependence. He must never be afraid to be the man of the house. And yet, he must never allow his position to make him proud and profane. The man is the man because God made him so. Thus, the man is utterly dependent in every way upon God's divine endorsement. The man does not represent himself. He represents the Creator. He is the image and likeness of God in the home.

Conclusion

Every man must consider all of this as he ponders his role as man, husband and father. He is created *like* God, but he is *not* God. His person, position and performance are all limited by reason of his creation. He possesses limited sovereignty and restricted free-will. Man's origin and destiny define his existence. He is authorized by God and accountable to God for the use of that authority. The man is the head of the family, the source of authority and responsibility. The man, as the representative of the family, answers to God for the whole family.

The woman must consider these things as well and recognize that God created the man in His image and likeness. The woman is also created in the image and likeness of God, but in a subordinate and derivative sense. Thus, man *exists* as the image and likeness of God regardless of subsequent action. He shall be judged as the man God made him to be whether or not he is living up to this great purpose. A man may fail to live up to the purpose of his origin and destiny, but it does not erase the fact of his existence: he is the image and glory of God because God created him so. He is the image and likeness of God based on his *person* not his *performance*. This fact must be confronted and accepted *now*, for this idea forms the basis of biblical understanding and godly submission.

Christian children must be taught this as well. They must be taught that their dad occupies the office of father as the image and likeness of God. This is the first point of the creation order, and it is the basis of a Christian family order: Dad is the image and likeness of God in the home because he is *the* man of the house, the one God created to represent God to the family and the family to God. And this has nothing to do *initially* with the actions of the man. Divine evaluation of his actions follows later. At first, the man does nothing to earn the image and likeness of God except be born a man.

2

Creation and Dominion

Genesis 1:28-30. "And God blessed them, and God said unto them, Be fruitful, and multiply, and replenish the earth, and subdue it: and have dominion over the fish of the sea, and over the fowl of the air, and over every living thing that moveth upon the earth. And God said, Behold, I have given you every herb bearing seed, which is upon the face of all the earth, and every tree, in the which is the fruit of a tree yielding seed; to you it shall be for meat. And to every beast of the earth, and to every fowl of the air, and to every thing that creepeth upon the earth, wherein there is life, I have given every green herb for meat: and it was so."

Dominion was promised to Adam when he was first formed from dust (v. 26). The passage above describes the moment when dominion was actually conferred (v. 28). This was Adam's official ordination. Indeed, this ceremony of blessing was Adam's regal coronation as prince of the earth.

This simple blessing upon Adam expands upon closer consideration into a powerful mandate. The blessing outlines the details of man's authority to rule. Adam's *coronation* becomes his *commission* as God elaborates the details of dominion. The Lord declares that worldwide dominion shall be achieved through the growth and expansion of the human family in the earth, and that man's dominion shall encompass sky, earth and sea.

Then, the Lord God concludes the coronation and commission of man by boldly promising to sustain them daily in their task. Each of these things has profound relevance to the family today. Let's consider each one in turn and apply them to our present situation.

Coronation

This first account of man's creation in Genesis 1 is somewhat abbreviated. The second account of creation in Genesis 2 gives much more detail. We shall consider those details below. But for now we are given the introductory summary of man's creation, coronation and commission.

The Genesis account simply says that "God blessed them...." However, Psalm 8 offers more background on man's coronation.

> O LORD our Lord, how excellent is thy name in all the earth! Who hast set thy glory above the heavens. Out of the mouth of babes and sucklings hast thou ordained strength because of thine enemies, that thou mightest still the enemy and the avenger. When I consider thy heavens, the work of thy fingers, the moon and the stars, which thou hast ordained; what is man, that thou art mindful of him? And the son of man, that thou visitest him? For thou hast made him a little lower than the angels, and hast crowned him with glory and honor. Thou madest him to have dominion over the works of thy hands; thou hast put all things under his feet: All sheep and oxen, yea, and the beasts of the field; the fowl of the air, and the fish of the sea, and whatsoever passeth through the paths of the seas. O LORD our Lord, how excellent is thy name in all the earth! (Psalm 8:1-9)

The Psalmist describes the wonder of creation and of man's dominion over it. God was "mindful" of Adam and "visited him." Adam was "created a little lower than the angels" and "crowned with glory and honor." Man was given "dominion over the works of [God's] hands," and all creation was put "under his feet." Psalm 8 lets us know that Adam's ordination to rule was a regal affair. It was a formal coronation. The Lord God "crowned him with glory and honor." At creation, Adam was enthroned as prince of the earth.

Adam's coronation occurred soon after Adam and his wife were married (which is described below). God summoned them before His presence for the final act in the drama of creation. Countless hosts of heavenly angels stood in hushed reverence on every side. They were arrayed in their glory as splendid courtiers of the King. As man and wife knelt somberly before His throne, the King of kings extended His hands over their bowed heads and proclaimed His blessing upon them. "Be fruitful, and multiply, and replenish the earth, and subdue it: and have dominion over the fish of the sea, and over the fowl of the air, and over every living thing that moveth upon the earth."

Thus the Lord God announced His approval upon Adam and his wife. He smiled upon them and granted them divine favor. Adam and his wife were ordained to live as the image and likeness of God, chosen by the Almighty to represent Him and His rule upon the earth. They were *blessed*. Thus, Adam was crowned with glory and honor and given dominion over all.

Blessing

Dominion was a *blessing*. This means then that dominion was a matter of free grace. It was a gift from God. Adam did nothing to deserve it. He had no résumé of good works to present. God gave Adam the responsibility of ruling over creation based on the goodness of God not the goodness of man. Man had not yet had the opportunity to be good. Dominion was not a merit-based promotion. Adam's rule was inaugurated by grace not by works.

Adam forfeited his dominion by forgetting this fact and grasping for dominion through human endeavor. He tried to obtain through works what could only be obtained by grace through faith. This was the folly of his sin at the tree of knowledge. Adam believed he could attain divine status through human education. Unbelievers still fail to see the fallacy of this idea.

When Adam sinned this blessing became a curse, and man's dominion was perpetually frustrated by sin and death. Dominion became a matter of cosmic struggle for control between man and Satan. Ultimately, the contest for man's frustrated dominion was won decisively by Jesus Christ. Jesus "…was made a little lower than the angels for the suffering of death, crowned with glory and honor; that he by the grace of God should taste death for every man" (Hebrews 2:9). Jesus was "crowned with glory and honor" and restored man's dominion. The work that Jesus accomplished in His death, burial, resurrection and ascension was done "by the grace of God." Jesus reclaimed the blessing.

So, dominion is a matter of divine blessing. Dominion cannot be obtained and maintained by the humanistic effort of man. Man cannot rule the world, even his own world, by fleshly effort. He cannot be saved by works. Dominion cannot be achieved by striving in the flesh.

Therefore, the Christian family that seeks dominion over their world, to rule it wisely for the glory of God, must come under the hand of God and receive His blessing. Otherwise, they are destined to struggle forever in the hopeless task of ruling in the strength of fallen man.

As the Lord spoke through the prophet: "Then he answered and spoke unto me, saying, This is the word of the LORD unto Zerubbabel, saying, Not by might, nor by power, but by my spirit, saith the LORD of hosts. Who art thou, O great mountain? before Zerubbabel thou shalt become a plain: and he shall bring forth the headstone thereof with shoutings, crying, Grace, grace unto it" (Zechariah 4:6-7).

If we intend to build a Christian home—to "bring forth the headstone thereof with shoutings"—then we must cry, "Grace, grace!" unto it. We cannot build our family in the might and power of man. We must build by the Spirit of the Lord. We need the blessing of God upon our family.

One other thing: dominion was a blessing and not a burden. Sinful man often views the task of dominion as an oppressive responsibility. Sinful man flees responsibility and abdicates his rule. He feels it is simply too much to ask of a man that he rule the world, even his own world. He is overwhelmed and just wants to get away from it all. But this craven desire is a result of the fall.

Sin causes man to forfeit his greatest opportunity for blessing by exaggerating the challenges of faithful leadership. Before the fall, however, Adam understood that dominion came as the blessing of the Lord upon him and was to be accepted as a great privilege. Christian men have the opportunity as husbands and fathers to rule with Christ upon the throne of God as the representatives of God to the family. This is a blessing, and faithful men must appreciate it as such.

Lower Than the Angels

Psalm 8 records another interesting fact about Adam's coronation. The Psalmist says that man was "made a little lower than the angels" (v. 5). In what sense was Adam made lower than the angels? Hebrews 2:9 explains that angels are superior because they are immortal: "But we see Jesus, who was made a little lower than the angels for the suffering of death" The angels possess ontological superiority; they are greater in being than man. Also, we are told that angels are superior to men in power and might (Psalm 103:20; II Thessalonians 1:7; II Peter 2:4). Angels are superior to man in being and ability.

But there is another way that man was "made a little lower than the angels." Angels were created to "minister to those who should be the heirs of salvation" (Hebrews 1:14). Though angels were created greater than man, yet they were created to serve man. They were like palace servants of a king who serve as guardians for the king's son, the prince, until the time of his maturity. Angels were ordained to serve man by assisting him in the task of dominion. Angels were created as the "principalities and powers" of the earth. They were set up in regional districts of the world to assist man as he expanded his rule through out the earth. Eventually, man would grow into full maturity before God and the angels would assist man in his universal rule. This seems to be the purpose against which Satan rebelled. Paul describes "the condemnation of the devil" as the pride of a novice who seeks glory for himself and refuses to serve (I Timothy 3:6). When Satan rebelled against his assignment, all of the principalities and powers of the earth fell with him. They were on his team. When Satan lost, they lost. This is how the principalities and powers became hostile to God. When Jesus came He subdued all principalities and powers and brought them under His perfect authority.

Now, we do not have space here for an in-depth discussion of principalities and powers. Suffice it to say, however, that Adam was created to serve God under the oversight of angels who would assist him in the task of dominion until he entered into the fullness of his sonship. The Lord God created Adam to serve for a time under the oversight of angels.

Just so, faithful men must be prepared to submit to biblical oversight. They must be prepared to receive instruction and correction from God's appointed servants. Godly men must be "made a little lower than the angels" before they can be "crowned with glory and honor." They cannot have authority if they are not under authority. In a practical sense, this means that men must accept their coronation and commission to rule under the direction of God's instituted governments and authority. Christian men must stand boldly in the office they have been given while seeking godly counsel and guidance from others. Men must lead their family decisively yet submissively. Men cannot expect their family to submit to them if they will not submit to others. Godly men must be *under* to be *over*.

Christian men must grow in leadership as Adam was intended to grow. They must mature as leaders of the family. Men must "go on unto perfection" (Hebrews 6:1). However, this does not mean that they cannot lead until they attain perfection. For then, as we noted above, no man could ever lead at all. Rather, it means that men must be prepared to grow in their leadership in the home. Every Christian father must submit himself to the "angels" (ministers) in his life: to family leaders (fathers, grandfathers, uncles), church leaders (pastors, elders, brethren), and political leaders (kings, governors, officers). This sort of submission leads toward perfection. As Paul said, "Let every soul be subject unto the higher powers. For there is no power but of God: the powers that be are ordained of God" (Romans 13:1). Every man must submit to political government, ecclesial (church) government and familial government. The man who seeks to wear the crown must bear the cross. Submission breeds submission. The man who resists authority teaches his family to resist authority. We shall reap what we sow.

Commission

The coronation of Adam included his commission for dominion. When God crowned Adam with glory and honor and set him over the works of His hands, He commanded: "Be fruitful, and multiply, and replenish the earth, and subdue it: and have dominion over the fish of the sea, and over the fowl of the air, and over every living thing that moveth upon the earth." This was Adam's commission.

The commission consisted of three parts: (1) to be fruitful and multiply in the earth; (2) to replenish (fill) the earth and subdue it; and (3) to have dominion over the sky, earth and sea. The goal was dominion. Adam was to rule over the sky, earth and sea. Every bird, every beast and every fish was to be identified and named, observed and subdued for the glory of God.

Dominion was the goal, but this goal could not be reached by one man alone. Global dominion would require the concerted effort of a global population. So, God gave man a helpmeet (an event described later) and endowed them with the creative power to have children, to "be fruitful and multiply" upon the earth. Adam was destined to achieve dominion as the earth was filled with his children and grandchildren. His posterity would develop human civilization and bring all creation under the oversight and stewardship of man. Dominion was the goal; the family was the means. Thus Adam's purpose was tied up with his family. He could not do it alone. And this was by divine design. It was completely necessary for Adam to submit to his role as father and husband in order to be fulfilled as a man. He could not avoid familial relationships and still achieve dominion. God made it so.

This has profound implications for the man today. The family is not just a convenient grouping of related people for the purpose of getting along better in life. The family is fundamental to the purpose of God in the earth. Man *cannot* exercise dominion over the earth apart from properly functioning family relationships. And this fact is true no matter how hard modern rebels try to prove it wrong. God made marriage and parenting necessary to Adam's *personal* fulfillment. He was created to rule over all, but he could not do so by himself and for himself. Further, the task of dominion would require a larger society, the global civilization formed by human expansion throughout the world. This means that man could not escape the exigencies and necessities—even difficulties—of human relationships. Adam was forced to climb up out of himself and relate to others.

The commission required Adam to develop relationships on three levels: (1) marital (his wife); (2) parental (children and grandchildren); and (3) civil (larger human society). Adam was required to accept his role in the world. He was expected to accept this responsibility as a blessing and not a burden. This meant that Adam had to accept the responsibilities of marriage. He could not be fruitful and multiply without a proper relationship with his wife. He also was required to embrace the idea of fathering children, even many children. He could not rebel against fathering children and providing for them without forfeiting his own destiny. Adam's destiny was tied up with his children. He needed children to realize his own purpose in life. Dominion was impossible apart from family. Further, Adam was required to embrace his larger role and responsibility in society at large. As Adam's children multiplied in the earth it would have been necessary to establish formal, familial government to regulate human interaction, commerce and trade. Adam could not refuse to face the demands of society at large. Adam was required to be a civic man, a man who would bring glory to God as local and global government developed. This government certainly would have been familial rather than merely political, but it would have been civil government nonetheless. Finally, Adam would be expected to exercise faithful dominion over his entire world, the sky, earth and sea. Adam was called to rule well.

This presents a startling idea. Man cannot attain dominion while in rebellion against the command to be fruitful and multiply and fill the earth. A man who abdicates his responsibility to his family cannot fulfill his purpose upon the earth. He may gain much in his quest for fulfillment, but, ultimately, man cannot succeed alone. The man that truly achieves success—as God measures success—is the man who submits himself to the Lord's directive to build a godly family. A man may work a lifetime, but if he does not invest himself in the generation to come, he really has accomplished nothing. (The only exception is the man that is gifted to serve the Lord in celibacy, but that is outside the scope of our discussion for now.)

This means that modern man's attempt to find fulfillment outside of fathering children and rearing them up to fear the Lord is doomed to fail. It is a tragedy that modern self-indulgent man has become the fiercest enemy of children. He encourages women to view sexuality as totally divorced from reproduction. If by chance unwanted conception interrupts their romantic recreation, he demands that the woman destroy the innocent child growing within her womb. He persuades the woman that there is no feminine fulfillment in being a wife and a mother—in other words, a *woman*—and leads her to believe that she can only be fulfilled in becoming a quasi-man. He leads her to faith in his god, the god of money and success. He challenges her to a duel between the sexes fought on the battleground of career advancement. He knows instinctively that the battle for gender supremacy is a fight he cannot lose. He offers her the illusive terms of equality and then laughs that she is such an easy conquest. Men will always have the advantage in the bedroom and boardroom, on the field and on the corporate ladder. Man was created to rule, and fallen man perverts this creation order to his warped advantage.

Feminism was invented by dissolute men. This is hotly denied by progressive women, but they simply demonstrate again how easily they are deceived. Rebellious men refuse to accept responsibility for their procreative power and try desperately to become all they can be apart from family. They cleverly devise self-serving schemes, such as feminism, to hide their craven abdication. But their scheming will never work. Fallen men cannot find lasting, genuine fulfillment apart from their role as husband and father. God designed it so.

Furthermore, the commission of Adam demonstrates that the man who does not submit to God's command to be fruitful and multiply will never have true dominion, over himself or his world. The man that fails to subordinate his own sexual drive to the necessity of rearing a godly family will never rule his own heart, much less the world. A man can either play the field or plow the field; he cannot do both. Dominion requires self-dominion. Self-dominion is self-discipline, and it cannot be attained as long as the man seeks it apart from the development of healthy, human relationships. We shall discuss more of this later in our study.

The Continuing Commission

So, how does all of this apply to our present concern? First of all, the Christian family today still lives under the command to be fruitful and multiply, for we do not spiritualize altogether the creation mandate. If we spiritualize the command to be fruitful and multiply, fill up the earth and have dominion, then we must

41

spiritualize marriage as well and "forbid to marry" (I Timothy 4:2). That will not be happening any time soon! The New Covenant does not spiritualize the original creation mandate. Rather, it reinforces it (I Timothy 5:14; Hebrews 13:4; I Corinthians 7). The sons and daughters of Adam are still expected to marry and grow their family for the purpose of dominion. The new birth does not obviate the need for the first.

Furthermore, our commission is expanded to include what we call the "Great Commission," the command to evangelize and disciple the nations (Matthew 28:18-20). The fall of man made the redemption of the human race necessary, and the rebellion of the angels made man's dominion a matter of spiritual warfare. Therefore, dominion now includes evangelism. The children of the Second Adam are expected to produce spiritual children, build the church in every nation and defeat the principalities and powers that are hostile to the gospel of Jesus Christ. We are commanded now to "be fruitful and multiply" through the conversion of unbelievers.

However, here is the salient point: just as the family was central to Adam's original commission, so the family is *still* central to the commission given by Christ to the church. The essential role of the family in gaining dominion in the earth has not changed. The family played a central role in the early days of the church. In the Book of Acts, the early church preached the gospel from house to house (Acts 2:46). This does not mean merely that they canvassed neighborhoods with door-to-door outreach. They may have done that, who knows. But that is not the point in Acts. The house-to-house evangelism that they engaged in was *family-to-family* evangelism. They preached the gospel from household-to-household.

There are several instances in the New Testament of entire households being converted at once. The angel instructed Cornelius to send for Peter, "Who shall tell thee words, whereby thou and all thy house shall be saved" (Acts 11:14). Paul preached the gospel to Lydia, and her entire household was baptized (Acts 16:14). The Philippian jailer and his house believed and were baptized (Acts 16:32-34). Paul speaks of baptizing "the house of Stephanus" (I Corinthians 1:16). These instances surely indicate that the early church expected entire families to be saved. The instances where some members of the family did not believe were rare and surprising. Paul and Peter both make it clear that the believer should expect their spouse and children to be saved (I Corinthians 7; I Peter 3).

Certainly the gospel is preached to strangers. The Holy Ghost is promised "to all that are afar off" (Acts 2:39). But this is where we often go wrong in our thinking. We think because the commission includes evangelizing strangers that it consists *primarily* of evangelizing strangers. We sometimes seem to think that evangelism has nothing to do with the natural family, that the children and relations of believers have no priority within the promises of God. This is wrong-headed thinking. The promise extended to the stranger is first offered "unto you, and to your children" (Acts 2:39). When the gospel comes to a man, it is a given that his family should be saved with him. If they are not, then it is a tragedy of unbelief. It is not the will of God that a man is saved alone. His family is *always* invited to come.

We too often pass by our own children in our haste to reach the stranger. We pound the streets, compass land and sea to make one proselyte, all the while hardly reaching for our own family. We teach Bible studies to all of our neighbors, friends and co-workers, but we rarely, if ever, crack a Bible with our own children. As James would say: "Brethren, these things ought not to be!" This neglect belies an underlying unbelief toward the promises of God made to us and *our children.*

The New Covenant that the prophet Jeremiah spoke about, which is the Christian Covenant (Hebrews 8), included this promise: "And they shall be my people, and I will be their God: And I will give them one heart, and one way, that they may fear me forever, for the good of them, and of their children after them" (Jeremiah 32:38-39). God plans to save the children of the righteous, so the righteous must plan for their children to be saved. Too often we treat the salvation of our family as a possibility at best rather than the promise from God it is intended to be. Our entire family *must* be saved. This is what we must expect by grace through faith. Anything less is unbelief.

The Psalmist says, "Lo, children are a heritage of the LORD: and the fruit of the womb is his reward. As arrows are in the hand of a mighty man; so are children of the youth. Happy is the man that hath his quiver full of them: they shall not be ashamed, but they shall speak with the enemies in the gate" (Psalms 127:3-5).

43

Our children are the Lord's heritage. They belong to Him. He blesses believers with children; they are His reward. Our children are as sharpened arrows in the hands of a mighty man. They are shot out into the earth for the purpose of dominion. Our children must be sent out as workers and worshippers, as missionaries and pastors, as evangelists and church planters. They must be sent out into the world to expand the boundaries of the kingdom of God. When the Lord promised to pour out His Spirit upon all flesh, He specifically declared what He would do through our children: "But this is that which was spoken by the prophet Joel; And it shall come to pass in the last days, saith God, I will pour out of my Spirit upon all flesh: and your sons and your daughters shall prophesy, and your young men shall see visions, and your old men shall dream dreams: And on my servants and on my handmaidens I will pour out in those days of my Spirit; and they shall prophesy" (Acts 2:16-18).

Believers and their children are integral to God's purpose. God intends to fill the earth with the gospel through the Christian family. God is building a church through believers and their families. Those who are strangers to the church and have no relations in the body of Christ are welcome. No righteous pedigree is required. But as soon as a man becomes a convert to the faith he should begin making plans to bring up his entire family in the fear of the Lord. His family, then, becomes an extension of the kingdom of God in the earth. Nothing less is acceptable.

Let us say it once more to drive the point home. God intended for the gospel to spread throughout the families of the earth. It is not the will of God for select individuals to be called apart from their families. It is God's pleasure to save us and our entire families. Certainly the gospel divides families (Matthew 10:34-37; Luke 12:51-53), but this is the tragic result of human unbelief, not the result of God's indifference to our loved ones.

Again, God promised to save our spouses (I Corinthians 7:16; I Peter 3:1), our children (Acts 2:38, 39) and our grandchildren (Deuteronomy 7:9; I Chronicles 16:15; Psalms 105:8). Of course, this promise is only reckoned and realized by faith, but when it is reckoned it *is* realized. The promise of salvation is to our entire house (Acts 11:14). Therefore, the dominion that the church is gaining in the earth through evangelism grows as we evangelize our families and the kingdom comes in our children. There is an intrinsic connection between dominion and family.

Adam was commanded by God to "*have* dominion" over the sky, earth and sea. He *had* dominion by divine decree, but now he was to *have* dominion by realizing the decree in practical experience. Adam failed to *have* what he *had* when through unbelief he chose to try to attain dominion through human effort. We *have* dominion as well through the gospel. All principalities and powers are subject to us in Christ through the gospel. We declare this reality by faith when we preach the Word of faith, the gospel of Christ's triumph over evil. The gospel is true whether or not we believe it. Unbelief does not dethrone the Lord Jesus Christ for even one fraction of a moment. Unbelief simply robs *us* of possessing the promise. When we refuse to believe, then we, like Adam, fail to *have* what we *have*. We must understand what Christ has done for the family at the Cross and what He is doing through the family even now. The Christian family is fundamental to the victory of the kingdom of God. We must *never* surrender this idea.

Provision

After Adam was crowned and commissioned, the Lord promised to provide necessary sustenance for Adam and his family. "And God said, Behold, I have given you every herb bearing seed, which is upon the face of all the earth, and every tree, in the which is the fruit of a tree yielding seed; to you it shall be for meat. And to every beast of the earth, and to every fowl of the air, and to every thing that creepeth upon the earth, wherein there is life, I have given every green herb for meat: and it was so."

There are several lessons to learn here. First, God *gives* the blessings, but we must *grow* them. Adam was promised that all fruits and vegetables growing from the earth were freely given by God as food for man and the animals. However, it becomes plain farther down in the story that Adam was expected to cultivate the earth and tend its bounty. The plenty that God promised was to flow out of man's dominion. The more man cultivated the earth, the greater the bounty would be.

There is much that God gives to the family as unearned largesse. We have all been endowed by God with certain talents

45

and abilities that are meant to bring provender and prosperity to the home both financially and spiritually. But we must choose what to do with all we have been given. Some waste their blessings and squander the grace of God in purely temporal and selfish pursuits. Others wisely develop their gifts in the pursuit of godly vocation and dominion. God *gives* the means for dominion; we *grow* them.

Second, God is the source of our provision. We should not disbelieve the Word of God and look around for other sources of provision. The Lord God caught Adam's attention when He said, "*Behold*, I have given…" God offered Adam a certain "vision for provision." Adam was compelled to see what God had done on his behalf. We must see the same today. We must "behold" the provision of the Lord for His people. We must focus on a biblical "vision for provision."

The failure to see the proper vision for provision has trapped many Christians into what Jesus described as a "Gentile" perspective on getting by and making do: "Therefore take no thought, saying, What shall we eat? or, What shall we drink? or, Wherewithal shall we be clothed? (For after all these things do the Gentiles seek:) for your heavenly Father knoweth that ye have need of all these things. But seek ye first the kingdom of God, and his righteousness; and all these things shall be added unto you. Take therefore no thought for the morrow: for the morrow shall take thought for the things of itself. Sufficient unto the day is the evil thereof" (Matthew 6:31-34).

Jesus warns us that we shall be tempted to wonder about the source of daily provision. He teaches us to "seek first the kingdom of God." He reproves our tendency to live just as the world lives, in the same desperate pursuit of material gain.

There is probably no greater enemy of the family in Western culture today than materialism. The biblical name for materialism is "covetousness." The greatest antidote to the poison of covetousness is contentment, as Paul explained in his first letter to Timothy (I Timothy 6:5-10). However, contentment comes only through complete trust in God's faithful care. We become content when we determine to trust that "God shall supply all [our] need according to His riches in glory by Christ Jesus" (Philippians 4:19). We become covetous when we question the wisdom of God's daily provision. Ask the children of Israel what happens when you murmur and complain. That sort of thing will leave you dying in a wilderness.

Modern Christians have succumbed to the slavery of debt, lured to their financial death on credit by the illusion of borrowed affluence. They have allowed the world to persuade them to send dad climbing the corporate ladder with mom scurrying quickly up behind him and the kids elsewhere—*anywhere* elsewhere—to be trained up by strangers. They have tolerated and defended such unnatural aberrations of family life in the blatant pursuit of wealth. The love of money truly has been the root of all evil for the family.

This sort of disaster can only be avoided by trusting the Word of God. God promised to provide, and He meant what He said. God is our source. Provision is a part of God's blessing on us and our family. God's Word to Adam from the start prevented covetousness as a motive for dominion. Why covet what belongs to someone else when everyone has been promised all that they will ever need?

We must not violate larger principles of righteousness in pursuit of provision. This is what Adam did when he ate of the forbidden fruit. It was provision, of a sort. But it was forbidden provision. It was sin and death. The woman saw that the fruit was "good for food" (Genesis 3:6), but it killed them dead. God had promised Adam all the food he needed throughout the entire earth. He did not need to seek provision another way. Adam was a fool to do so. However, we often do the same. We follow Adam's folly when we seek provision apart from God's instructions. We imitate Adam's unbelief when we fracture our home to seek material wealth. We also do so when we enslave our family to creditors in order to live a lifestyle we cannot afford. We must repudiate the world's "vision of provision" and seek to provide for our family according to the principles of the Word of God. Maybe this is why we seek prosperity and cannot find it. If we would seek the kingdom of God first, then possibly, just possibly, the Lord might keep His Word and prosper our house. It may be worth a try.

Moreover, God's provisions are enough. He has promised to supply all of our need according to His riches in glory (Philippians 4:19). That should be plenty. This, of course, assumes that we trust God to determine what enough is. And that can be a problem for fallen man beset by the lust of the flesh, the lust of the eyes and the pride of life (I John 2:16).

God's providence extends to all of our life. In God's promise to Adam, even the animals are cared for. The herb of the field and the fruit of the tree are cultivated as food for beasts of the field. This helps man in his task of dominion as he uses food to domesticate the animals. Jesus tells us that God's concern for the animals is an indication of His greater concern for us (Matthew 6:26). There is no member of the household left out of God's gracious provision.

As noted, provision and dominion are directly linked. Thus our lack of trust in God for provision is one of the greatest hindrances to Christian dominion. It seems certain that much of God's promised provision for the righteous is held back because of our covetousness. The kingdom of God could experience tremendous growth far beyond what we are now experiencing if we could be trusted to administer the blessings of God properly and wisely. This is a constant difficulty. And it is one we are not struggling very hard to overcome. Many Christians have succumbed completely to the world's invitation to join in the quest for pride, pleasure and power—all made possible by the benevolent trinity of currency, credit and capitalism.

Covetousness refuses to be satisfied with God's provision. Rather, covetousness demands more, much more, than God has allotted. Certainly, the desire for more is acceptable, but it must be sought acceptably. Jesus outlines the biblical path to gaining more:

> After a long time the lord of those servants cometh, and reckoneth with them. And so he that had received five talents came and brought other five talents, saying, Lord, thou deliveredst unto me five talents: behold, I have gained beside them five talents more. His lord said unto him, Well done, thou good and faithful servant: thou hast been faithful over a few things, I will make thee ruler over many things: enter thou into the joy of thy lord. He also that had received two talents came and said, Lord, thou deliveredst unto me two talents: behold, I have gained two other talents beside them. His lord said unto him, Well done, good and faithful servant; thou hast been

faithful over a few things, I will make thee ruler over many things: enter thou into the joy of thy lord (Matthew 25:19-23).

The biblical path to success and prosperity in all things is faithfulness "over a few things." However, the covetous spirit cannot be content to accept little, even for a little while. The covetous man refuses to be thankful for the little he has received. He spends his lifetime chafing over what he lacks rather than appreciating what he has gained.

God endowed man with a powerful ambition for dominion. However, this driving desire must not be confused with covetousness. The distinction between godly ambition and covetousness lies in its motive. Godly desire for dominion seeks to subdue all creation for the glory of God, whereas covetous seeks to own it all for the glory of man. When man accepts the call to rule the world, he does so understanding that God is the provider and proprietor of it all. When man rejects God's invitation to rule under His oversight and seeks to build an earthly empire for his own glory, then man rejects the provision that God offers and seeks to finance his schemes according to his own economic principles. This is why the financial systems of debt-driven, consumerist-oriented capitalism are destined to fail. Man cannot attain dominion over the world on borrowed capital.

The Word of God calls such financial futures speculation "boasting about tomorrow." The Apostle James rebukes our boasting thusly: "Go to now, ye that say, Today or tomorrow we will go into such a city, and continue there a year, and buy and sell, and get gain: Whereas ye know not what shall be on the morrow. For what is your life? It is even a vapor, that appeareth for a little time, and then vanisheth away. For that ye ought to say, If the Lord will, we shall live, and do this, or that. But now ye rejoice in your boastings: all such rejoicing is evil. Therefore to him that knoweth to do good, and doeth it not, to him it is sin" (James 4:13-17).

The will of God must be paramount in every financial decision that we make. We must see all provision as flowing from the hand of God, and thus flowing out of His will for our family. Too many foolish commitments are made as we rush recklessly into financial agreements we cannot keep. We often make unwise boasts about tomorrow—we call them "terms"—without considering the direction of the only One who actually sees tomorrow. We must not allow covetousness to dictate our financial future. This is the short path to financial slavery.

Covetousness is one of the greatest problems facing the Christian family today. We must reckon with it and repent of our sin. We must accept the Lord's provision, however great or small, with a thankful heart, and pledge that, by the grace of God, we shall be the best stewards we can be with the little we have until the reckoning shall come and we are given more. This sort of contentment and thankful spirit would liberate the family from the evil pressure of materialism.

Covetousness is overcome by contentment, and contentment flows out of thankfulness. We must "behold" (as Adam did) that God has given us everything we need to survive and thrive. He has promised to provide for us and our family. A thankful spirit sees God in the details, in the smallest "herb bearing seed." Thankfulness sees God's provision in the smallest crumbs of bread. Thankfulness takes it seat at the table and offers gratitude to God for the daily bread He has provided. This is why our giving of thanks at mealtime must be more than mere formality. It must be a profound recognition of a daily miracle wrought right before our eyes. Our daily bread is from the hand of God, even though wrapped in cellophane and bought at the store, and He deserves our thanks. Those who seek to build a godly house would be well advised to spend time here reflecting on how covetousness threatens their own families. We must trust that God's provision is enough. Let's work to manage wisely what we have until He is pleased to bless us with more.

It is also interesting to note that God gave the promise of provision as He commanded Adam to "be fruitful and multiply." Adam and his wife were commanded to grow their family in the earth, and God promised *in that specific context* to provide for them. This is an important consideration because so many Christians today limit the size of their family because of financial concerns. They refuse to have children because of budget constraints. And yet, God explicitly promised provision to those who are fruitful and multiply. So, it a particularly egregious form of unbelief to claim that we cannot bring children into the world because of economic considerations.

God's promise to provide for the family was specifically related to His command to grow the family. This is *not* to say that Bible commands that every family must have a certain number of children, whether three or twenty-three. But it *is* to say that we should never buy into the lie that we should avoid having children because of a lack of money. That is absolute nonsense. Poverty is the result of sin and poor stewardship (except in the case of providential poverty for the gospel's sake—I Corinthians 4:11, 12; II Corinthians 11:27; Philippians 4:12), not the result of many children. That posterity equals poverty is a persistent superstition of credulous moderns. The number of children is not the point. Every Christian family must prayerfully consider the will of God for their house and plan accordingly. The Bible does not expressly forbid all forms of family planning. But it does condemn an attitude of unbelief that scorns "the heritage of the Lord" (Psalm 127:3) as poor financial planning. There is no better financial planning than to trust in God. And God has promised to provide for those who obey His command to be fruitful and multiply.

Furthermore, we must not refuse to fulfill the commission because we are afraid of financial failure. And this is true both in a spiritual and physical sense. We must not limit the natural family and its growth because of financial concerns. Neither should we allow finances to cripple our evangelistic mission. We must believe, as one minister said, that the will of God is always affordable. God always provides for those who are doing His will in the earth. The quest for dominion is guaranteed full provision by God. Jesus promised to be with those who fulfill the commission all the way to the end of the age (Matthew 28:20).

3

Work and Worship

Genesis 1:31-2:6. "And God saw every thing that he had made, and, behold, it was very good. And the evening and the morning were the sixth day. Thus the heavens and the earth were finished, and all the host of them. And on the seventh day God ended his work which he had made; and he rested on the seventh day from all his work which he had made. And God blessed the seventh day, and sanctified it: because that in it he had rested from all his work which God created and made. These are the generations of the heavens and of the earth when they were created, in the day that the LORD God made the earth and the heavens, and every plant of the field before it was in the earth, and every herb of the field before it grew: for the LORD God had not caused it to rain upon the earth, and there was not a man to till the ground. But there went up a mist from the earth, and watered the whole face of the ground."

After God had commissioned Adam for dominion in the earth, He stepped back and surveyed all He had created. The Lord "saw everything He had made." The Lord took account of all creation and found that "Behold, it was very good." Everything God had made was beneficial. Everything had its purpose and was fruitful in its own way. Everything the Lord made contributed to the larger good of creation. Nothing existed alone and apart from everything else. Prior to this final moment of creation God declared that all He had created each day was "good." But now, the Lord pronounces all "very good."

Surely the Lord invited Adam to "behold" with Him and consider the goodness of creation. Possibly Adam lifted holy hands in worship as he beheld the glory of God revealed in creation. And it was in this moment of beholding that the "evening and the morning were the sixth day" and the seventh day, the day of rest and worship, began. Adam was invited to take account of all that God had done in six days of labor so that he might bring with him into the day of worship a fresh awareness of God's works. "Thus the heavens and the earth were finished, and all the host of them." All of the creatures of heaven and earth, both celestial and terrestrial, stood in their proper place for divine evaluation. God beheld the stars in their courses, the sun, moon and planets beginning their first orbit through the heavens, and the earth spinning perfectly on its axis. God beheld every creature He had made, the fowls of the air, the beasts of the field and the fish of the sea. All were *very* good.

As the Lord beheld all He had made His gaze rested finally upon Adam. The Lord must have smiled as Adam tried with wide-eyed innocence to see all at once what his Creator had made. Adam surely was breathless with wonder as evening began to fall, as the darkness deepened, and the shimmering night sky came into focus. The Lord pointed out the stars to Adam and called each one by name. The glory of the Lord was brilliantly displayed upon the purple canvas of the evening. Adam listened in reverence and awe as "the morning stars sang together, and all the sons of God shouted for joy" at the wondrous world God had made (Job 38:7). "Thus the heavens and the earth were finished, and all the host of them." What a beautiful picture of creation!

So, the work was finished. Creation was done. This is the resounding theme of Scripture: It is finished, it is done (John 19:30; Revelation 16:17; 21:6). God completes whatever He begins. The Lord God established this pattern at the outset of history. God never leaves an unfinished task. We are reminded in Hebrews 12:2 that Jesus is "the author and the finisher of our faith." Paul spoke about God's determination to finish a task: "Being confident of this very thing, that he which hath begun a good work in you will perform it until the day of Jesus Christ" (Philippians 1:6). The Lord set this example for Adam to follow, that man might learn to complete what he started.

Failure to follow through is a besetting sin for fallen man. Indeed, it was Adam's original sin. He did not "endure to the end" (Matthew 10:22). There is no greater lesson for Christian men today. We must be finishers. The building of a Christian family is a good work that must be followed through to completion. We cannot be like the man that failed to count the cost when he set out to build a tower and thus did not have the resources to finish what he had begun (Luke 14:28). This is often the case with men who fail to make the commitment necessary to finish building a godly marriage and family, and they bail out of unwanted relationships at the first opportunity. We must "behold" the fact that God finishes His work and learn to imitate His perfect example.

"And on the seventh day God ended his work which he had made; and he rested on the seventh day from all his work which he had made." The seventh day was the end, the objective, of the six days of labor. And God *rested* on the seventh day. The idea of divine rest includes several shades of meaning. First, it means what it obviously says: God ceased from His labor. He did no more work on the seventh day. The efforts of creation were at an end. Second, the *rest* of God means that He settled down upon His creation much as a king ascends the dais and is seated upon his throne. God was enthroned upon all creation in regal splendor. This is seen again when the Spirit of God rested upon Sinai and upon the mercy seat in the Tabernacle and Temple (Exodus 24:16; Exodus 40:34; I Kings 8:10; Ezekiel 43:7; Revelation 21:3). God finished the Temple of the cosmos to be the dwelling place of the Most High, and on the seventh day, He rested upon the world that He had made. The Lord God ascended up to the heaven of heavens behind the veil of the firmament and was seated upon His throne in the Holy of Holies.

Third, the *rest* of God means that He performed consecrated labor. The idea of rest in Scripture does not always mean inactivity or idleness. When we think of rest, we sometimes think only of stretching out to sleep or relaxing in an easy chair. And certainly that can be the idea of biblical rest. God does want His people to be refreshed with sleep (Psalm 3:5; 4:8; Ecclesiastes 5:12; Jeremiah 31:26; Ezekiel 34:25). But there are other instances where rest includes certain forms of work. Jesus spoke of the priests performing labor in the Temple that is perfectly acceptable on the Sabbath. In the new creation, the people of God "rest from their labors" (Revelation 14:13), and yet, "his servants shall serve Him" and they shall "reign forever and ever" (Revelation 22:3,5). This is consecrated labor, labor that is devoted to God in worship, and it is the ultimate rest.

"And God blessed the seventh day, and sanctified it: because that in it he had rested from all his work which God created and made." God set the seventh day apart from other days and made it the ultimate objective of the six days of labor. The six days of work reach their conclusion in the seventh day of worship. As the Lord spoke to Israel, "Six days shalt thou labor, and do all thy work: But the seventh day is the Sabbath of the LORD thy God: in it thou shalt not do any work, thou, nor thy son, nor thy daughter, thy manservant, nor thy maidservant, nor thy cattle, nor thy stranger that is within thy gates: For in six days the LORD made heaven and earth, the sea, and all that in them is, and rested the seventh day: wherefore the LORD blessed the Sabbath day, and hallowed it" (Exodus 20:9-11).

In the New Covenant, the Sabbath is ultimately fulfilled in Jesus Christ. He *is* the Christian Sabbath. And yet, we do still have a consecrated day of worship, the first day of the week, our Christian Sunday. Some misunderstand the biblical teaching on the Sabbath and conclude that there should be no designated day for worship. They mistakenly hold that, since all days belong to the Lord, there is no particular day that God hallows for worship. That is not the case. The New Testament makes it clear that the Christian church gathered for worship on the first day of the week. Indeed, the church recognized that the Sabbath had been transformed and reborn into a first-day celebration by the resurrection of Jesus Christ, which happened on the first day of the week (Matthew 28:1; Mark 16:2,9; Luke 24:1). John pointedly emphasized that the disciples were gathered on the first day of the week when the resurrected Christ appeared to them (John 20:1,19,26). Pentecost occurred on the first day of the week (Acts 2:1). Paul taught the church to gather on the first day of the week (Acts 20:7; I Corinthians 16:2). The church eventually came to call the first day of the week, "the Lord's day" or the day of the Lord (Revelation 1:10). So, the Christian Sabbath is the first day of the week, the Lord's Day.

Now, of course, we do not observe the Sabbath according to all of the strictures of the law of Moses. The Mosaic Sabbaths were a type and shadow of Christ. We must not reduce the Lord's Day into a day of imitating shadows. Paul taught that Old Covenant Sabbaths were to be seen as fulfilled in Christ, and we should never allow anyone to impose the old Sabbaths on us again (Colossians 2:16,17). The writer of Hebrews confirms the same idea (Hebrews 4). And yet, we must not accept the notion that there is no longer a consecrated day of worship. God rested from His labor and consecrated the Sabbath as a holy day for consecration and celebration. Later, this day was described as a "holy convocation" (Leviticus 23:3). This holy convocation was a weekly gathering to worship, pray and hear the Word. This was the beginning of the weekly Sabbath celebration in the synagogue.

The weekly celebration is carried over into the New Covenant as our weekly Sunday services. God commanded the people to serve Him weekly, and the command is not weakened in the New Testament. For the writer of Hebrews warned us: "Not forsaking the assembling of ourselves together, as the manner of some is; but exhorting one another: and so much the more, as ye see the day approaching" (Hebrews 10:25). The church has a specific time for "assembling" (synagogue-ing) together. Our Sunday worship is our holy convocation where gather to worship, pray and hear the Word. With the rebirth of the Old Covenant world into the New, the seventh-day Sabbath progresses to the eighth day, which is the first day of the new week, the Lord's Day.

On the Lord's Day, we follow the Lord God's example and rest from our labors. We do so in the same ways that He did in the beginning. First, we *rest* by ceasing from our "servile work" (Leviticus 23:7, *et al*). This means that Sunday is a day of rest when we cease from our labor. And we should take advantage of this time to rest and recoup our energy for dominion. However, God is interested in more than just giving us a much-needed, well-deserved break. The Lord commands man to appear before Him once a week to give an account of his work. The Lord's Day is "the Day of the Lord," the day of reckoning and judgment when God hands down blessings and curses.

Second, we *rest* by ascending together with Christ—and *in* Christ—into heavenly places where we are seated together with Him on His throne as He rules the nations (Ephesians 1:3, 19-23;

57

2:6; Colossians 3:1). We are the body of Christ, hidden together in Christ, and we rest with Him upon His throne of dominion. We *abide* with Him, and we *rule* with Him. Christ has ascended up far above all principalities and powers, and once every week we ascend up with Him to declare His rule over all creation. We then return to the "real world" and announce His authority as we work and witness in every nation. Indeed, our work is a part—perhaps the greatest part—of our witness. This is why our work must honor God. We are taking dominion over the earth as we proclaim the Lordship of Christ in everything we do. Hence, sloppy, shoddy work is mockery of Christ's rule over sin and death. Lazy, tardy labor is a reproach to the Christian faith and witness. We are called to *rest* with Christ each Lord's Day so that we may be reminded to serve Him every other day.

Third, we *rest* on the Lord's Day by performing consecrated labor. We serve the Lord in His temple on the Lord's Day as we worship God with reverence and rejoicing. We do not worship the Lord according to the dictates of our own heart, but rather as the Lord has commanded us to worship Him in His Word. We are called to worship as citizens of the realm compelled to do obeisance to our King.

There is no rest outside of true worship. The soul of man came into being when the Spirit of God breathed into Adam the breath of life. Therefore, the human soul cannot rest apart from the rest that Christ promises to those who come to Him (Matthew 11:28). Rest is not mere idleness. Rest involves much activity. But it is activity consecrated to the Lord's service in the sanctuary.

The Lord's service is a holy convocation of consecration and celebration. We sing, pray and hear the Word of God. We fellowship together and enjoy the communion of the saints. As we worship on the Lord's Day we are "compassed about with so great a cloud of witnesses," the faithful of all the ages, gathered together with an "innumerable company of angels" and "the spirits of just men made perfect" (Hebrews 12:1,22,23). We stand with Isaiah and behold the Lord Jesus "sitting upon a throne, high and lifted up, and his train fill[s] the temple" (Isaiah 6:1). There is no rest like this rest.

Every Christian family needs the rest of the Lord's Day. We need to cease from our labors, to ascend with Christ to reign and to perform consecrated labor in the service of the Lord. Each of these is necessary to the spiritual well-being of the family. Furthermore, God has commanded that we do these things. To forsake the assembling of the church and the fellowship of the saved is to forfeit the purpose of God and to condemn our family to a lifetime of restless toil.

Work and Worship

The Sabbath highlights the integral relationship between work and worship. We have been given six days for mundane labor. Then, on the first day of the week, we bring our labor before the Lord for His review and evaluation. We work all week and then bring our labors before the Lord each Sunday. As we stand together before the throne of the Lord, we look back over the past week with thanksgiving and look forward to the coming week with anticipation. The Lord's Day is the culmination of labor past and the expectation of labor to come. The Lord's Day stands as the fulcrum of all our efforts. Accomplishment and hope meet together here to be judged and blessed. This idea is fundamental for dominion. It cannot be overemphasized. There is an intrinsic connection between work and worship. Indeed, work has no motive or meaning apart from worship: we work to serve and glorify God.

When understood in its relation to worship, work is totally transformed. A mere job becomes a vocation, a calling to work for the glory of God. Then, we see our everyday work as being holy unto the Lord. This means, then, that even the secular becomes sacred. Christians often fall into the trap of separating life into a sacred/secular dichotomy. This radical division of life is unbiblical, and it has the effect of shutting God out of everyday life. We cannot separate work and worship into two disparate realms of endeavor. Each flows out of the other. We work as worshippers and we worship as workers. Work linked together with worship finds its motive and meaning in the glory of God.

Work as vocation is an idea that must be reclaimed among Christians. It really does not matter what particular type of work we do. It all must be done in the service of the Lord. Every man is called to work for God in the earth. Thus, every man must consider work as a calling—a vocation—and carefully consider the work that God would have him do in life. We have limited the idea of Christian vocation to only a calling to Christian ministry. But this is clearly unscriptural. Paul explicitly connected a man's relationship with God to his work in the earth. Indeed, he taught that Christian workers are truly serving the Lord as they serve their employers (Ephesians 6:5-9; Colossians 3:22; I Timothy 6:1; Titus 2:9; I Peter 2:18). In another instance, Paul defined a man's faith by his faithful provision for his family (I Timothy 5:8). There is no artificial separation in Scripture between faith and life. The sacred and the secular must be brought together under the lordship of Jesus Christ. Work was given to man by God to exercise dominion and bring glory to the Creator. This is the ultimate meaning of work. Work done apart from this purpose, the purpose of giving glory of God, becomes mere drudgery and sours with *ennui*, the weariness and dissatisfaction with life that results from a loss of interest or sense of excitement. There is no deeper meaning to work, regardless of our vocation, than to serve the Lord in all of life.

Work was not created as punishment for sin. Adam was given work to do before the fall. Work was not imposed as a part of the curse of sin on Adam. The curse made work painful, and now work ends in futility and frustration (Ecclesiastes 1:1-3), as we shall discuss below. But originally, God created man to work. Work is not a temporary misfortune made necessary by the fall of man. Work was man's original purpose, and work shall be man's eternal destiny (Revelation 22:3). The new heaven and new earth will be a place of everlasting, infinitely satisfying labor.

The relationship between work and worship has tremendous ramifications for the form and function of the family. The family that understands its purpose in terms of work and worship shall be blessed of God in every endeavor. God blessed the family to have dominion in every area of life, to rule successfully as God's servants and agents in the earth. God blessed our families, and this blessing is realized in our lives through work and worship. Dominion is accomplished through work and worship. All work is ordained for God's glory whether or not we recognize it. Every man and every family must maintain a balance of work and worship and serve the Lord in both.

Conclusion

Finally, this portion of the text concludes: "These are the generations of the heavens and of the earth when they were created, in the day that the LORD God made the earth and the heavens, and every plant of the field before it was in the earth, and every herb of the field before it grew: for the LORD God had not caused it to rain upon the earth, and there was not a man to till the ground. But there went up a mist from the earth, and watered the whole face of the ground." Consider a few final points before we continue to the next section of scripture.

Created by the Word of God

The story rehearses the foundational fact of biblical history: "The LORD God made the earth and the heavens." Thus, we are reminded of our divine origin and divine destiny. We are not here by some freak cosmic accident. We were created for the purpose and glory of God.

The family that forgets this is destined to live without motive and meaning. God created the worlds (*aeons*) by His Word (Hebrews 11:3). Thus, any part of the world, including the family, that is not founded upon the Word of God and built up by the structure of Christian doctrine is sure to fall into chaos and ruin. The family that is established on principles other than those by which God made the universe is destined to careen as a world out of its orbit and crash into spectacular destruction. It may take several years, or even generations, for the full effect to be observed, but the decline and fall of the disobedient family is inevitable.

Husband: A Man to Till the Ground

The earth was uncultivated and barren before the third day of creation when God spoke the produce and fruit of the land into existence. After God made it fruitful, He placed a man in the earth to "till the ground."

Just so, the family is like a plot of uncultivated ground until a godly man puts his hand to the plow and brings the earth under his dominion. This is why the man is called the "husband." His work in the home is the work of "husbandry." The man is ultimately responsible (with the help of his wife and children) to bring order out of chaos in the fertile field of the home. An unfruitful family is the result of failed husbandry.

Consistent Blessing: A Mist to Water the Ground

In the first days of creation, God caused a mist to come up from the earth and water the ground. The uncertainty of the seasons and varying periods of bounty and barrenness came later. They were the result of the fall of man and the curse of sin upon his efforts. God mitigated the curse somewhat after the Flood and established cyclical seasons with some semblance of predictability (Genesis 8:20-22). But in the original creation the earth was watered every morning with a gentle mist.

The family that lives under the blessing of God sees the curse broken in Christ. Though the fullness of that victory awaits the resurrection, the Christian family should expect consistent and continual blessing upon their home now. We should not live with sporadic and occasional downpours of spiritual blessing. Too often our homes are either awash in a flood of spiritual fervor or parched in the barrenness of carnality and disobedience. We are either doing family devotions three times daily, praying every hour on the hour and tithing everyone's allowance at thirty percent, or we are quarreling, cursing (in a quasi-Christian cussing-lite sort of way), skipping prayers, devotions and even regular church attendance and failing for weeks to tithe and give offerings. It is often either feast or famine at our house. But this is not God's created order. God created us to have the consistent blessing of God's Spirit upon our homes.

4

The Creation of Man

Genesis 2:7-17. "And the LORD God formed man of the dust of the ground, and breathed into his nostrils the breath of life; and man became a living soul. And the LORD God planted a garden eastward in Eden; and there he put the man whom he had formed. And out of the ground made the LORD God to grow every tree that is pleasant to the sight, and good for food; the tree of life also in the midst of the garden, and the tree of knowledge of good and evil.

And a river went out of Eden to water the garden; and from thence it was parted, and became into four heads. The name of the first is Pison: that is it which compasseth the whole land of Havilah, where there is gold; and the gold of that land is good: there is bdellium and the onyx stone. And the name of the second river is Gihon: the same is it that compasseth the whole land of Ethiopia. And the name of the third river is Hiddekel: that is it which goeth toward the east of Assyria. And the fourth river is Euphrates.

And the LORD God took the man, and put him into the Garden of Eden to dress it and to keep it. And the LORD God commanded the man, saying, Of every tree of the garden thou mayest freely eat: But of the tree of the knowledge of good and evil, thou shalt not eat of it: for in the day that thou eatest thereof thou shalt surely die."

The narrative so far provides only a thumbnail sketch of Adam's creation. But now, we are taken back through the story of man's creation with closer attention given to the details. Each of these details has particular relevance to our study on the family.

A Living Soul: Both Physical and Spiritual

"And the LORD God formed man of the dust of the ground, and breathed into his nostrils the breath of life; and man became a living soul." Adam was first formed from dust, and then the Spirit of God breathed life into his hollow form. The soul of man came into existence as a result of the union of spirit and body. Therefore, man was created to experience life both in the physical and spiritual realms.

Adam was perfect when he was formed from dust, but he was a perfect corpse. This is the same sort of life that unbelievers scrape together in their sandbox of life. Every minute detail of their dream world may be perfectly arranged, but their world is dead. Anyone can make castles in the sand, but only God can make dust come alive. It is impossible to experience full, authentic humanity apart from the indwelling Spirit of God. The soul of man was created by the breath of God, and nothing less can satisfy.

This is also true for the family. We may strive from daylight to dark forming the perfect little family, but if our family is not filled with the Spirit of God, then it is dead. It is family without soul. Such families are afflicted with dead marriages, with dead parenting, with dead stewardship, on and on—all because they lack the breath of God in their homes. We need more than the dust of earth; we need the breath of heaven. As Christian families, we must seek the balance between physical and spiritual pursuits. We do not follow the example of Gnostics and ascetics and deny the value of the earthly realm altogether. Adam *was* made from dust. But neither do we follow the example of materialists, and other assorted fools, and deny our need for heaven. We were made to live at once in both realms.

God Planted the Garden Eastward in Eden

After God formed Adam from the dust of the ground and filled him with His Spirit, He "planted a garden eastward in Eden." God created a place for Adam to live and flourish, an environment where he could attain his destiny for dominion. The Garden of Eden was a prototype of what the Lord wanted the entire world to become. God took the fruitful bounty of the earth and placed it in careful rows for efficient cultivation and harvesting. The Lord God planned to teach Adam how to tend the garden so that, as his family grew, he might expand the garden through the entire earth. Thus, the garden was the original model for all creation. The world beyond the garden was a pristine jungle, a place of profuse vegetation and exotic creatures made to be brought under cultivation and domestication. The garden was to be the first test of man's dominion.

Adam's basic needs were met in the garden. He worked and worshipped there. He was fed and sheltered there. Adam rested there and enjoyed the communion of his wife in the garden. The garden would have been a place of security and safety for his children, a center for training and teaching. They would have been prepared there for their future task of dominion. Every day, as Adam learned from God the principles of effective husbandry, he would have taught them to his children. Then, his children would have been prepared to go into the world and enlarge the boundaries of man's dominion.

Most importantly, the garden was the first earthly temple. It was a tabernacle where Adam approached God as king and priest. The garden was a place of work and worship. It was the first "mountain of the Lord" where God descended to meet with man. The four rivers flowed out from the garden to the farthest corners of the world watering the earth with worship as Adam ministered daily before the Lord. This opening "temple-motif" echoes throughout the rest of Scripture. God created the universe to be transformed by work and worship into the eternal dwelling place of God. The entire universe is the temple of the Lord. The garden, as the first temple, was the beginning of this purpose.

This applies marvelously to the Christian family. Just as God created the garden to be the fruitful field of the family, so the household today is a sort of garden. The home is like a vineyard or an orchard where the family can be fruitful to the glory of God. The family, like Eden, is a garden/temple where the man ministers as king and priest and trains his children to exercise dominion in the earth. The home should be a safe place where the family can work and worship and bring glory to God through fruitful dominion. Our family is our "Garden of Eden."

God Placed Man in the Garden

Next, the Lord God "put the man" in the garden. Adam was placed, or positioned, in the garden as its keeper and guardian. The Garden of Eden was Adam's first task and test. It was there that man was given his first realm of stewardship. God set man in a position of authority and gave him responsibility over a vast expanse of land. When Adam was placed, or ordained, as the ruler of the garden, he was formally authorized to rule. Though Adam's authority was immature and untested at first, God would have developed Adam's leadership as He walked with him every day. The servants of God, the angels, would have tutored Adam in their particular areas of expertise and responsibility. Adam would have been trained to accomplish the divine mandate with grace and glory. Adam was God's man, placed in the garden to do the will of God.

Just so, God created the family and placed the man in the family as the head of the home. God gave the woman to be his helpmeet. The family is a divine institution. The husband and wife both occupy divinely ordained "offices": the office of husband and the office of wife. These positions are where God placed us. God ordained marriage and made it "honorable in all" (Hebrews 13:4). The man may be inexperienced and untested in his rule, but he is fully authorized to rule the garden where God placed him. The man must grow in his office and authority as he walks with God every day. His rule will be tested and perfected as he cultivates his garden and expands the boundaries of his dominion.

The man of the house should never be nervous about standing in his place. God placed him there in the first place. Dad has a place, mom has a place and the children have a place, each of them designated by God. Unbelievers often reject the idea of "individual place" (offices) within the family and attempt to blur the distinct roles that God ordained. However, they are struggling futilely against nature. It was God who placed Adam and Eve in the garden. He set them where they belonged, and the world is simply fleeing the inescapable order of creation. We must humbly discover our own place and then boldly stand in it.

God Made Provision for Adam and Eve

When God placed the man and woman in the garden, He gave them adequate provision to live and thrive upon the earth. God is a generous God. He does not place His people where they cannot survive and grow. God graciously supplied every need.

The same is true for the Christian family. God has promised to supply the material needs of the family that serves Him (Philippians 4:19). This promise offers a powerful hope for the family that trusts in God. The family that lives in fear of never having enough will be pulled apart in a selfish pursuit for provision and sustenance. They will become the sort of people that Paul describes as "they that will be rich" (I Timothy 6:9), those who live in a frantic quest for "enough." And yet, if we do not learn to be content with God's faithful provision, we shall never have enough. God was and still is Jehovah-jireh, our provider. We must trust Him to provide, to bless our faithful efforts and godly stewardship.

God Placed the Tree of Life and the Tree of Knowledge

God placed two trees in the center of the garden, the tree of life and the tree of knowledge. The entire garden was arranged around these two trees. It seems that all the other trees radiated out in perfect concentric patterns from the trees in the center. Man was invited to eat freely of the tree of life. The tree of life sustained man's immortality. The breath of life was renewed within them daily as they ate of the tree of life. Man's daily fellowship with God at the tree of life held back the power of sin and death, which is the inevitable result of distance from God. As long as they ate of this tree they would be renewed daily in the life of the Spirit.

Of course, Jesus is our tree of life, and we enjoy the fruit of His Spirit every day as we are renewed in the Holy Ghost. And, just as the tree of life was in the center of the garden, so Christ must be the center of the Christian household. We must make

Him the central purpose for all that we say and do. Jesus cannot be shoved off to the periphery of our life. He must remain the center. When Jesus is the center, then He is visible to all and available to all within our house. Our children are not forced to search high and low for Jesus in our life when He is at the center. He is always as close as the mention of His name. We hold Christ at the center through daily devotions and family prayer. We hold Christ at the center by maintaining a constant spirit of praise and worship in our home. We hold Christ at the center by demonstrating the Spirit of Christ in all that we do. Our kind words become a tree of life to our family (Proverbs 15:14). Just as God placed the tree of life in the center of the garden, so Christ, our eternally-blooming tree of life, must remain in the middle of all that we do.

The other tree in the center of the garden was the tree of the knowledge of good and evil. Many wonder why God placed the tree of the knowledge in the garden. It seems to some that God was just setting man up for a fall. However, the Bible clearly states that God will never tempt a man to do evil (James 1:13). And yet, God does "tempt" men to do right. To be tempted is to be tested, and God's tests men to see if they will walk worthy of His glory. Abraham is a good example of such testing. God's test for Abraham required him to be willing to offer his son as a sacrifice (Genesis 22:1). God's glory cannot be shared by those who have not passed the test of perfect obedience. Even Jesus, the sinless Lamb of God, "learned...obedience through the things which he suffered" (Hebrews 5:8). Everyone who shares in the glory of God shall pass the test of obedience. This was the reason that God placed a forbidden tree in the middle of the garden. Adam had to be tested before he could share in the fullness of the glory of God.

Furthermore, there is no reason to believe that the tree of knowledge of good and evil, the knowledge of right and wrong, was to be forbidden forever. Hebrews 5:14 makes it clear that discernment of right and wrong, of good and evil, is the mark of maturity, the prerogative of the obedient. God simply did not want Adam and Eve to attempt to gain this sort of knowledge before it was time. We do the same with our children. Every parent wants their child to learn right from wrong, but not too soon. We want them to learn right from wrong only when they are mature enough to handle such knowledge safely and properly.

Adam was not ready for the gift of discernment yet, but he would have been after the proper time of probation had occurred and he grew beyond spiritual infancy. When the time was right, God would have given him the responsibility to cultivate and eat of every tree. Adam would have been given the authority as a judge over the earth to discern right from wrong and make proper judgments for his children as they filled the earth and established human civilization.

This lesson applies to the Christian family. Every family will be tested by God. God will prove us to find out if we are obedient under pressure. We cannot share in the glory of God as a faithful household if we are unable to pass the test and remain faithful when tested. We must understand that testing comes from the hand of God to perfect our faith and endurance into Christian maturity. We must pass the test.

God made the River from Eden to Flow through the Garden and to Divide into Four Rivers to Water the Whole Land

God caused the river that flowed through Eden to flow out in four separate streams so that the entire land of Eden could be watered. Apparently, Eden was upon a mountain, and the river flowed through the portion that God had set aside and cultivated to be the prototype of the earth under man's dominion. As it flowed through the garden, it broke into four divergent streams and flowed down the mountain into the valley and plains below. Therefore, the entire land of Eden was blessed by the abundance of the garden.

The river of Eden is a great type of the gospel and how it flows through the garden of the church and divides through our Christian witness into streams that flow to the four corners of the earth. Every nation is watered by the streams of the gospel. We see this same imagery used in Ezekiel when the prophet observed that the water of the holy place flowed out from the temple and became an ocean that filled the entire earth (Ezekiel 47).

This image also applies to the influence of grace within the Christian family. God's grace flows into our family from the headship of a godly husband through the union of man and wife, and then flows out into the earth to water the land through the faithfulness of our children. God intends for our families to wield considerable and distant influence through our children and grandchildren.

God Placed Adam in a Land of Vast Natural Resources

The Garden of Eden was in a land of tremendous natural resources. It is interesting that these resources were placed in the ground long before man knew what to do with them. This affirms the idea mentioned above that man was born physically mature but mentally and spiritually immature. God intended for Adam to grow in grace and knowledge. Seeking knowledge apart from grace caused man's sin, but growing in knowledge was not wrong of itself. God had already made preparation for the time when man would develop human civilization from earth's natural resources and build the world the God had in mind. The heavenly city, the New Jerusalem, is the ultimate example of what man was created to build. At the end of human history, Jesus will succeed where Adam failed. But the point here is that God had already placed the materials necessary for growth and maturity within the ground. Adam and Eve walked each day over a field of tremendous treasure without a true understanding of the riches they possessed. The understanding of their boundless potential could only come as God taught them daily how to develop all their resources. Then, they could bring forth from the earth its wonderful riches and use them to build civilization to the glory of God.

It is difficult to imagine the endless potential that our universe holds. Indeed, modern man cannot even begin to fathom all the wonders hidden within the depths of the sea, much less the wonders of outer space that remain to be explored. Science fiction pales in comparison to reality God has made. Adam was given all of this so that he might rule over creation and be "crowned with glory and honor." Adam forfeited the right to rule, but Christ redeemed this cosmic purpose, and the church will enjoy God's wondrous creation forever when we are glorified in the resurrection.

This is a wonderful lesson for the family. When God forms a godly Christian home and blesses a couple with children, He places within the soil of that family boundless potential for greatness and glory. There is no way to really measure the possibilities that God plants as seeds within our souls. We have been given "all things that pertain to life and godliness" (II Peter 1:3), and these things are just waiting to be drawn out and developed by the Spirit of grace as He teaches us to "live soberly, righteously and godly in this present world" (Titus 2:12). The gold and the silver are there. The precious stones of Christian glory are there, resident within those who are in covenant with Christ. But the gold and the silver, the precious stones and minerals, must be mined out of the sanctified heart by the on-going work of the Holy Spirit. This process of purification and perfection takes time, but the potential is already there.

This is especially true of our children. They are like a priceless piece of ground full of gold, silver and precious stones overflowing with potential for the kingdom of God. God gives us children with eternity latent within them (Ecclesiastes 3:11). Their destiny is simply waiting to be drawn out and perfected by parents wise enough to see the beautiful future God has planned. We must not waste the potential God has given us. It would be a pity to die with the gold and silver lying undiscovered, still hidden beneath our feet. We must not allow sin to rob us, as it did Adam, of the incredible potential God has carefully planted within our world. Our marriage, our children and every generation to come must dig out the precious gifts of God and develop them for the Master's use. Our family is the ground of limitless opportunities for the glory of God.

God Placed Man in the Garden to Dress it and to Keep It

God placed Adam in the garden with particular responsibilities. He was charged to "dress it" and "keep it." To "dress" the garden meant to cultivate the garden, to serve in the garden by plowing and working it. To "keep" the garden meant to protect and maintain the garden. Adam was ordained by God to be the cultivator and protector of the garden. The language of "keeping" the garden is echoed in the commands given to the priests of Israel to serve as keepers of the house of the Lord. Again, we see the idea of Adam serving as king and priest in the garden.

The garden was a place of bounty and beauty, but this excellent state of affairs could not continue without effort on Adam's part. It is a common misunderstanding to think that work was not required before the fall of man. The work of cultivating and protecting the garden was man's task long before sin ever became a factor. Man's work only became a matter of futility and frustration when his work was cursed after the fall. Adam was called to be the steward of the garden in perfect righteousness. The blessings that God had given were to be multiplied by Adam's diligent husbandry.

This is true in the Christian family. The man is placed by God in his particular garden of life, career and family. He must accept God's direction in every area. God plants the garden and directs the man to dress and cultivate it. The man of the house, as husband and father, is charged by God to be the cultivator and provider of the family. God commands the man to keep his garden, to guard, protect and maintain it as the king and priest of the home. The man is called to be the guardian and protector of the family. So, the man has the dual task of serving (dressing) and guarding (keeping) the garden of his home. He must preserve the purity of his house. The home is a sacred place, a place of worship unto the Lord. The man must guard the sanctity of his home. This pattern shall emerge fully later on as we consider the responsibilities of the husband and father to his wife and children. The man must serve and guard, provide and protect.

The Tree of Life and the Tree of Knowledge

After God had placed man in the garden to dress it and keep it, He gave man detailed instructions on the two trees in the midst of the garden. The Lord "commanded the man" concerning the tree of life and the tree of knowledge. The tree of life was freely given while the tree of knowledge was forbidden. The tree of life represents the grace of life, which is freely given to believers. The tree of knowledge represents the law of God, which cannot be fulfilled apart from the power of divine life. When Adam sinned, he attempted to obtain righteousness (God-likeness) through a mere intellectual knowledge of right and wrong. And, while the knowledge of right and wrong is a good thing (Hebrews 5:14), we must never seek knowledge apart from the direction and instruction of God.

As we noted above, it seems evident that God created man to grow in knowledge of right and wrong. However, God intended for this knowledge to be the fruit of Adam's relationship with Him as they walked together in the cool of the day. It is worth noting again that God probably never intended for the tree of knowledge, the tree of law, to be forbidden forever. Surely the Lord God would have personally led Adam and Eve to the tree when they were mature enough to receive it. The knowledge of right and wrong can only truly be understood in the light of fellowship and relationship with God. Otherwise, knowledge takes on a self-centered, anthropocentric orientation. This is exactly where man loses his bearings and plunges headlong into sin and death.

The tree of life was the tree of salvation by grace through faith. The tree of knowledge (apart from relationship with God) was the tree of attempted salvation by works. The same choice exists in our homes today. We make a choice every day whether we shall attempt to live in the grace of God by faith or whether we shall attempt to earn our own righteousness through knowledge of right and wrong gained apart from relationship with God. We cannot save our family by self-righteous works any more than we can save our soul by self-righteous works. We must choose life over law. This problem becomes much clearer later on when we consider Adam's fall.

Obedience

Though Adam was instructed not to eat of the tree of law and judgment between right and wrong, it is wrong to assume that there was no place at all for the law of God prior to man's sin. The Lord God "commanded the man" concerning the tree of knowledge, and God's commands are to be obeyed. And yet, obedience came natural to Adam, for he was filled with the Spirit of God and had not yet been tempted to disobey.

The conflict between obedience and disobedience still rages in the family. The choice to do right must be made every day all day. Obedience is the root of order and disobedience the root of disorder in the home. All problems in the family can be traced to disobedience to the commands of God. We must see our marriage and child-rearing problems as problems of disobedience. Too often, we excuse our behavior problems as personality traits, mood swings, tiredness, etc. But, actually, our behavior problems are disobedience to the law of God and should be recognized and confessed as sin. *This changes everything.* When we begin to view our follies and foibles as sins rather than excusable quirks of fate and fancy, as disobedience to God's law rather than minor unpleasantness that everyone must overlook, then we begin to transform the attitudes and actions in our home from division and anger to peace and harmony. It all begins with recognizing God's authority and His command in our home.

Grace and Law

God commanded man to partake freely of God's gracious provision of life while refusing to seek a form of godliness through intellectual knowledge apart from the grace of God. This applies directly to the family. We must understand the importance of building our families by the grace of God. We cannot build our families by simply learning the ABC's of family-building. And yet, too often this is exactly how we go about it. We spend our time reading self-help manuals and how-to books that analyze the human condition and point to man as the solution for the problem. But this only amplifies and compounds the problem. For the answer to the problems in the family do not lie within man or the ideas of man. The answers to our problems lie within the Word of God. *The just shall live by faith.*

We must first of all recognize our dependence upon God and His grace to see us through. We must hear and accept by faith the promises God has given to our families. Only then can we realize the promises of God by faith in our lives and in our homes. The promises of God cannot be realized by simply learning a formula. We build up our families through a daily, dynamic interaction with the Spirit of God by the grace of God, hearing the promises of God and accepting them by faith. This dynamic interaction of faith occurs as we walk with God everyday, as we learn from Him what our families need and how that need is graciously supplied. This kind of family-building is building by grace through faith. We cannot forsake the tree of life (grace through faith) and eat from the tree of knowledge (self-righteous knowledge apart from relationship with God).

Death

God warned Adam that he would die in the day that he ate of the tree of knowledge. Any time a man seeks righteousness apart from the life of God he begins to die. The same is true of our marriages and families. When we build our families on the sinking sand of humanistic effort, our homes begin the slow, agonizing descent into chaos and death. Disobedience to the law of God produces death in the home, which is manifest in many different ways. This is how a marriage dies. This is how the relationship between parents and children dies. It all begins with either an ignorant or deliberate disobedience to the law of God. We must recognize the importance of careful, faithful obedience.

5

Creation and Marriage

Genesis 2:18-25. "And the LORD God said, It is not good that the man should be alone; I will make him an help meet for him. And out of the ground the LORD God formed every beast of the field, and every fowl of the air; and brought them unto Adam to see what he would call them: and whatsoever Adam called every living creature, that was the name thereof. And Adam gave names to all cattle, and to the fowl of the air, and to every beast of the field; but for Adam there was not found an help meet for him. And the LORD God caused a deep sleep to fall upon Adam, and he slept: and he took one of his ribs, and closed up the flesh instead thereof; And the rib, which the LORD God had taken from man, made he a woman, and brought her unto the man."

After the Lord God placed Adam in the garden and gave him detailed instructions, He declared, "It is not good that the man should be alone." It was still somewhere in the middle of the sixth day, and God was placing the finishing touches on His creation as He prepared for the seventh day of rest. The world was filled with every kind of plant and animal. Each star in its constellation traced its orbit in the sky. To the farthest reaches of outer space, the faintest twinkling star declared its shining testimony of the handiwork of God. The planets had begun their maiden voyage around the sun. The angels were positioned around the earth as principalities and powers, as "ministering spirits sent forth to minister for them who shall be heirs of salvation" (Hebrews 1:14). The sea was filled with every sort of exotic creature. The towering waves of the world's great ocean pounded the sandy shores of earth, and yet, not one drop of water dared venture a hairsbreadth farther than the Master had decreed. Man, created in the image and likeness of God, stared in wide-eyed wonder at the world around him, absorbing its breathtaking beauty in childlike innocence. What a glorious creation! And still, creation, with all its beauty, with all its wonder and perfection, was incomplete. For man had no companion, no bride to stand alongside him as a fitting helper. It was time for Adam to get married.

God created the world with Christ and the church in mind. The idea of marriage was an idea foreordained in Christ and the church. Adam and Eve would be living expressions of an eternal plan, written before the foundation of the world (Ephesians 1:4,5,11). Marriage was created to be the physical, temporal expression of the eternal relationship between God and His people, between Christ and His church. God would be one with a people taken out of His side. "It is not good for man to be alone" was a powerful statement about God's essential nature of self-expression. God is love, and love requires an object. The church was the eternal object of that love (Ephesians 5:25). God determined to reveal Himself and "fulfill" Himself in the creation of a holy people called to be His church. The church was predestined to become "the fullness of Him that filleth all in all" (Ephesians 1:23), the "habitation of God through the Spirit" (Ephesians 2:22). God refused to be alone, so the man formed in His image and likeness could not abide alone.

Adam was the image of God in Christ, and his wife would be the image of God in the church. With all of the abundant beauty of creation, the work was not complete until the angel choir sang the first wedding chorus. Every creature of heaven and earth arose and stood in reverent silence as they witnessed the ultimate goal of all creation—a wedding.

It Is Not Good For Man to Be Alone

The worst thing that can happen to a man is to live for self alone. Of course, both Christ and Paul made an exception for the man or woman who is celibate in service to the Lord (Matthew 19:11,12; I Corinthians 7:7). Those who are celibate in service to the Lord are not truly alone, for they are living to serve others. But, "aloneness" is condemned by God as "not good." To be alone and cut off from God and man is to be cast into hell, into "outer darkness" where there is "weeping and gnashing of teeth" (Matthew 8:12, etc.). Indeed, there is nothing worse about hell than the utter and ultimate isolation suffered there. The rich man in hell was surely surrounded by fellow sufferers, and yet there is no indication that he was aware of anyone there but himself (Luke 16:19-31). To be fully and completely turned in upon one's self is to be sentenced to the harshest punishment a man can endure, the solitary confinement of the soul. And yet, this is the awful fate that selfish people pursue when they foolishly seek to live for self alone. No wonder they are infinitely unhappy. No wonder they are depressed. No wonder they are suicidal. They are rebelling against their own created nature. "It is not good for man to be alone."

Paul tells us that no man lives to himself or dies to himself (Romans 14:7). We are related to God and man essentially by reason of our creation. We cannot escape relationships. Americans have fallen for the myth of radical independence, the idea that man exists for and by himself. This is unnatural nonsense. We come into this world attached to another, and when the cord is cut, the attachments have just begun. Having been reared in a democratic republic, we have learned to prize our "individual liberties" very highly. But the Word of God places a premium on the willing surrender of such liberties and demands that every Christian live for the good of the body, the group, and not for the good of himself alone (Romans 15:2; I Corinthians 8:9; 10:29,33; 14:26; Galatians 5:13; I Peter 2:16, etc.). And the irony of the matter is that living for our own selfish good is never good for us.

The man who is given a wife is a man who must learn that he cannot live for self alone. God wants to teach men the fullness of experience that only comes from a selfless relationship with another. And in the case of marriage, the "another" is truly "other." The woman is different from the man in every way, and lives as a feminine complement to his masculine identity. The godly husband understands that the woman is his opposite, but she is not his mirror image. She is more than just a reverse reflection of him. She is an individual pulled out of his side to become one with him again through the union of a lifelong relationship. The man is fulfilled in the woman and her in him. This is *good*.

It is also "not good for man to be alone" because man needs a helpmeet to assist him in his task of earthly dominion, in work and worship. Not only does the woman fulfill the man, she helps him fulfill his vocation. For as the Preacher said,

> Then I returned, and I saw vanity under the sun. There is one alone, and there is not a second; yea, he hath neither child nor brother: yet is there no end of all his labor; neither is his eye satisfied with riches; neither saith he, For whom do I labor, and bereave my soul of good? This is also vanity, yea, it is a sore travail. Two are better than one; because they have a good reward for their labor. For if they fall, the one will lift up his fellow: but woe to him that is alone when he falleth; for he hath not another to help him up. Again, if two lie together, then they have heat: but how can one be warm alone? And if one prevail against him, two shall withstand him; and a threefold cord is not quickly broken (Ecclesiastes 4:7-12).

God was good to give man a fitting helper. She walks beside him. She is his confidant and best friend. Man was created to exercise dominion through work and worship, to fulfill his divinely ordained vocation. The woman was created to be his helper in fulfilling this task. The purpose of the man is dominion; the purpose of the woman is to help her husband fulfill that purpose. This emphasizes man's headship, but it also clarifies the purpose of the wife: she is created to help her husband in his godly vocation. The wife helps her husband by supporting him in his daily task of work and worship, by managing their household responsibly as he works in the field. She rears his children and teaches them to fear his God. She is his co-worker and fellow laborer in the pursuit of dominion. The woman joins the man in his work, and they labor together to build a godly household to the glory of the Lord. In the kingdom of God, everyone is called to work. However, the man and the woman were not intended to pursue their own vocations apart from one another. Rather, the woman works together with the man to fulfill the purpose of the entire family before God. She works and worships by his side. She is truly a "fitting helper."

It is impossible for a man to know the fullness of loving service without a covenant companion (unless he is gifted for celibate service). A man loves his wife in a way that he loves no one else. The relationship is unique and exclusive. And *it is good!*

Furthermore, the task of dominion requires children. This is another reason why it was not good for man to be alone. The only way that Adam could fill the earth and take dominion over it was to bear and rear children. This required a wife. Children were given to Adam and Eve to propagate and perpetuate their mission through work and worship. The man who abides alone has no posterity to carry on his work. He has no one to preserve his name, his identity and his legacy in the earth. God saw that it was not good for man to be alone, for the task of cultivating the earth for the glory of God could have never been accomplished by one man alone. The task of dominion through work and worship requires families, dad and mom and children. And *it is very good!*

This is why Jesus told His disciples, "It is expedient for you that I go away" (John 16:7). The work of spiritual dominion through evangelism that Jesus came to accomplish never could have been done as long as the ministry of Christ consisted of just one man alone. But when He ascended up on high and gave gifts unto men (Ephesians 4:8), He multiplied Himself through the gift of His Spirit in His bride and children. And now the earth is filled with the gospel of Jesus Christ. This is the power that a man attains when he is willing to lose himself and multiply himself in others. Jesus said that a grain of wheat "abides alone" until it falls into the ground and dies. But when it surrenders its form and dies to itself, then it arises in the power of new life and brings forth an abundant harvest (John 12:24).

What a lesson to self-centered man! If we could only see that God has declared that it is not good for man to be alone and make up our minds to surrender ourselves to a larger cause, to the larger purpose of spiritual dominion through work and worship. Then, we could see the eternal significance of our marriage, our children and our extended family. We could understand that life is not about "me." It is about learning to live for God and others. Then, we could truly see what God meant when He said, "It is not good…."

As we noted above, marriage is a living, visible symbol of the eternal relationship between Christ and the church. The man who lives alone, who lives and dies unto himself, is rebelling against this eternal purpose. The man who spends his time, his effort and his money on selfish pursuits is living a lie. He is denying his own nature and creation. Marriage should remind us daily that we are ultimately destined to dwell together forever with the Lord as His body and bride.

Marriage is God's idea. God created the institution of marriage, and everything God created is good. We must never succumb to the modern temptation to denigrate marriage. "Marriage is honorable in all and the bed undefiled; but whoremongers and adulterers God will judge" (Hebrews 13:4). We must revere marriage. Our attitude toward marriage will determine the kind of marriage we have. We cannot look at those who have failed marriages and conclude that there is an inherent flaw in the concept of marriage and family. The modern attack on the family is based on just such a willful misunderstanding. Because terrible things have happened in some homes and because many fathers have abused their authority and abdicated their responsibility, some have concluded that the problem is woven into the fabric of marriage and family. Thus, the critics of the family have advocated the total abolition of marriage and family. But God declared that it was *not* good for man to be alone, and He created marriage and family and called *that* good. We must not call good what God has declared is *not* good.

Relationship with God Comes First

One final thought here before we move on to the next passage. God did not lead man into a consideration of marriage until after he was properly oriented in his relationship with God and aware of the dire consequences of disobedience. This is fundamental to our approach to marriage and family relationships: a man must develop his relationship with God before he attempts a relationship with a wife and children. Family relationships must be built on the firm foundation of relationship with God.

The man must learn obedience by grace through faith before he considers taking a wife. The failure to do so has produced countless heartaches and broken relationships. Too many young men contemplate marriage much too soon, and some even contemplate marriage as a solution to their ongoing problem with disobedience, which comes in many forms. They seem to believe if they can just get a wife, then suddenly they will become obedient and responsible. Of course, it does not work that way. Learning obedience should precede consideration of marriage. If we wish to build a godly family, then we must develop a relationship with God. Seems simple enough.

Vocation

Just as the wedding bells were set to ring, God interrupted the procession and called Adam to the side. The Lord had a preliminary task to require of him before he was married. Certainly, it was not good for the man to be alone, and help was on the way. Quite possibly, the man felt that he could not wait another moment longer. He just *had* to get married. But before the ceremony could get started, there was work to be done. The man needed a job before he married a wife. In fact, he needed more than just a job; he needed a vocation. God pressed Adam to get a head start on his vocation before bolting down the garden path to embrace his blushing bride. The job comes first.

God stood Adam in his place in the garden and brought to him all of the beasts of the field and fowls of the air that He had made. He marched them past Adam one by one, and they passed under Adam's hand. And the Lord stood by watching "to see what he would call them." This was the initial test of Adam's amazing perception and insight. God brought each animal under Adam's hand to be named and subdued. Adam was being proved in the task of dominion, to see if he could work a job. God was like the concerned father who interviews the potential suitor seeking his daughter's hand in marriage—"What do you do for a living, son?" God made sure Adam could keep a job. Adam was required to demonstrate responsibility before he could be married. Apparently, he did okay, for the wedding carried on as planned.

Naming the animals was a matter of *ability*. Adam was required to recognize the traits and characteristics of each animal and select the name that would convey an enduring identity for it. Adam demonstrated that he could recognize the disparate parts and components of his world and organize them into their categories. Adam was able to take account and reckon correctly. This ability is fundamental to stewardship. Naming the animals was also a matter of *authority*. By placing his hands on each animal and naming it, Adam demonstrated his dominion over the beasts of the field and the fowls of the air. He was bringing them under his oversight. By naming them, he brought them under his rule and placed them in his domain. He was their ruler, for they obtained their identity from him. A man who gives a name to anyone or anything is announcing his dominion.

Adam was required to exercise his *authority* and his *ability* as a man. This was the purpose of requiring faithfulness in vocation prior to marriage, to preview the man's authority and ability as the head of the home. Adam was required to learn stewardship, to learn how to take account of his tasks and manage them properly. He was required to be in command of everything under his dominion. Adam was expected to develop the necessary skills to get the job done. And his task required considerable skill and acumen. But Adam did not shrink from his task and flee responsibility. He did his job, and he did it well. Then, and only then, he was ready to get married.

Adam also viewed his task as a responsibility before God. God brought the animals to him and required him to complete the job. Thus, Adam viewed work as working for God. Adam viewed vocation as a divine calling, even though it involved "secular" work. God trusted Adam to do a good job, and Adam justified God's confidence with perfect competence. God delegated the task and Adam met his obligation willingly and expertly.

This has tremendous bearing upon the way we make plans for marriage. A man must demonstrate faithful stewardship in vocation before he can even consider getting married. Part of the reason that men were required in various cultures to pay a dowry to the father of the bride (which was often kept by the bride as her own inheritance) was to demonstrate financial stability. The father of the bride has every right to require a potential suitor to demonstrate faithful stewardship. God certainly required it of Adam.

A man must be able to "name" everything under his dominion. He should be able to place his hands on the members of his family, bless them and call them by name in order to bring them under his oversight and authority. He should be able to put his hands upon his property and possessions and name everything he owns. One of the purposes of tithing is to force us to give a proper account before God of all He has entrusted to our oversight and stewardship. Diligent tithing requires diligent management of financial resources. The man must bring everything in his life under his authority and responsibility. The man must develop complete command of his resources.

When Adam had finished naming the animals, it was obvious that no helpmeet was found for him among the animals. Adam had demonstrated faithfulness in vocation, but he also proved that work alone was not enough to satisfy his need for a helpmeet. God not only proved Adam's authority and ability as a man, He also proved that a man who is consumed and content with work alone is not complete. It is not enough to work; a man's work must go on and grow in the earth. The fullness of human relationship cannot be found in work alone. It is amazing how many men try to find fulfillment in work alone. Adam proved that it cannot be done.

Every Christian man must avoid this trap. Those who lose themselves in their work lose sight of the bigger picture. They tend to forget their origin and destiny. The project becomes greater than the purpose. We must see the bigger picture, and marriage and family help keep it all in proper perspective. Work must have meaning beyond itself.

The Marriage of Man and Woman

After work was over, God put Adam to sleep and took a rib out of him and made him a fitting helper. This process of providing a wife for Adam offers many lessons for the family.

God Did the Operation

Possibly, the last thing Adam remembered as he dozed off was God's promise of a wife. He had put in a day of hard work, and nothing is better after work than a refreshing nap. Then, Adam was sleeping like a baby, at rest in the hand of God, and God was performing surgery. The lesson to be learned here is that Adam was not in control of choosing his wife. God was in control. Adam was not given the option of selecting the girl he wanted from a line-up of attractive women. God gave him a "fitting helper" while he was asleep.

This is the attitude that we must take when we approach marriage. We must recognize that marriage is a spiritual matter, and that we cannot trust in the flesh and its desires to guide our decision in choosing a wife. We cannot trust the deceitful dictates of our own heart. We must be guided by the direction of the Word and Spirit, considering all options in light of godly counsel and biblical purpose. We must place our trust in God and rest in His sovereign grace. God knows the perfect helpmeet for every man. We must allow God to be the one who puts us together with our mate. Rest easy, though. The woman that God chooses for a man will never be an unattractive disappointment. She will be the most beautiful woman in the world. The love of God makes it so. We must go to sleep.

This may sound much too pragmatic for some, but it is the only basis for a healthy marriage. Too many marriages are built on an exaggerated idea of romance as the basis for relationship. Certainly romance is important. God wants couples to enjoy one another and be affectionate. Christian men are taught to be "ravished" with the love of their wife (Proverbs 5:19). But never should this "romantic ideal" replace a practical and wise emphasis on finding the will of God for our life. Romance is the fruit that grows on the tree of a good relationship, and a good relationship is rooted in a mutual submission to the will of God. God knows the mate we need, and He will direct our steps if we will be faithful to Him. We must trust in God.

God Took the Rib Out of Man

The woman that God made for man was exactly the woman that man needed, for she came out of him. She matched him perfectly. The Lord could have created the woman from the dust as He did man, but He chose to take her out of her husband so the man and woman could see the essential relation between the husband and wife. They are truly one flesh before God.

Seeing God as the sovereign matchmaker affects the attitude of both the man and woman. The man must not complain about the woman he has married, for she is the woman that God pulled out of his side. He was given the helper that was fitting. A man may rebel against this idea and complain that he did not realize what he was getting, but God knew all along, and He placed the perfect bride in his life. God knows what every person needs, and He will give grace to discover the purpose in the choice. The woman must recognize that God drew her out of the man (her husband) by His own sovereign hand. She must see the hand of God in the choice of her mate. God drew her out of the man to whom she is married, and she must submit to God's sovereign choice and trust God to show her how to be a godly helpmeet. Thus, her dependence and confidence is ultimately in God. The woman who sees her marriage as her own free decision or as the whim of fate will have no assurance before God concerning the salvation and destiny of her home. But the woman who trusts God and His choice for her has the assurance that God will work everything together for her good. Even when the situation at home seems hopeless, the woman who trusts in God is the one who truly has hope. God works out His purpose in us, even in the free choices that we make in life. We must trust God that our situation is firmly in His control. Accepting God's sovereign will for our marriage is the first step toward turning defeat into victory.

This may seem like a radical idea to some, but this is actually the basis of the most successful and blessed marriage possible. When a man and a woman harbor doubts about whether or not their mate is their "right rib," they are guaranteed resentment and contention. We begin to view our spouse differently when we accept that God knows what is best and gives us what we need rather than what we want. Accept the will of God and be thankful.

God Brought the Woman to the Man

When Adam awakened, God brought his bride to him. This is the way godly marriages should occur. We often rely on every means of getting a wife other than the right one: waiting on God. We must trust that God will bring the right woman at the right time in our life. Until then, the man should be concentrating on vocation. When the godly man finds his bride, he will discover to his surprise that God was at work while he was sleeping.

A godly man should look for God's direction in choosing a mate by conferring with his parents, grandparents, other family advisors and Christian leaders in his life. Once a Christian man is ready for marriage—he has proved himself in vocation and he has "slept" for awhile to practice the discipline of waiting on God and refusing to marry on impulse—then, he will trust the Lord to let him meet the young woman God would bring to him. Once he is introduced to a young woman he thinks may be a suitable mate, he should confer with his counselors and get their input on the matter. If they agree with his assessment that she very well could be a "fitting helper," then he should approach her father and request the authority to court the daughter. The young man, then, does so with her father's approval and under his watchful eye.

God brings a woman to a man through the proper channels of family authority. The young man should expect the hand of God to be extended in the hand of the father who gives the hand of his daughter in marriage. Here is another radical concept: the Bible plainly teaches that the father of the daughter is the one who confers the authority upon the man to receive the daughter in marriage. The young man should understand that the Lord God seeks to bring him a wife under the authority of her father (or her guardian) so that the authority of the kingdom may flow into the newly established household. God gave Eve to Adam just as the father now gives the daughter to her new husband. "Who giveth this woman to be married to this man?" we still say in our wedding ceremonies. Sadly, we mean very little by the phrase these days. That must change. We must recover the idea of the father's authority and responsibility to "authorize" the young man to marry the daughter. This does not mean that we should practice arranged marriages, *per se*. Rather, we should recognize the proper flow of authority and submit to it. This is how God brings a man his wife.

6

Creation and Family

Genesis 2:23-25. "And Adam said, This is now bone of my bones, and flesh of my flesh: she shall be called Woman, because she was taken out of Man. Therefore shall a man leave his father and his mother, and shall cleave unto his wife: and they shall be one flesh. And they were both naked, the man and his wife, and were not ashamed."

After Adam awoke and God brought him his new bride, Adam recognized what God had done and accepted that the woman should become one with him. He called her "bone of my bones and flesh of my flesh." Adam demonstrated the same authority and ability that he had already shown in his vocation as he named his wife. He called her "*Isha*" because she was taken out of man. She came under his authority when he named her. The same is still true today when a woman takes the name of her husband: she is coming under his authority. This is why women who resist submission to their husband often refuse to accept his name. They are instinctively, even if only sub-consciously, aware of the spiritual principle involved.

For This Cause

After Adam named his wife, he was so moved by the wonder of the moment that he broke out into a grand soliloquy about marriages to follow. Indeed, his words were quoted later by Jesus and Paul and equated with prophetic utterance (Matthew 19:5; Ephesians 5:31). Adam was speaking the mind of God about how a man should be married. He spoke about the new relationship that is established when a man goes out from the house of his father and mother to establish a new household with his new bride. Adam says that the man will go out from his father's house "therefore"—*because* he is made one with his wife. This oneness of relationship is unique, and it requires "forsaking all others," as the wedding vows say. This is not to say that the relationship with parents is broken, but rather it is transformed into something entirely new. The child moves from "obey your father and mother" to "honor your father and mother." The parental relationship is now one of counsel rather than command. It is now up to the son to lead his own house in the fear of God.

When a man goes out from his father and mother's house, he should go out with his parents' blessing and approval, for they are authorizing him to exercise authority in his new household. Indeed, he is being sent out, or commissioned, to marry and build a house. When the man leaves his father and mother and cleaves to his wife, he is establishing a new government before God. He is enlarging the jurisdiction of the kingdom of God in the earth. This is one way that the kingdom of God grows in the earth as Christian parents send out their sons to establish new households of faith.

The New Testament rendering of Adam's statement says that a man should leave his father and mother "for this cause" (Matthew 19:5; Ephesians 5:31). This sheds even further light on the Lord's statement, "It is not good for man to be alone." When a man goes out of his father and mother's house, he should go out for the cause of building a godly family. Of course, there is the exception of the man who is called to singleness and is sent out of his father's house to serve the Lord continually "without distraction" (I Corinthians 7:35). However, generally, the man should leave home for the cause of marriage.

This means that the common practice of young men leaving home to seek their fame and fortune, to find their own way in the world, is one of the worst possible things that can happen to a young man. "It is not good for a man to be alone," as we have emphasized repeatedly. The man who goes out to be his own man will find it very difficult to surrender his selfish "freedom" when he does settle down. The responsibilities of marriage and family will be bitterly oppressive to his wild and wayward heart. He will be forced to root out an ingrowing selfishness in order to ever find fulfillment in marriage. The young man who goes out of his father's house for any cause other than this cause could very well become "a rebel without a cause." A man needs a purpose beyond himself. The man who fails to understand this will seek his own way in everything, including marriage when he does settle down. And the sort of marriage that he will seek is the sort of marriage that often ends in divorce.

We must repudiate the myth of independence. The world encourages their young men and women to seek their own ways, to be his own man or her own woman. But this is simply setting them up for tremendous frustration in the future. For no one lives unto himself (Romans 14:7). We are all connected to others. Paul speaks thus of the interdependence of man and woman: "For man was not made from woman, but woman from man. Neither was man created for woman, but woman for man. That is why a wife ought to have a symbol of authority on her head, because of the angels. Nevertheless, in the Lord woman is not independent of man nor man of woman; for as woman was made from man, so man is now born of woman. And all things are from God" (I Corinthians 11:8-12 ESV). God never intended for any man or woman to live in selfish independence. We could just as easily say, "It is not good for man to be *independent.*"

When a man or woman goes out into the world to live the independent life, he or she is reinforcing his or her immaturity. Maturity grows out of selfishness into selfless service. But when we go out into the world to serve self, then we are making it even more difficult to adjust to the sacrifice that marriage and parenting relationships demand. This is why so many young people have so much difficulty adjusting to married life. They have lived for themselves too long. Adam had it right: we should go out "therefore." Why for? For the purpose of marriage and family. Go out with this purpose from the start, and you will be much better prepared for the life ahead.

The Higher Cause

Furthermore, not only should marriage be "the cause" of a young man's departure from home, but the young man must understand as he leaves what the ultimate cause of marriage really is. He must understand why God created marriage in the first place. God made man and woman to become one flesh for the purpose of filling the earth with believers for godly dominion. God created marriage to bring the earth under man's dominion. This is the overarching purpose for marriage.

It is also evident from the later witness of Scripture that God created marriage to populate the new heaven and earth. God made man so He could glorify him and indwell him forever. God created the human race to be the living stones of His eternal habitation, the temple of God through the Spirit. This shall be realized fully after the resurrection. Therefore, temporal marriage participates in this eternal purpose. After the resurrection, we shall no longer marry and be given in marriage. The propagation of the human race will be finished. Thus, we are populating the new heaven and earth now, as every soul who stands on the celestial shore will have passed through the womb of an earthly mother. This is the grand cause of marriage. Paul speaks of this heavenly purpose for earthly marriage when he speaks about the mystery of marriage in Ephesians 5. He teaches that earthly marriage is a manifestation of the relationship between Christ and the church. And those who make up the bride of Christ are people, people born to a man and woman joined together in marriage. Marriage has a purpose far beyond personal gratification. Marriage is the plan of God to build a holy nation of people redeemed by the blood of Jesus Christ.

The Lord God tells us that he married the first couple "that He might seek a godly seed" (Malachi 2:15). This is the higher cause of marriage. The purpose of the Lord is godly children reared in the fear of the Lord. And yet, so few seem to understand today the true cause of marriage. Marriage is not for selfish gratification. It is not to find someone to meet our needs and satisfy us emotionally and physically. Marriage is for the glory of God. This understanding radically changes the way young couples approach the wedding altar.

Jesus addressed a group of men who failed to see the higher cause of marriage (Matthew 19). They asked the Lord if they could divorce their wife "for every cause." Jesus responded that they did not understand that marriage was "for this cause" from the very beginning. Marriage was made for a higher cause than the whim and desire of man. The Pharisees revealed a conflict of causes: the cause of God revealed in marriage and the cause of selfish man revealed in divorce. When a man goes out from his father and mother and marries for the correct cause, then there is no question of divorcing "for every cause." The cause of marriage is greater than the cause of divorce. The grounds for staying together are firmer than the grounds for splitting up. Men who live and die unto themselves are men who murder relationships and "cover violence with a garment" (Malachi 2:16). One must leave his father and mother and cleave to his wife for the proper cause.

One Flesh

Then Adam declared that the man and woman would become "one flesh," or one body. The married couple is made one body in three ways: (1) legal oneness; (2) sexual oneness, and (3) reproductive oneness.

Legal oneness is corporate, covenantal oneness. This legal oneness is like a corporation, a legal entity that is generally formed by the agreement and union of more than one party. Adam recognized that he and his wife were one legal entity before God with man as the head. The family becomes a team with the man as captain. This is the idea of headship we spoke about earlier. Adam recognized the need for a man to sever ties (in a jurisdictional sense) with his parents and form a new household beginning with him and his new bride. The household is a separate, legal entity before God. It is a corporation, a government, with sovereign authority and jurisdiction under God. This means that the legal oneness of marriage unites the man and woman into a joint effort. They cannot live for self alone. They must live for the good of the house, the one body joined together in love.

Sexual oneness, of course, refers to the intimate relationship between man and woman that God has given for loving pleasure. Paul makes it clear in I Corinthians 7 that the relationship of sexual love has tremendous spiritual and physical value. Christians should never shrink blushing and giggling into the corner when sexual relationship is mentioned. We are sexual creatures, and God made us so. There is no shame in the oneness of sexual union between a man and woman in honorable covenant. "Marriage is honorable in all and the bed undefiled; but whoremongers and adulterers God will judge" (Hebrews 13:4).

Sexual union produces oneness. It is the sacrament of marriage itself. The man and the woman are brought together in a very real way when they make love in holiness. When a couple abstains from love, or when they make love in a superficial and selfish way, their marriage is pulled apart (I Corinthians 7:1-6). The physical union is an emblem of the spiritual union that occurs in marriage. God has joined the man and woman together, and He has given an ongoing expression of this union in sexual love. Sexual union must never be reduced to a merely physical act. Those who try to do so simply frustrate their own spiritual nature. Hence, fornicators are never satisfied. They are satiated for a moment, and then, begin lusting again for another, more exciting encounter.

Reproductive oneness is the oneness that is realized in our children. Our children are us. They are one person from two. They share in the nature of both father and mother. No child is ever influenced by just one parent, even if one parent is absent. The absent parent still influences whether from a distance or from the grave. The child cannot deny his own nature. He may overcome his nature, if negative, or develop it, if positive, but he cannot deny the nature given to him by his parents.

In the process of childrearing, nurture is added to nature, which, again, is a product of two becoming one in the life of a child. Parents must recognize that the life of their child is determined by the nature and the nurture that they give him. We are determining the destiny of a soul when we bring a child into the world. Everything he becomes is affected by who we are and how we rear him. In reproductive oneness, children become the final product of our legal and sexual oneness. Our household authority and marital love shapes who they are and what they become. They can be better or worse, depending on the investment we make in them. We exert our dual influence for good or evil. By the grace of God, we "twain shall become one flesh" in godly children.

Covenant and Compatibility

The married couple is one flesh in a covenantal relationship. The married couple is "what therefore God has joined together" (Matthew 19:6). The *covenant* is the basis for their oneness and unity before God. This is an important concept that must not be overlooked. Too many couples have an "eharmony.com" attitude toward their union. They mistakenly think that *compatibility* is the basis for marital unity. They fail to see that harmony in marriage flows out of the grace that God gives when He joins a couple together. It is *God* that joins a couple together. They are made one by the grace of God. If they cheerfully submit themselves to the Word of God, then the blessings of unity and harmony will flow out of the covenant they made. If they refuse to submit to the Word of God, then the curses of division and strife shall flow out of the covenant they made, for they are rebelling against the covenant and the God who honored it.

The answer to marital division does not lie in personality assessment and psychological self-analysis. The answer lies in looking to the God of the covenant and the Word He has given to govern the covenant. Those who are divided in their marriage often wonder, "Are we really meant for each other? Are we really compatible?" But they are asking the wrong question. The question they should be asking is, "Are we *married*? Did we enter into covenant before God and did He make us one?" For if they are married—and they obviously are—then *God* has joined them together, and if God has joined them together, then they are right for each other on the basis of that union alone. It is because of the covenant that they are one. Marital union flows out of the grace promised in the covenant. God honors marriage. God blesses those who make a covenant together, and God curses those who live faithless to their covenant: "Whoremongers and adulterers God will judge" (Hebrews 13:4). Compatibility flows out of covenant. God makes us compatible as He joins us together. No two people are perfectly compatible, personality profiles notwithstanding. God makes us compatible over time as we submit to one another in love. Marriage requires both the man and woman to surrender individual self and become one in holy matrimony. And this oneness flows out of the *fact* that they are one. God has made it so.

Those who seek to find unity on the basis of personality arrogantly assume that they are fine just like they are and need no change whatsoever. They are simply looking for someone to complement who they are. They seek someone to serve their personality type, to bow before their throne and humbly worship.

Compatibility driven match-ups are sought by those who are looking for someone to meet their needs. This assumes that marriage is made for selfish benefit, and this is generally the root of the problem with troubled marriages. However, if the man and woman both recognize that marriage serves a higher purpose than the cheap gratification of self, then they can look toward the purpose of God revealed in the marriage covenant and submit to it.

If we simply find someone who is compatible with us, then we have not found the one we need. Now, certainly we should seek for those with whom we have much in common. "Can two walk together except they be agreed?" (Amos 3:3). But if all we find is compatibility, then we can never grow. God uses marriage to challenge us to grow out of self, out of individual existence into the corporate relationship of selfless service. Remember, "It is not good for man to be alone." The man and woman should be seeking to lose their own identity in the new identity of the marriage and family. Thus, compatibility flows out of covenant, out of a steady commitment to oneness, not the other way around.

God made man and wife one, and on the basis of this union, the man and woman should be confident in the fact of their ability to overcome all conflict and division. It has nothing to do with compatibility. If God has joined you together, then the grace for compatibility is in the spiritual oneness God has made. God promised to join the married together. Those who claim that they cannot be one are lying against God. God clearly and publicly made them one in their marriage vows. They are one because God said so. Now they simply must accept it and live like it.

This sort of oneness is by grace through faith. God gives the gift of unity in covenant, and we appropriate it by faith. As with everything else in the Christian walk, we must reckon it so by faith. Our faith is in the work that God did when we were married. If we are divided, then it is because we are rebelling against the promise that God has made. There is no division that cannot be corrected if both man and wife would be willing to look toward the promise God made them in their marriage covenant—to join them together as one—and humbly submit themselves to the chastening and correction of the Word.

Those who divorce are betraying their covenant. The basis for oneness and unity is covenant, and God will judge those who break it. It is a question of faith: Do we believe what God has said and done in marriage? We must trust that God has made us one. And this is not merely a matter of pragmatism. It is a matter of faith in the covenantal union that God made when He joined a couple together in marriage. The power to be one is in the fact of marriage, for God honors marriage and joins two in one.

Naked and Unashamed

Finally, the Bible says that Adam and Eve were naked and unashamed. Just so, the godly marriage begins with perfect trust and complete innocence. It begins with openness without shame. There should be nothing hidden or concealed between a man and his wife. The physical condition of nakedness that is necessary to godly union typifies the perfect transparency of spirit that should unite the man and the woman together. When sin comes into a home, the first instinct of the man and woman is to hide from one another, to withdraw into subterfuge and dishonesty. Sin's first casualty is the innocence of a godly union.

Conclusion

Too often the basics are overlooked. A godly marriage must be built upon submitting to the sovereign hand of God and accepting His will in the woman given; recognizing the intrinsic, organic unity of the one body that God joins in marriage; and establishing the marriage upon the authority and submission of the husband and wife. Then, the marriage must be established upon the new orientation of relationships with regard to parents and other former relationships. And finally, the man and the woman must be open and naked with each other and completely unashamed.

The order of relationship established in the creation of the family is very important, for it shows how a successful family is established. A man is established first of all in his personal relationship with God; second, he learns to balance the spiritual/physical realms; third, he accepts the responsibility of work and worship; and fourth, he learns how to apply the law of God in the arena of life by grace through faith. Only when these

97

things are established is the man ready to consider a husband/wife relationship. Then he must establish relationship with her, with others (particularly family and friends he has forsaken for her) and finally with his children and grandchildren.

We must consider the pattern of the family as God created it if we wish to recover what has been lost through sin and rebuild the Christian family according to the purpose for which it was created. But we can also avoid the pitfalls of sin in the family if we consider the fall of the family and how we came to be where we are today. Let's continue on with the narrative of Adam's fall and see how the human family fell with him.

PART II

The Fall of the Family

7

The Scheme of the Serpent

Genesis 3:1-5. *"Now the serpent was more subtle than any beast of the field which the LORD God had made. And he said unto the woman, Yea, hath God said, Ye shall not eat of every tree of the garden? And the woman said unto the serpent, We may eat of the fruit of the trees of the garden: But of the fruit of the tree which is in the midst of the garden, God hath said, Ye shall not eat of it, neither shall ye touch it, lest ye die. And the serpent said unto the woman, Ye shall not surely die: For God doth know that in the day ye eat thereof, then your eyes shall be opened, and ye shall be as gods, knowing good and evil."*

The fall of the family began when the serpent entered the garden. It seems that the serpent was an actual snake that Satan possessed for the purposes of temptation. How all of that worked is beyond explanation, but it seems unavoidable that the serpent was an actual animal, for it was counted among "the beasts of the field" (v. 1). And yet, the serpent was clearly more than just an animal, for Scripture describes Satan as "that old serpent called the devil and Satan, which deceiveth the whole world" (Revelation 12:9). So, it shall be our working assumption that the serpent was an animal used by the devil.

The introduction of the serpent brings the introduction of numerous problems for the first family. The first problem is that the serpent was a "beast of the field." The field was the land outside the garden where the animals roamed free, the open wilderness where man had not yet imposed cultivation and dominion. Thus, the serpent, as a beast of the field, had no business in the garden. He belonged on the outside with the other beasts of the field. However, the woman did not seem to be surprised by his presence in the garden. Perhaps the serpent was a frequent guest, which could have been the beginning of the problem.

Apparently, God made the serpent capable of speech and possessing wisdom far beyond the capacity of the other beasts, for, once again, the woman seems completely at ease with the intellectual capacity of the serpent. Of course, we do not know if the beasts of the field were created as dumb beasts, or if they were created able to speak and lost the capacity for speech at the fall of man. We know that God once "opened the mouth" of a donkey, and he spoke to Balaam (Numbers 22:28). But whether or not beasts could speak before the fall is unknown. Regardless, the problems in the family all began when the woman started visiting with a beast that should have been out in the field.

Satan is always looking out for some way to gain entrance into our home. He may enter subtly through the doorway of entertainment, through television, movies, books, internet, etc. Or he may insinuate himself into our homes through unhealthy friendships and associations. He may quietly introduce us to those who do not share our values or convictions. Any one of these things could become a serpent in the garden of our life. If we permit such satanic intrusions into our home, we will ultimately be deceived by them. Anything that questions the Word of God is a serpent that must be seized by the tail and hurled back out into the field where it belongs—figuratively speaking, of course. We constantly must be alert for serpents whatever their form.

It was Adam's responsibility to keep the serpent out of the garden. Adam was given authority over all the beasts of the field. Therefore, sin made its inroads into the family when the man permitted things in the house that did not belong there. It is the man's job to hunt down serpents and cast them out. What kind of man would leave the task of snake-killing to his wife or children? The man must accept personal responsibility and drive out the serpent.

Too often modern Christian men imitate Adam and stand by watching as the devil does his dirty work in the home. Sometimes, men are shamed into reluctant silence by the pleading demands of their family. Thus, they end up tolerating activity and entertainment that is obviously harmful. On the other hand, sometimes it is the man who has a selfish lust for pleasure. This sort of man brushes aside the concerns of the wife, and even the children, to indulge his sin. Regardless of who let the devil in, however, it is the man's responsibility to cast the serpent right back out, right now.

Approaching the Woman

When the serpent set out to deceive and destroy the first family, he fixed his narrowed gaze upon the woman. The devil understood that Eve was vulnerable to his wiles. Satan recognized that God created the man to be the leader of the home. Thus, the quickest way to destroy the foundation of the home was to undermine the authority of the husband by isolating the woman and deceiving her. Paul confirmed this when he taught that the woman is susceptible to deception when she steps out from the covering of headship and authority (I Timothy 2:14).

Two things went bad wrong when Satan persuaded the woman to visit with him for awhile: First of all, the woman conversed with the serpent without her husband's oversight. Second, the man did not assume and assert his proper role of leadership when the conversation began. These are the same two things that still go bad wrong in the Christian family today.

Paul made it clear that the man must be the teacher and spiritual leader in the home (I Corinthians 14:35). The woman should have immediately turned to her husband and asked him what he thought about the serpent's question. And Adam should have immediately intervened when the serpent began to speak to his wife. The man apparently was standing nearby while the conversation was going on (the woman gave the fruit to the man "with her" – v. 6), but he remained silent while the serpent brazenly deceived his wife. Two things were wrong with this picture: the woman was not asking, and the man was not teaching.

Paul addressed this problem in the church at Corinth (I Corinthians 14:35). The wives were bringing confusion into the services by interrupting while the prophets were speaking and asking questions of the men as they spoke. Paul rebuked this practice and commanded the women to remain silent in such settings and to ask questions of their husbands at home. The idea that every man must teach his wife at home is a principle largely lost among Christian men today. And yet it is still vital to the health of the family—and the church. Most men abdicate their responsibility to teach to the "professional" ministry of the church. This must be corrected. The man cannot expect preachers and Sunday school teachers to do what he is called to do.

We must reclaim the home as the center of our religion. The man must come before the Lord each Lord's Day as the head of his household, and the ministers of the church teach him and his family. Then, the man of the house reinforces the teaching of the church to his wife and children at home (II Timothy 2:2), and the wife reinforces the teaching of the father to the children with daily instruction. This is how the home is made the center of Christian instruction once again, and serpents are uncovered and cast out.

Godly pastors recognize the need for men to lead at home and vigorously promote such leadership. However, false teachers are afraid of the strong leadership of faithful husbands and seek to undermine it at every turn. False teachers are always intimidated by men of discernment who are cautious in the teaching they receive and share with their families (as they are instructed by God to be – Luke 12:57; Acts 17:11; Romans 16:19; I Corinthians 14:29; I Thessalonians 5:21; I John 4:1; Revelation 2:2). However, a true man of God recognizes the need for the man of the house to hear the Word of the Lord and lead his entire household into the faith. The gospel is preached to whole houses beginning with the man (Acts 11:14; 16:31, *et al.*). One of the first signs of a serpent is the subtle, or even blatant, attempt to sidestep the man and deceive the woman. Paul spoke about this sort of "creepy" preacher in II Timothy 3:6. He described their craven attempt to sneak around the husband's authority and exploit the weakness and emotional nature of the woman. In Titus 1:11, Paul lamented that false teachers "subvert whole households." The word "subvert" means "to overthrow," or literally, "to turn upside down." This is what false teachers do when they go around the man to exploit and deceive the woman.

We must be careful to promote the leadership of men in the home. Furthermore, we must take this approach even when evangelizing sinners. We must seek to evangelize households. We must imitate the example of Jesus when He witnessed to the woman at the well (John 4). He spoke with her for just a moment before asking her about her husband. Jesus and the apostles always followed this pattern of "household evangelism" where the conversion of the entire house, beginning with the father, was the goal. We should do the same.

Men as Leaders in the Home

The proper role of leadership for the husband cannot be overemphasized. Until Christian men reclaim their rightful role as the spiritual leaders of the home, the Christian family will be vulnerable to spiritual assault as Satan exploits and deceives the woman at the tree of knowledge. The rise of feminism and so-called "women's liberation" in our country is an indication of women who refuse to ask and men who fail to teach. The woman must submit to her husband's spiritual leadership, and the man must exercise that spiritual leadership.

The family is the basic unit of Christian instruction. Indeed, the elders of the church who govern the church and teach the congregation and the deacons who serve the presbytery must be men who have demonstrated their ability to lead their own families (I Timothy 3:4,5,12). We have mistakenly relocated Christian discipleship's center of gravity to the congregation when it should be centered in the home. The instruction that occurs at church is designed to spring out of the family as the church is taught by godly fathers and husbands who are ordained as elders of the church. The leaders of the church speak as men teaching men, as fathers teaching fathers, as husbands teaching husbands, and the men who are taught are expected to teach their own families at home.

We have already noted this pattern in Acts where the early church evangelized and discipled Jerusalem "from house to house"—or, from household to household. The family is the center of Christian instruction. Of course, this does not diminish the importance of the local Christian congregation. Indeed, it heightens it. For the local church is an assembly of faithful families, a congregation of Christian households. And yet, Paul made it clear that home and the church cannot be separated. We must reclaim this biblical idea.

In the instances where a woman is the head of the home due to divorce, desertion or death, she must submit herself to an older woman who is subject to her own husband and given the task of teaching the younger women (Titus 2:4). Thus, when questions arise, the widow or single mother can appeal to the elder sister who can in turn ask her husband for guidance and counsel. If her husband needs further instruction, he may appeal to the elders of the church for instruction. When we follow this pattern, there is no danger of any man or woman trespassing beyond the bounds of their household authority.

Family instruction was central under the law of Moses. God commanded the people to instruct their children in the law of God every day all day long:

> Now these are the commandments, the statutes, and the judgments, which the LORD your God commanded to teach you, that ye might do them in the land whither ye go to possess it: That thou mightest fear the LORD thy God, to keep all his statutes and his commandments, which I command thee, thou, and thy son, and thy son's son, all the days of thy life; and that thy days may be prolonged.
>
> Hear therefore, O Israel, and observe to do it; that it may be well with thee, and that ye may increase mightily, as the LORD God of thy fathers hath promised thee, in the land that floweth with milk and honey.
>
> Hear, O Israel: The LORD our God is one LORD: And thou shalt love the LORD thy God with all thine heart, and with all thy soul, and with all thy might.
>
> And these words, which I command thee this day, shall be in thine heart: And thou shalt teach them diligently unto thy children, and shalt talk of them when thou sittest in thine house, and when thou walkest by the way, and when thou liest down, and when thou risest up.
>
> And thou shalt bind them for a sign upon thine hand, and they shall be as frontlets between thine eyes. And thou shalt write them upon the posts of thy house, and on thy gates (Deuteronomy 6:1-9).

God commanded Israel to teach their children, and He promised that their faithful instruction would be the basis of their dominion in the land. God's method has not changed. We are still instructed to teach our children at home every day. Jesus referred to this passage in Deuteronomy as the first and greatest commandment of all (Matthew 22:34-40; Mark 12:28-34). The family and the home must be reclaimed as the center of Christian instruction. The church does not replace the family, but rather the church is where the men are taught how and what to teach their families. Men are taught by men to be *the man* of the house.

Satan knows that the foundation of Christian instruction is based upon the role of godly fathers, and he slithers into the garden of our homes looking for ways to displace and destroy the father's teaching authority. He seeks to instigate disrespect and rebellion in the heart of the woman and the children against the man's authority to teach. He tries to paralyze the man in ignorance and insecurity and prevent him from learning what he needs to know and sharing it with his family. Men have been denied their rightful place of leadership. They have been displaced by domineering women, by spoiled children and by godless government. God describes this state of affairs as a judgment and a curse (Isaiah 3:12). We must repent of our sins and appeal to God to restore the godly leadership of faithful men.

Submitting to the Word

So, first of all, the serpent had no place in the garden. Second, he subverted the man's authority by approaching the woman directly apart from the man's loving oversight. Next, the serpent questioned the authority of the Word of God. He did so by introducing a seemingly innocent question: "Hath God said?" The serpent knew that woman would never sin unless he could get her to question the Word of God. The woman naively responded to the serpent's subtle question. She said that God commanded that they could neither touch the tree nor eat of it. Actually, this is bit more than what God said. God commanded Adam not to eat of the tree, but He did not tell him that he could not touch it. The woman added this requirement. There is much speculation as to why she did so. Some say that she erred by going beyond the Word of God and adding unnecessary requirements to the law of God. Others say that she was echoing a stipulation that Adam had added to prevent the possibility of ever eating of the tree, supposing that if they did not touch it they certainly would never eat of it. But whether the woman's response was right or wrong, the question had the tragic effect of drawing her into a dialogue with the devil about God's Word and His motive for restricting man's freedom. She began to question God.

Whenever the serpent infiltrates the home and subverts the authority of the man of the house, his next objective is always to raise subtle questions about the Word of God. The devil wants to stir up a lust for divinity and an arrogant resentment for the restraints of God's law within the Christian family. Many homes have been destroyed because the husband or wife succumbed to Satan's flattery and believed that they knew better than the Word of God what was right for their family. We must reaffirm often our fundamental commitment to the Word of God as the rule of faith and life for our family. The husband, wife and children must never permit Satan to raise impertinent questions about the Word of God. The Word of the Lord is right, and we must humbly submit to it.

One common trick of the devil is to relegate the Word of God to a distant and irrelevant past by insisting that its specific requirements were only for the ancient culture of Bible times. Satan whispers that the Word of God is "culturally conditioned" and no longer binding for us. This is one of the most effective ploys Satan has used. Thereby, he cuts the family loose from its biblical moorings and set it adrift on the sea of moral relativism.

God's law is timeless and relevant to every generation. We must learn how to apply it to our unique time and situation. This may present a considerable challenge now and then, but we cannot shirk the task. We must accept by faith that the Word of God speaks to our current situation and offers hope and help for our families. It is a lie of Satan to say otherwise. We must not allow the serpent to raise questions in our mind about the validity and relevance of the Word of God. When the serpent whispers, "Did God say?" we must respond, as Jesus did, "It is written!" The Word of the Lord is right.

The family is under tremendous pressure today to yield to what the world around us thinks is best for the family. Humanity has been eating at the tree of knowledge since the fall of man, but never has there been an age more subservient to the idol of knowledge than this present age. Paul described the intellectual knowledge of the world as "science falsely so called" (I Timothy

6:20, 21). We have been intimidated by those "in the know," the "experts" who profess to be highly educated and knowledgeable about the working of the family. We have allowed psychologists and psychiatrists, family planners and government officials to define what is normal for the family until they nearly have destroyed it.

We must repudiate the world's view of the family and return to the tree of life, the Word of God. Do not be impressed by the "experts." If these supposed authorities do not submit to the Word of God, then they are fools. And we do not sit at the feet of fools. We do not learn their folly. The world has demonstrated the bankruptcy of their ideas. We should refuse to imitate them and their vanity. We must eat of the tree of life and refuse the tree of knowledge. The *life, law* and *love* of God will teach all that we need to know through daily fellowship with Christ and obedience to His Word. We must resist the tempter's call to replace the Word of God with an idolatrous false knowledge.

The Consequences of Sin

The serpent also minimized the consequences of sin. He mocked God's promise of judgment upon disobedience. He assured the woman that they would not die. Indeed, he convinced her that, rather than face death, she would attain divinity. This refrain sounds so familiar. Satan's lie has not changed. He still seeks to persuade men and women that God's promise of judgment is an outdated superstition. The experts insist, "We now know better." Intellectuals believe they can reshape the family and relationships in the light of their own superior knowledge. This presumptuous arrogance is utterly astonishing. And when their social experiments fail, the humanists just demand more education, more money and more time. Their mistakes are repeated over and over *ad infinitum*, and anyone who questions their humanistic orthodoxy is viewed as a threat to their claims to divinity. Their detractors must be silenced and destroyed. Fools such as these are desperate to deny the consequences of their actions, but history plods on recording their perpetual folly. The serpent may wink and whisper that we should shake off the restraint of traditional, biblical values, but even fools should see by now that the serpent's way is the way to hell. The church must summon the courage to obey the Word of God in the face of every lying devil and prating fool.

It is amazing that humanists do not hesitate to experiment with people's lives. Radical and reckless theories produce disastrous, even deadly, social engineering. And yet because it may seem to work for awhile, they boldly proclaim success and declare the end of all religious restriction on social and familial behavior. Thus, divorce is accepted and promoted as a viable option for those unhappily married. Feminism, which is a moral and physical aberration where women seek to become more masculine than the men they despise, is held up as the preferred ideal. Homosexuality is paraded openly as an alternative lifestyle that only bigots can condemn. The traditional "nuclear family" is derided as the bastion of oppression and abuse. Men abandon their families, mothers murder their babies and children spit in the face of their fathers and mothers, and all of this is called progress. But this is the kind of progress we cannot afford. All of these things are sin, and sin has consequences.

The consequences of sin are not always immediately apparent. Sometimes it takes a generation or two before the sins of the family began to get in the fabric and structure of that family and the culture. But sin that is not exposed and corrected will inevitably produce death. If we are intimidated by the world's reckless and deluded self-confidence and become slaves to a politically correct culture, then we should expect to share in the consequences of sin that come upon the world. If the church is a partaker of the world's sins, then the church shall be a partaker of the world's judgment (Revelation 18:4). We must choose blessing rather than cursing by choosing God's way rather than the way of the world.

8

The Tree of Knowledge

Genesis 3:6. "And when the woman saw that the tree was good for food, and that it was pleasant to the eyes, and a tree to be desired to make one wise, she took of the fruit thereof, and did eat, and gave also unto her husband with her; and he did eat."

God's instruction to Adam was straightforward: In the day you eat of the tree of knowledge you will die. What is so hard about that? It actually seems rather simple. In fact, this simplicity was the serpent's greatest obstacle. If he was to succeed in enticing man to sin, he had to find a way to overthrow the simple command of the Lord. The devil had to complicate the issue. The serpent's scheme was ingenious. He intended to tell the woman that God was lying. But he did not come out and say it just like that. He hinted at it. In fact, he raised the subject as an innocent question. "Did God say?" Satan's approach started out by shifting the woman's mental perspective on the Word of God from declarative (God *did* say) to interrogative (*Did* God say?). He had to get her in a questioning frame of mind.

After Satan succeeded in getting the woman to scribble questions marks in the margin of her Bible, he led the discussion into an open challenge to God's command. He brought up the delicate matter of God's motives: *Why* in the world would God make such an outrageous statement, that you would die—*die!*—for eating such a harmless little piece of fruit? That does not make sense, does it? Unless, that is, God is holding back the whole story. Maybe He is not telling you all there is to know about this fruit.

The serpent's subterfuge introduced a little trick that he has since perfected. Satan distracted the woman from *what* God said by a discussion on *why* He said it. Together they brought the Word of the Lord under critical and intellectual scrutiny. They delved into God's motives and sought to understand and explain His mind. It was right there in the garden that the serpent introduced the defiant impulse of rebellious humanity that still refuses to obey what it does not understand. Unbelievers look away from the plain *what* God said to the obscure *why* God said it so they can justify their reluctance to obey altogether. They explain in ponderous and sophisticated language all the reasons they will not obey: We simply *cannot* embrace what we do not fully understand, they complain. They cannot deny *what* God said. *What* He said is rather obvious to even the meanest intelligence. Instead, they underscore the difficulty of understanding *why* God would impose such harsh requirements.

This refusal to accept and obey what we do not understand is the root of all spiritual deception. If God said it, then we must obey it regardless of our personal understanding of God's motives. His ways are above our ways, and His thoughts above our thoughts (Isaiah 55:8). We must simply obey.

This is still how sin is introduced into the family. Men and women forget *what* God said and question *why* He said it. Many Christians have joined in with unbelievers in asserting that people cannot be expected to obey what they do not fully understand. Christians who succumb to this idea are in for a tremendous shock. They shall find to their utter amazement that God spends very little time explaining *why*. He just tells us *what* to do and expects us—wonder of wonders!—to do *what* He said. Imagine that.

The essence of Christian experience is faith, and faith submits to the Word of God even when there is little or no intellectual understanding of *why*. For now, we must simply do *what* God said. We shall understand *why* better by and by.

Further, Satan knew the reason, he said, for *why* God was holding them back from eating of the tree of knowledge. God was jealous of His precious divinity, and He did not want man to share in it. Indeed, the serpent whispered, if man would eat the fruit, he would be like the gods, knowing good and evil. His eyes would be opened, and he would be wise concerning right and wrong. Simply by grasping forbidden knowledge he would lay hold on the divine. The serpent was the first liar to assert that knowledge produces divinity—modern intellectuals still believe this lie today.

God promised death, while the serpent promised divinity. Of course, the serpent was wrong. However, there were a couple of things that seemed to indicate at first that he was right. The fruit of the tree did appear "good for food," and "pleasant to the eyes" (v. 6). This made the serpent's argument all the more convincing. The fruit's harmless appearance gave credence to the serpent's assertion that God was trying secretly to prevent them from sharing in divinity.

After a moment of hesitation the woman began to be persuaded by the lies of the serpent. She may have plucked a piece of the fruit and held it in her hands. Possibly she pulled it apart and smelled of it. It did not seem so different from other fruit she had enjoyed before. In fact, if anything, it was more beautiful than the other fruit, brilliant in color, exotic in appearance. It was certainly very pleasing to the eyes. *How interesting.*

Maybe the woman had been curious about these things before. She may have even examined the fruit from a safe distance at earlier times. Possibly she had wondered why such harmless looking fruit could be so deadly. For, as Paul notes, prohibition produces desire (Romans 7:7). But now that charming serpent had opened up a new train of thought: the fruit was not only beautiful—it would make her *wise.* Not only was the fruit obviously edible and unusually beautiful, it was the source of divine wisdom. Could God really forbid something as good as that? The woman began to think that the Word of God was somewhat outdated, even irrelevant. In fact, the more she thought about it, the more the Word of God seemed downright mean-spirited and oppressive.

The serpent persuaded the woman to focus on how edible and beautiful the forbidden fruit really was. However, God's original instruction about the forbidden fruit made no comment whatever on whether the fruit was edible or beautiful. He said nothing about it making them wise. The Lord simply said it would kill them. Period. All that the serpent said about the fruit was completely irrelevant. It was right, but it was irrelevant. What good is edible, beautiful fruit if it kills you? Satan succeeded in making the Word of God seem irrelevant and unnecessary, but in reality, it was the evil philosophy of the serpent that was rooted in irrelevance. The serpent turned the woman's attention to matters that really did not matter at all. God commanded them not to eat of the tree of knowledge and that should have been enough.

The Family at the Tree of Knowledge

What vs. Why

Consider several things with regard to the family before we continue on with the story. First of all, the Christian family must consider *what* God said and ignore altogether questions about *why* He said it. It is simply amazing today how few Christians will simply accept the Word of God at face value. We are told these days that this modern generation cannot just be told *what* to do— they must be told *why*. No doubt this is true of this generation, but it is not at all because they are modern. Questioning God is not a modern problem. It is an ancient problem that goes all the way back to the garden.

Now, of course, we should never be discouraged from seeking a clearer understanding of *what* God says. But there is a world of difference between seeking to understand clearly God's instructions and arrogantly demanding to know His reasons *why*. God does not seem to care much for being hauled before a court of human inquisitors to offer trembling explanations for His Word.

This affects the family profoundly. The Word of God is filled with detailed instructions for the family. However, very few modern Christians practice anything anywhere near what the Bible actually says about family life. We allow the intellectuals— which is just a big word for "fool"—of our world to persuade us that they, the professionals, the elites, the scientists, the academics, know so much better than God how we should live. They speak with us in the shade of a modern tree of knowledge. Will we eat the fruit?

The only way Satan can get us to eat the fruit of disobedience is to get us thinking about the *why* rather than the *what*. Did God say that men should be providers and women keepers at home? Why? Did God say for parents to train up their own children in the way that they should go? Why *that?* Did God say that children should be chastened with a rod? Why spanking? Is that not rather brutal? And so out-of-date. Time-out works so much better. The list could go on and on. We have abundant instructions that tell us *what* to do, but we dismiss them as irrelevant because we fail to see the rationale, the *why*. We have fallen into the same trap as Eve. We have been convinced that the path to wisdom departs from the Word of God and arrives at the opinion of experts, who really have no expertise except folly. We eat of the fruit of knowledge that does not flow from the life of God and then wonder why our families are dying. It is time to get back to *what* God commands for the family and refuse to waste time asking *why*.

The Appearance of Innocence

Secondly, the woman was deceived by the appearance of innocence. The fruit looked harmless, and the more she considered it, the more harmless it appeared. Indeed, the more her desire for the fruit increased, the more she calmed her irrational fears, suppressed her doubts and reassured herself that it was okay, really okay.

We do the same. Here is just one example: we convince ourselves that it really is okay for our children to be educated by pagans in government schools. It really *is* okay. Quit worrying about it, silly. Remember, all the experts agree that parents are not really capable of educating their own children. Leave it to the professionals and do not try this at home. It really will be okay. But very few of our children survive this evil indoctrination, and it really is *not* okay.

There are countless examples of how we are deceived every day by the appearance of innocence. The world makes it all look so normal. We are persuaded by the serpent that daycare really is *good* for our babies. They need that time away from mom, anyway. They need the socialization. Come a little closer, Eve. Eat the fruit; it will not hurt you. God must have been dreaming when he instructed Israel to teach their own children all day every day (Deuteronomy 6). Besides, that was way back then when people were sort of dumb anyway, and now people are so much smarter. See our degrees, the ones hanging there on the wall? We are *smart*.

Come on, Christian! Come with us into the twenty-first century. What can it hurt?

Knowledge and Relationship

The serpent tempted the woman to seek for wisdom apart from God. But wisdom apart from God is folly. The knowledge of good and evil, discernment between right and wrong, is a good thing (Hebrews 5:14). However, knowledge apart from relationship with God is *never* good, for knowledge that is not rooted in the knowledge of God becomes a self-referential and idolatrous knowledge. Once we reject God as the source and guide of true knowledge, our knowledge becomes purely subjective knowledge. Human knowledge cannot help but be limited to the finite boundaries of the knower's understanding, which distorts his knowledge.

However, God's knowledge is boundless. His wisdom is infinite. Moreover, God is truth, so when we learn from God, we cannot help but learn the truth. God knows all things about all things. Those who learn from God are guaranteed right knowledge. But those that learn apart from a relationship with God have no controls for their learning except their own limited perspective and understanding. And this limited knowledge makes learning the whole truth about anything impossible. Every man, then, develops his own "truth," and the earth is filled with competing truths. This has occurred among philosophers, the "lovers of wisdom." Relativists and pluralists even allow that every man's truth is equally valid, which, of course, is a tacit admission no man's truth is valid at all. Man simply cannot know truth within himself. Therefore, the quest for knowledge apart from the knowledge of God inevitably ends up in self-deception.

We must be careful about this even as we seek greater knowledge about building a godly family. If we fill our heads with knowledge of the family without filling our hearts with knowledge of God, then everything we learn becomes a form of self-deception. Family relationships can only be truly understood through a deep relationship with Jesus Christ. We must resist the temptation to use any instruction on the family as a sort of tree of knowledge from which we may pluck facts like fruit and learn in a few bites all we need to know about childrearing or marriage. Too often, we end up seeking knowledge for knowledge's sake without seeking the knowledge of the Lord. We search for a formulaic, color-by-the-numbers approach that reduces truth down to a list of rules and regulations that can be obeyed in the flesh. But, of course, we cannot fulfill God's righteousness in the flesh. We must be empowered by the life of God. We must eat from the tree of life and allow God to teach us His knowledge through a deep, daily relationship with Him.

It is possible to get just enough of an understanding of the Word of God to make us dangerous. Proud, sinful man tends to misinterpret and misapply Scripture to fit his own ambitions and agendas. We must guard against emphasizing certain teachings of Scripture because they reflect biases and opinions that we hold dear while ignoring others that may serve to balance our outlook and rebuke our own failings. A proper relationship with God will keep us under the constant reproof and correction of the Word and Spirit of God and prevent this sort of deception.

It is also evident that the woman was persuaded by the serpent to seek knowledge prematurely, before she was ready for it. The Lord God would have taught Adam and his wife right from wrong through a daily, personal relationship. Then their knowledge would have been rooted in the fear of the Lord, which is the beginning of knowledge and wisdom (Proverbs 1:7; 9:10). The woman was compelled to seek instant gratification rather than waiting patiently on the Lord to teach her what she needed to know when she needed to know it. The demand for instant gratification is the curse of the modern family. Our technological age has made us incredibly impatient. But God cannot be forced into a hurry. He moves at His own pace according to His own will, and no amount of petulant whining can rush Him along. God has a reason for His decision to move slowly. We must simply trust and obey.

The Desires of the Flesh

Before the serpent could persuade the woman to join him in his subtle rationale for sin, he had to get her wanting the fruit really badly. If he could get her to want it badly enough, she would talk herself into disobeying the Word of God. So, he appealed to the desires of her flesh. He successfully internalized the impulse for sin. The serpent tempted her from without, but her own desire tempted her from within. "Every man is tempted when he is drawn away of his own lust and enticed" (James 1:14). Sin arises from the twin impulses of temptation *within* and *without*. Jesus proved that temptation without is never enough to cause a man to sin (Luke 4:1-13). The devil never succeeded in getting Christ to desire what he offered. But with the woman, he found a way to provoke covetousness within her.

The serpent still uses the same tactics on the modern Christian family. He must stir up a desire for the things of the world so that we shall go along with his arguments against the righteousness of God. Once he gets us longing for the world and its ways, the job is done.

The Decision to Sin

The woman stood by the tree considering what the serpent had to say. He made such perfect sense. God's prohibition did seem a bit like divine overkill. Surely she would not die. The fruit was obviously edible, unusually beautiful—and besides, it would make her as wise as the gods. Then the fateful moment came. She decided to do it. She brought the fruit up to her face as the serpent winked encouragement and urged her on. Go ahead. Do it. You will never regret it. She put the fruit to her lips, and then, with an unexpected boldness, she happily sunk her teeth into the ripe, juicy fruit and experienced her first taste of exhilarating freedom from the bondage of God's oppressive rules. She felt so free, so alive!

Now, stop here for a moment and think about this: before the woman ever put the fruit to her mouth to eat, she *decided* to do so. That seems obvious, and yet the point bears further consideration. There was a particular moment in time when the decision was made. At that point, the deed was as good as done. Eating just acted out what she had already set out to do. Decision produces action.

We must confront this fact. Sin is a decision. Sin is a decision to disobey the Word of God. But we do not like to look at it that way. Avoiding blame is a booming business. We point fingers at every other possible cause for failure rather than our own decision. We excuse disobedience by every means possible. We blame our sins on circumstances beyond our control. We insist that we were caught in the grip of remorseless fate. We ignore the fact that there came a point in time when we *decided* to sin. We focus on the overall stream of events rather than the spring of decision. We camouflage our decisions to sin by renaming and redefining our actions. We call them everything *but* sin. We describe our unpleasant and unkind actions as "moods," "personality quirks," "being tired," "hormones," etc.—whatever we can do to avoid responsibility for our own actions.

However, we must identify sin as what it really is: a willful decision to disobey the Word of God. If we are unkind, then we have chosen, because it is convenient for us, to disobey the command of the Word of the Lord to "be ye kind one to another" (Ephesians 4:32). If we are angry without cause, then we have made a decision to disobey the command of the Lord against being angry without cause (Matthew 5:22). If we speak harshly to one another, then we have made a decision to disobey the command of the Lord to speak the truth in love (Ephesians 4:15). We can defeat the power of sin in our home only when we properly identify our actions as sin and recognize that sin prevails when we decide to disobey.

Repentance and Restoration

Furthermore, if our actions are *sin* rather than just personality quirks and mood swings then we must deal with problems in the home just like sin should be dealt with everywhere else. We know (at least everywhere but at home) that there is only one remedy for sin: repentance. Repentance includes confession of sin and restoration through forgiveness. Of course, this sounds pretty serious, and some may be tempted to take a lighter view of family transgressions. But this has been our problem in the Christian home. We have failed to take our problems seriously enough and then confront our disobedience as sin. When we hear the Word of the Lord and realize that we have allowed a pattern of sinful habit to develop in our home, we must confront the sin honestly, repent and confess that sin both to God and those against whom the sin was committed. Finally, we must seek the restoration of the blood of Jesus by faith in His sacrifice at Calvary.

This process of *repentance* and *restoration* must begin with fathers and mothers, and then trickle down through the family into the lives of the children. Too often, parents begin with their children and fail to correct their own sins first. This guarantees disciplinary failure. We are not qualified to discipline if we are not disciplined. Our discipline must come from the Word and the Spirit of God. We must submit to biblical authority and accept the chastening of God that is administered by the preaching of the Word of the Lord and the conviction of the Spirit of the Lord in our daily lives. We first must consider our actions as parents and then look to the behavior of our children to reprove faithfully the sin that is taking root in their thoughts, words and deeds.

As parents, we are responsible before God to be the agents of God's discipline and chastening in the lives of our children. Our goal is that they may be convicted and convinced of their sins and find repentance and restoration through the blood of Jesus. A spanking is never enough. Chastening should turn the hearts of our children toward the righteousness of Christ revealed in the Word of God. Chastening should highlight the mercy and forgiveness found in Christ. Chastening should purge them of sin and produce holiness in their lives. This is not some sort of idealistic super-spirituality. It is the Word of God. "Foolishness is bound in the heart of a child, but the rod of correction shall drive it far from him" (Proverbs 22:15). This is a promise that God has made, that faithful chastening will drive out the folly of sin from the hearts of our children. We should use every instance of correction and chastening to point our children toward the Lord, toward His goodness and mercy.

And this brings us back to the need to see disobedience in the home as *sin*. Only when we see our children's disobedience as a *sin* against God and man can we truly take seriously the task of disciplining our children. Our children are not only sinning against us and others; they are sinning against God. These patterns of sin are broken only through the power of the Cross, which finds its first expression to them in our unconditional love for them. Otherwise, they will bring these sinful patterns with them into adulthood. As their heart is hardened in old age and their youthful tenderness is lost, repentance and restoration will become increasingly difficult. Our children must be taught to remember their Creator in the days of their youth.

We cannot make excuses for ourselves and our children. Sin is a decision, a decision to disobey the Word of the Lord. Ignorance is no excuse. We must not remain ignorant of what the Word teaches. We must meditate on the law of God day and night, learn these things and pass them on to our children. The consequences of sin are inevitable regardless of how much or how little we know and understand. We cannot excuse ourselves or our children on the basis of ignorance. Indeed, discipline is designed to teach us and our children and banish ignorance from our minds. Every instance of chastening in the home should have as its goal teaching a lesson in righteousness. We must learn and teach our children that we *decide* to obey or disobey, and every decision has consequences, good or bad. The woman decided to take the fruit and eat of it. Likewise, we make *the decision to sin* when we disobey the Word of the Lord.

The Delayed Effects of Sin

The woman hungrily finished the piece of fruit she had plucked from the tree. She licked her lips and wiped her mouth with the back of her hand. She looked around with just a tinge of anxiety about God's promise that she would die. She felt no different. The world around her looked the same. The breeze was still blowing through the trees, the birds singing softly. She seemed none the worse for her decision. The serpent was right. She would not—she did not—die!

Her eyes widened as she looked around with a new perspective on life. She was free now, free to become like one of the gods in her new-found knowledge of right and wrong. And yet, oddly enough, she did not seem to know all that much more than she did before she ate. Regardless, the main thing was that she did not die, *she did not die!*

The woman was overjoyed at the prospect of growing in her boundless divinity. She looked over at her husband who was watching her reaction to the fruit from a little distance. She beckoned him to come closer. It is okay, she nodded. I am fine. God was wrong, and the serpent was right. We now *know*, Adam. This forbidden fruit is wonderful, and we were destined to be like the gods. Adam walked a little bit closer. His mind was racing. It seemed like the woman was fine. He reached out and took the fruit quickly before his doubts could overcome his decision. The woman stared intently at the man as he took the first taste of sin, and the serpent laughed softly under his hissing breath. The deed was done. The human race would follow him in defiance against God.

The dramatic details aside, it is noteworthy that the woman ate of the forbidden fruit and seemingly suffered no immediate ill effects from it. The serpent told her that she would not die, and she did not, at least not in any obvious sense. She "took the fruit thereof, and did eat" (v.6), and then she gave it to her husband, and he ate with her. Sin very rarely affects the sinner immediately.

Just so, the effects of sin on the family are not often immediately apparent. It takes a while, sometimes a generation or two, before the effects of sin become obvious. This gives the deceptive illusion that sinners are getting by with their disobedience to the command of the Lord. Generally, the Lord does not permit Christians to get by with as much for as long as He does unbelievers. However, even Christians must remember that the wheels of God's justice may grind slow, but they grind fine.

For example, look at the slow deterioration of American culture in the twentieth century as it rose in full-throated rebellion against God's law on the family. The unisex movement that sprouted in the Roaring Twenties came to full flower in the hippie culture of the 1960s. The entertainment culture of Hollywood became a household demon through movies and television. An entire generation of baby-boomers was pampered with unparalleled self-indulgence, which culminated in the enculturation of radical selfishness and suicidal nihilism. We have suffered the rise of the feminist movement and the mass exodus of mothers from the home into the workplace. We have reached the place now in America where we are not even sure what the definition of a family really is.

But it has taken many, many years for these dramatic changes to become visible, and only now are we truly seeing what the revolt of sinful man has wrought. And many still refuse to look at what they are seeing. Their eyes are open, but they cannot see. We may eat the fruit of disobedience and feel certain that we are getting by with it. But do not be deceived: God is not mocked

Whatever a man sows, he shall reap. It is inevitable—the wages of sin is death.

This is also very true in the Christian family. We may buy into the world's philosophy of family and childrearing and think for awhile we are doing fine. But eventually the reality and results of our sins will set in, and we shall watch in horror as our families plunge headlong into hell just a step or two behind the world. If we desire families that are blessed of God, then we must take the commands of God seriously and refuse to eat at the tree of worldly knowledge.

Conclusion

We could multiply lessons forever from the woman's single act of disobedience. However, consider three final points before we go on:

The Woman Gave the Fruit to her Husband

The woman was created to be a helpmeet for her husband, but she became a hindrance and his worst enemy when she served him a meal of forbidden fruit. Now, obviously the man was responsible for his own sin, and God does not allow the man to place the blame for his disobedience on the woman. Man is not allowed to excuse himself on any basis, including ignorance. But it is certainly tragic when the woman becomes the instrument of a man's downfall, when the woman created for loving service serves the man a helping of disobedience. Godly Christian women should avoid being the agent of sin and disobedience in the home.

Her Husband Was With Her

We noted earlier that Adam was standing nearby when the woman engaged in dialogue with the devil. The man abdicated his responsibility to lead the home when he stood silently by and allowed the conversation to proceed. Adam should have intervened at several points throughout the scenario, but here is the last chance the man has to take a stand and refuse to partake of the woman's sin. Husbands will have many opportunities to stand for righteousness, even down to the last moment when the final decision is made to permit sin in the home. Somewhere, hopefully, long before that point, the man must take a stand.

Adam Ate the Fruit

We do not know what would have happened if Adam had refused to eat the fruit. But we must consider if possibly Adam could have stood before God when He visited and confessed the sin of his wife and received mercy for his household. It is impossible to know now what Adam could have done then. But we do know what *we* must do now in the case of sin: the man must confront the wife with her sin and command repentance in the name of the Lord. The man must stand before the Lord as the head of his house and confess the sins of the house as the woman confesses her personal sin before the Lord. The man must refuse to partake of sin and lead the family to repentance and restoration.

9

The First Effects of Sin

Genesis 3:7. "And the eyes of them both were opened, and they knew that they were naked; and they sewed fig leaves together, and made themselves aprons."

The first effects of sin were felt after Adam ate the fruit. Nothing happened when the woman ate, but when the man ate "the eyes of them both were opened and they knew that they were naked." This is interesting. This is exactly the sort of thing we see all of the time in the Christian home. Certainly sin affects the home when mom or the kids are disobedient. That is undeniable. But sin does not really get a foothold in a house until the man gives in to it. The faithfulness of the father provides a solid bulwark against sin even in the face of the wife's sin and disobedience. Dad may not prevent sin from happening, but he can prevent it from gaining dominion over the family. And when dad disobeys the effects are far greater than when any other does so.

Most Christian men underestimate the full power of their authority and responsibility. The man is the federal head of the family, and God reckons sin against the home based on the actions of the husband and father. The wife and children will not be judged personally as sinners based on the sin of their father (Ezekiel 18:20), but the household *as a household* will suffer the curse of God's judgment against it when the man persists in sin.

Once the man sinned, the effects of sin were felt by *both* the man and the woman. It is striking that sin in the home never affects only one member of the household. When there are marriage problems between a man and woman, it never fails that both are wrong to some degree. One party may be guilty of greater crimes against God and against the family than the other, but never is one completely wrong and the other completely right. *Never!*

When there is discord between parents and children, invariably there is sin on the part of both the parents and the children. If we can accept this reality, that each party to the problem shares some blame for the problem, then we are well on our way to solving the problem and redeeming the situation. We should confront every problem in the household by honestly examining ourselves and seeking to discover what we have done wrong and what we can do to make it right. As we shall see, this is exactly the opposite of how Adam and his wife responded.

They Knew They Were Naked

When Adam and Eve ate of the tree their eyes were opened and they saw that they were naked. They *learned* that they were naked. God certainly would have given them this knowledge later. Nakedness was never intended to be the final condition of man. They were created naked in their innocence, but God would have clothed them in righteousness later on. Never are the angels, the saints in heaven or even Christ Himself portrayed in Scripture without clothing. Nakedness is a sign of innocence and immaturity. So, God would have clothed Adam and Eve later on. But they should have learned about clothing and nakedness in God's time and in God's way. They sought knowledge apart from relationship and ended up learning what they were not capable of correcting. The man and woman discovered they were naked, but could not know apart from God's instruction how to be covered adequately in righteousness.

It is also quite possible that they would have eaten of the tree of knowledge later at God's instruction and with His oversight. But they rushed into premature knowledge without God's direction, and the forfeiture of relationship through sin and disobedience caused death. They were cut off from God by disobedience, and this spiritual death made their physical death inevitable. Adam and Eve lived by the Spirit of God within them, and they were created to learn through the counsel of His Holy Spirit. But they rebelliously sought knowledge apart from relationship and ended up dead.

The Shame of Nakedness

Although Adam's eyes were "opened" when he sinned, he was not blind before. Rather, the opening of Adam's eyes indicates two things: first, Adam's understanding was opened and he saw that he was naked. This is sight in a metaphorical sense. Second, Adam apparently suffered a reduction of physical sight when he sinned. It seems likely that before the fall Adam was able to see as the angels see with a form of spiritual sight. This ability was lost and now the spirit-realm is entirely invisible to man though it exists all around him. His eyes were "opened" in the sense that his sight was limited to the physical world.

Sin still affects our eyes. It affects how we see things. When a father and mother allow sin into their home, their eyes are "opened" and they begin to see things in a different way, albeit in a wrong way. One's vision is affected by disobedience. This is why we must pray continually that God will open the eyes of our heart and permit us to see things the way they really are.

Adam's new understanding allowed him to see rightly that he and his wife were naked. However, this was a fact learned much too soon. They were not ready for this knowledge. The newfound knowledge made them desperately ashamed. If Adam and Eve had waited and allowed God to teach them about their need for covering, they would have been covered in righteousness without the bitter experience of shame. They would have been led gently by the Creator into His perfect righteousness. They would have moved steadily from the ignorance of innocence to the confidence of maturity. They would have gained a healthy self-awareness in the light of their knowledge of God and would have stood confidently before God and each other. But they foolishly chose to seek knowledge apart from relationship with God and were introduced to the stunning embarrassment of an immature and insecure self-consciousness.

Ignorance, they say, is bliss. Adam and Eve lived in this bliss until they sinned. They were naked, but they did not know it and were not ashamed (Genesis 2:25). They were completely open with one another with nothing to hide. But when they sinned, they started hiding from one another and from God. They began searching frantically for anything within reach to cover up. They reached for fig leaves and improvised a crude apron, a sort of loin-cloth, to cover up. Of course, this was an inadequate covering at best. But they were desperate to do something, anything, to prevent their openness and exposure to one another. They retreated into their own pitiful little hiding places and peeked out warily to see if the other was looking. It was the first game of marital hide-and-seek. Men and woman have been playing that ancient game ever since.

The Covering of Love

Sin still affects marriage just like this. God intends for the newly married couple to begin their relationship in the innocence and ignorance of wedded bliss. They are created to grow in their relationship with the Lord and one another. Their knowledge of one another should grow slowly out of ignorance into intimacy. Their knowledge of one another is intended to be a loving knowledge rooted in relationship. In this sort of relationship, the man and woman's nakedness—their weakness and vulnerability—is covered by love, the unconditional love that covers a multitude of sins. God intends for the Christian couple to discover the truth about each other, to really get to *know* each other, and still love one another in spite of all they know. This covering hides their nakedness as they are clothed together in the love of Christ.

Loving knowledge is rooted in the knowledge of God. Our relationship with one another grows as our relationship with God grows. The Bible plainly shows that our relationship with one another is intertwined with our relationship with God. Thus, the marriage, as it is clothed in the righteousness of God, will grow in the awareness of the other, clothed in humility and love.

Marriage begins in innocence. The man and woman are open with one another, trusting and secure. They are "naked and not ashamed." Then, before the wedding bells have quite stopped ringing, the serpent comes calling. He slithers quietly in to entice someone, anyone, to start the awful cycle of sin and shame. It matters little who sins first, or how the sin is first manifested. All that matters to the devil is that sin occurs. Sin is inevitable because of our fallen nature, and when it comes, the eyes of the man and the woman are opened. They become critically self-conscious, aware of themselves and one another. This critical self-awareness, this sinful self-consciousness, makes a couple defensive and dishonest. They become self-conscious about their relationship and begin hiding themselves from the critical scrutiny of the other.

Just as Adam and Eve attempted to cover their nakedness with fig leaves, so men and women today, so cruelly exposed by sin and disobedience, try to hide their weakness and vulnerability with various masks and disguises. Husbands and wives often develop sophisticated defense systems to guard against unwanted intrusion and exposure. They withdraw stealthily and steadily from loving fellowship with their mate into well-fortified positions of self-imposed isolation. Then, sporadic hostilities break out into all-out war using all available fire-power. And the nuclear family has nuclear war.

The only covering for sin is the love of Christ. We can either run and hide in shame from one another or we can clothe one other in the garments of Christ's tender mercy. Our fig leaves are never enough. We need the full covering of love, the love that covers a multitude of sins.

10

The Day of Judgment

Genesis 3:8-13. "And they heard the voice of the LORD God walking in the garden in the cool of the day: and Adam and his wife hid themselves from the presence of the LORD God amongst the trees of the garden. And the LORD God called unto Adam, and said unto him, Where art thou? And he said, I heard thy voice in the garden, and I was afraid, because I was naked; and I hid myself. And he said, Who told thee that thou wast naked? Hast thou eaten of the tree, whereof I commanded thee that thou shouldest not eat? And the man said, The woman whom thou gavest to be with me, she gave me of the tree, and I did eat. And the LORD God said unto the woman, What is this that thou hast done? And the woman said, The serpent beguiled me, and I did eat."

After Adam and Eve covered themselves with fig leaves, they heard the voice of God as He came walking in the garden in the cool of the day. This part of the story often evokes in our mind a tranquil image of the deep, reverberating voice of God carried softly on a gentle breeze as the Lord came down for His daily visit with Adam. But the phrase "heard the voice… in the cool of the day" probably means something much more serious.

The phrase "the cool of the day" can be rendered "the wind of the day" and is likely a reference to the mighty wind of the Spirit of God. Moreover, the images of "voice," "wind" and "the day" are images of judgment throughout scripture. When the Voice thunders, the Wind blows and the Day of the Lord comes, it is a day of fierce judgment. This was likely the case on that dreadful day. Surely Adam and Eve scattered like frightened animals into the undergrowth around them as the thundering voice of God blasted through the trees with a rushing mighty wind, ripping leaves and limbs from the trees, scattering debris throughout the garden with the deafening roar a powerful hurricane. No wonder Adam says, "I was afraid" (v.10)!

God Enters the Garden

The foregoing scenario is a perfect example of events that follow the intrusion of sin into the home of a Christian. First of all, God does not prevent sin from occurring. He often stands by while we take matters into our own hands and end up making a total mess of it. Thereby, God teaches us essential lessons about trusting in Him rather than trusting in ourselves. Of course, God does not cause sin, but He does allow it to occur. God could have intervened and prevented Adam and Eve from sinning, but He did not do so. And He did not come into the garden until after the deed was done. Just so, the Lord will not prevent willful sin in our homes. He may work by His Word and Spirit to convict our heart before we go astray, but if we insist on having our own way, then He will step aside while we rush headlong into disobedience.

Thankfully, however, the Lord will not remain outside forever. He will not abandon us entirely to our sinful self-will. God may have waited outside the garden while Adam and Eve succumbed to Satan's spell, but He refused to leave them in their hopeless condition once they had done so. When the moment was right for confrontation, God burst into the garden, thundering His disapproval and judgment upon their sin. The assurance that God will not abandon us to our own devices is a bulwark against despair. Every Christian soon discovers that he cannot build his house through his own strength. We inevitably make serious mistakes in marriage and child-rearing that can have eternal consequences. But God has demonstrated again and again that He will not stand by and watch us destroy our hopes and dreams through sin. He graciously will intervene to save us.

Of course, God saves us through a bold confrontation of our sin, and we must humbly submit to His correction. We must never resent the intrusion of God's chastening hand. We must simply seek repentance and restoration by grace through faith. This is the only hope of salvation for the Christian family.

Judgment upon Sin

It is interesting that God's judgment came as the voice of God upon the wind of the day. As we noted, the voice, the wind and the day are images of judgment used throughout Scripture signifying the Word of God, the Spirit of God and the Judgment of God. The Word and the Spirit of God bring men into judgment before the throne of God. This is exactly how God works to judge sin in the home and bring repentance and restoration: He speaks by His Word and Spirit, and judges our sin by the offering of Christ at Calvary. When we are judged under the blood of Christ, then we are forgiven on the basis of His offering. We receive in a continual sense the imputed and imparted righteousness of Christ to justify and sanctify our family. God rebukes and restores us by the teaching of His Word (through public preaching and private study) and by the direction of His Spirit (through prayer and a sensitive conscience). Every family must be sensitive to the judgment of the Word and Spirit of God. It is our only assurance of salvation.

We must receive daily judgment for daily sins. We must develop the habit of confessing our sins before the Lord every day. The proper response to sin is immediate repentance and confession. As we confess our sins before the Lord daily we are judged daily under the blood of Christ. Thus, our sins will not pile up against us reserved for the Day of Judgment on the last day. We are taught by Paul to live under continual judgment so that we are not judged with the world at the last judgment when the opportunity for repentance and restoration has passed (I Corinthians 11:31, 32).

This principle of on-going judgment is incredibly important for the family. Too often we refuse to recognize our need for daily confession and correction and end up pushing our sins far ahead into the future. Thus, we face our mistakes when our children are grown and bitter and it is too late to do much about it. It is a dreadful thing to postpone repentance until long after you have sown the seeds of disobedience and cultivated ever-growing transgressions with the brackish irrigation of anger and selfishness. Those who do will gather in the horrifying harvest of a bitterly divided family. This sort of failure can be avoided if we would determine to submit to the daily judgment of the Word and Spirit of the Lord. We must welcome God into our garden to confront our sins. We must never postpone confession and correction.

Hiding from God

Adam and Eve hid from God when they heard His voice. We often do exactly the same thing. When the Word and the Spirit thunder into our home to rebuke our sin, we run in terror and hide from the presence of the Lord. But this is exactly the wrong response. We should run *to* the Lord, never away from Him. It is interesting to consider what may have occurred if Adam had come running to the Lord for repentance and restoration. Instead Adam set the precedent that the human race has followed ever since: we try to play hide and seek with God. Of course, this is a game that God always wins, though some will be found only at the final judgment when it is forever too late. But rest assured, every sinner will be found. No one can hide from God. The Lord knew where Adam and Eve were hiding all along. But their hiding separated them from fellowship with God. It is impossible to be located physically where the Spirit of God cannot see us, but it is possible to be separated covenantally from God and to be out of fellowship with Him.

We become separated spiritually from God when we "hide" from Him and withdraw from fellowship in His presence. We do this by adopting a carnal attitude of unbelief and trusting in the flesh, by refusing to pray and study our Bibles, by missing church and breaking fellowship with fellow Christians. Some hide from God even as they continue attending regular services. They simply learn how to remain aloof in their hearts even as the preaching, worship, prayer and Christian fellowship surround them. There are many different ways to hide from God when we sin.

We must make the decision in advance to steadfastly refuse to hide from the Lord in those times when we are disobedient to the Word of God and sin enters the home. We must immediately call out unto the Lord for mercy, confessing and confronting our sin.

134

This is the only remedy. We cannot simply ignore the sins within our marriage, our children and family relationships. Running to hide from sin is never a proper response. And yet, this is so often how we respond to sins of the family.

We avoid unpleasant issues and uncomfortable topics and learn to live with sin in our home. We learn to wear the mask, to patch together our own fashionable aprons made from fig leaves, embroidered and sewn in the latest styles. We take a trip, go shopping or buy a new car, anything to avoid confronting the problem. Our family problems are all relationship problems, and they all begin with a breakdown in our relationship with God. As long as we avoid confronting the sin in our life, our relationship with God and others continues to deteriorate. The only way to heal the relationship is deal with the sin.

Hiding among the Trees

Adam and Eve hid among the trees of the garden. The trees were the domain of their labor, the work God had called them to do in cultivating the garden. In a sense we could say that Adam and Eve retreated into their work to hide from God. This is exactly what so many disobedient Christians do. They busy themselves with their work trying to hide from the searing glare of God's light. Men give themselves over to work extra hours, taking additional assignments on the job and accepting excessive overtime. Wives busy themselves with chores around the house, running errands and marking off an ever-growing list of mundane tasks. So often when we are so frantic to stay busy, we are simply hiding from God. We are hiding among the trees of our garden to avoid confronting the problems in our house and the sins that haunt our minds.

Refusal to confront sin compounds the error. Sin leads to sin, and disobedience piles up like rotting mounds of garbage in our house. Our children are reared in this atmosphere of hypocrisy, and they add their own sins to an ever-growing mountain of family transgressions. We pretend that the problems are just normal irritations of everyday life, just the stress of the daily grind. But the problem is not *just life*. The problem is un-confessed and uncorrected sin from which we flee into the darkened jungles of daily responsibilities. And the problem will never be addressed until we confront that our problems are *sins* that we have hidden in our house.

Set aside the laundry. The dishes can wait. Getting away for a week or two is not the answer. Refuse to work away the weekend. It is not time to go fishing with the boys. The family is in trouble. The Word and the Spirit of God are present to judge now so that judgment is not delayed until there is no remedy. God is here, calling your name. Come out of the trees. Confess your sins and the sins of your family. Confess the sins of unkindness and disrespect. Confess the anger and the resentment. Confront and confess the sin whatever it is. God is merciful and quick to forgive. God is ready and willing to restore, but we must quit hiding from Him.

Calling for Adam

When the Lord God burst into the garden, His mighty voice thundered the summons to judgment: "Adam, where are you?" Consider the following.

God Insisted that Adam Respond

God did not make a cursory inspection of the garden, and then leave mildly frustrated. God did not demonstrate a casual, "Oh, well" attitude toward sin. The Lord knew from the start the serious consequences of sin, and He was determined to confront man with those consequences. This confrontation of consequences is what made salvation from the consequences possible.

Sins that are ignored and allowed to continue un-confronted will inexorably grow into much deeper problems. Ignoring sin is like ignoring weeds in a garden. Looking away will not make them go away. We are often like little children who think that if they close their eyes the monster disappears. Closing our eyes to sin does not fix the problem. It is not going to get better by itself. We must allow God to confront our sin.

So God put Adam on the spot, called him by name and demanded a response. We should be thankful that the Lord is insistent about confronting sin in our home, and that He does not leave matters as they are. The Lord chastens those He loves, and the chastening is given to bring us to repentance and restoration.

God Called Adam as the Man of the House

Adam was the federal head of his family and the human family, and God called him to give an account of the family for the sin that had been committed. As we noted earlier, the man is the federal head of the house, and he is called by God to give an account of all the activities of the house. The man is the king and priest ordained by God to "keep" the garden, the temple of the home.

The man cannot avoid this responsibility. Every man must give account of his leadership in the home. Men cannot pass the blame for the sins of their house upon others, not even upon those who were personally guilty of committing the sins. Every sin committed in the home is both God's business and dad's business. God will call every man into account to answer in judgment for the sins of his house. God calls the man by name and expects a response of responsibility.

God Demanded that Man Acknowledge his Position and Condition

Adam was required to reveal his hiding place. God still requires this of godly men. We must take inventory of our lives and give an account to God. We must reveal our hiding places, the places where we run when we have sinned. God demands an honest reckoning before Him. "Adam, where are you—where do you stand?"

We must give an account for where we stand in prayer and daily devotions, for where we stand in holiness and separation from the world, for our lifestyle and the habits of our family. Sin can only be addressed when there is a complete and honest disclosure to God of everything good and bad.

Adam's Response

Adam responded to the Lord's call and came slinking out of the bushes. You can run, but you cannot hide. Every man and woman must come before the Creator of all the earth and give an account for their sins. How much better it is to come when the Savior calls and pray for mercy, rather than running deeper into the woods hoping that God will never discover you there. Adam responded to the Lord thusly:

"I heard your voice."

Though Adam had sinned, he could still hear the voice of the Lord when He spoke. This is one of the greatest gifts God has given fallen man: the ability still to hear the Word of God even after we have sinned. Otherwise, we would perish without hope. We must be ready to hear the voice of the Lord when He calls.

"I was afraid."

When Adam disobeyed through unbelief, he became fearful in the presence of the Lord. Fear is the inevitable result of sin, and it is why we are so reluctant to come running when the Lord calls. We are afraid. Of course, this is not "the fear of the Lord," the fear that produces a holy reverence and awe. Adam's fear was a fear of judgment and damnation, the fear of death. This fear is the root of insecurity that threatens every relationship. Only the perfect love of Christ (unconditional love, the self-sufficient love of God) can cast out this fear. Sin brings fear, and fear erodes our relationship with God. This erosion of trust and confidence toward God affects our relationships as husband and wife, parents and children, and as brothers and sisters. Sin causes fear, and fear destroys the peace of the home.

"I was naked."

Adam recognized that he was naked even though he had tried to cover himself with fig leaves. At least Adam had the good sense to admit that his attempts to cover himself were inadequate. Those who trust in their own efforts can never be saved, and their family can never be saved. We must admit that sin has exposed our weaknesses and left us insecure before God and man. Only God knows what we need to be truly covered. Pretending that everything is alright in the presence of the Lord only perpetuates the problem and ensures that we remain naked and insecure. Confidence before God is the root of confidence before men. We must recognize that our fig leaves of self-righteousness still leave us naked.

"I hid myself."

Adam admitted that he was hiding. Again, the man had the presence of mind to be honest about his futile attempts to escape divine scrutiny. Christians often perfect their disguises and stubbornly pretend that no one knows the truth. Some have worn a mask for so long that they have nearly convinced themselves that it is their true appearance. But God knows the truth. He knows who we are deep down inside beyond the mask. God is calling us to open our hearts and admit we are hiding from Him. This is the first step to repentance and restoration.

God's Response to Adam

God listened to Adam as he explained that he was hiding from God because he was naked and afraid of His voice. God then asked two questions: (1) "Who told you that you were naked?" and (2) "Have you eaten of the fruit of the tree that I commanded you not to eat?"

God did not deny the obvious, that the man and woman are indeed naked before Him, and He made no attempt to lessen their shame and discomfort. The only hope for man at that point was his ability to confront his sin honestly in the presence of the Lord. All God wanted to know as who had been talking to them and whether they had disobeyed. Of course, God knew the answer before He asked, but it was necessary that man answer the question and confess his sins before the Lord.

Adam explained that he hid because he was afraid, and he was afraid because he was naked. This is exactly how sinful man responds to God every time. Man tries to turn the focus on the fact of his nakedness, on his weakness and vulnerability. Sinners try to hide behind their emotional problems, psychological scars and existential weakness. We often try to explain our problems in terms of personality flaws, insecurities and inferiority complexes. We say that we are sick, maybe that we were abused as children, anything to turn the gaze of God's righteousness away from the free choice that we made to disobey, away from our sinful deeds to our helpless human condition. We can be very creative when excusing our sins.

We sometimes even become defiant in our attempt to convince God and everyone else that we cannot help our condition, that we have an excuse. We end up developing a prolonged and pitiful self-analysis and self-defense. Sinners will pay outrageous sums of money, wallowing self-indulgently on a therapist's couch in a darkened room, to be consoled ever so gently and have it carefully explained to them that in fact *they* are the real victims, that their behavior could not be helped, and no one should be allowed to blame *them* for the problem. Whatever it takes to avoid facing the reality of their sins.

Marriages are destroyed and relationships are shattered because people waste so much time in introspective navel-gazing. Solutions for the problems cannot be found because each partner in the crisis insists on analyzing and defending themselves as naked and helpless. Sinners claim they cannot *do* differently because they cannot *be* different. They insist that the problem lies within their flawed psyche. This is the fundamental problem with humanistic solutions to human problems: humanists (psychologists, psychiatrists, self-help gurus, etc.) turn the eyes of man upon himself rather than upon God and His Word.

We need less self-centered introspection and more awe-struck repentance as we behold the holiness of the Lord. Repentance occurs when men lift their eyes from their unholy selves to the Holy One. We must acknowledge that the root of the problem does not lie in our existential, personal and emotional problems, but rather the root of the problem lies in our disobedience to the Word of God.

God went directly to the heart of the matter: "Adam, did you eat of the fruit of the tree that I commanded you not to eat?" God ignored their nakedness. He would deal with that issue later. It is amazing how God refuses to waste time on side issues. He laid bare the root of the problem: *"You have sinned!"* If we wish to confront the problems in our home, then we must get to the heart of the matter. The problem is that we have hearkened to lying voices and disobeyed the Word of God. The problems in our home are always a result of disobedience. The problem is sin.

Responsibility for Sin

When God insisted on going to the heart of the matter, Adam started pointing fingers. He pointed one finger at the woman and one finger at God: "The *woman* that *You* gave me…." Adam admitted that he ate the fruit, but only because the woman gave it to him. And furthermore, if God had not given him this woman in the first place, then he would have never disobeyed. So the man claimed that both the woman and God were responsible for man's failure, not him. That refrain sounds familiar to anyone who has ever met a man caught in sin.

Adam refused to accept personal and federal responsibility for his sin and the sin of his house and offered feeble excuses. This has been the man's habit ever since. Men are accomplished at making excuses. Women also make excuses, but men are especially good at it. When men are caught in a sin, they will point stubbornly at everything and everyone but themselves. Men are loath to accept personal responsibility for their actions and quickly pass the buck. This tendency must be conquered before we can attain the restoration of the Christian family. Men must accept their God-given responsibility for leading the home. We cannot waste time pointing fingers and making pitiful excuses.

Jesus reversed this trend when He accepted responsibility for the sins of His bride and died in her place. The Cross is the ultimate emblem of a man's love for his wife, of his willingness to be the responsible party. The man must be willing to face God for the sins of the home regardless of who is guilty. The man stands before God for the home and must give an account to God for the deeds done in the "body," the corporate body, the family that he leads. Redemption begins here with man's willingness to accept responsibility for his entire house.

God did not deny that the man was correct when he protested that the woman gave him the fruit. However, He did not allow that fact to exonerate man, as the later judgment upon man shows. God turned to the woman and asked her, "What have you done?" The woman imitated the folly of the man and passed the blame to others. She complained that she was deceived by the serpent. She recognized that she had a problem, that she was deceived, but she insisted that it was the serpent that was to blame. The man pointed fingers at God and at his wife. The woman pointed fingers at her own personal weakness and the devil who exploited it. Thus, they attempted to justify their sin by blaming it on God, on others, on physical, emotional, or mental conditions beyond their control, and on the devil.

We often do the same. We blame God for our situation. We point fingers at others, our spouse, our children, or other family and friends. We hurl curses at the devil and think that now we surely are safe in pointing fingers, for the devil deserves the blame even if he is innocent. We blame our minds, our bodies, our hormones, moods, sickness, weariness, our personalities inherited from obviously culpable parents, the weather, the area where we live, the neighbors who live around us and mow their grass at seven in the morning, going on and on creating an ever-growing list of people, places and things that deserve the time for our crime. In short, we blame everything and everyone other than the one who is truly guilty, the one who freely chose to disobey the command of the Lord—namely, *us.*

The clearest sign that a man has not truly repented is when he still insists on confessing everyone's sins but his own. God is not to blame, our spouse is not to blame, our physical circumstances and conditions are not to blame, and the devil is not to blame. We are the guilty ones, and we must confront this fact and confess our own sin before God. This is the only hope we have for rooting sin out of the home and rebuilding our families on a holy foundation.

11

The Curse upon the Serpent

Genesis 3:14, 15. "And the LORD God said unto the serpent, Because thou hast done this, thou art cursed above all cattle, and above every beast of the field; upon thy belly shalt thou go, and dust shalt thou eat all the days of thy life: And I will put enmity between thee and the woman, and between thy seed and her seed; it shall bruise thy head, and thou shalt bruise his heel."

The Lord God ignored Adam and Eve's stammering excuses for the moment and turned His fierce anger toward the serpent. God gave the serpent absolutely no opportunity for explanations. He simply launched into a fiery denunciation of the serpent's devious treachery. "Because you have done this, you are cursed." The Lord wasted no time doing dialogue with the devil.

By cursing the devil first, the Lord God identified the primary front in the battle for the family. The fight for the family is a spiritual one. We are arrayed against "principalities, against powers, against the rulers of the darkness of this world, against spiritual wickedness in high places" (Ephesians 6:12). The serpents that we allow to slither into our garden prove to be much more than friendly beasts of the field, much more than just culture and custom, much more than just harmless entertainment. The "harmless" little serpents that we let loose in our house grow into deadly vipers that poison the minds and hearts of our children. The battle for the family is a spiritual battle with deadly and eternal consequences. We should learn this first of all.

Notice that it was *God* who addressed the serpent. We need this sort of divine response today. As we deal with sin in the family and seek for repentance and restoration, we must allow the Lord to step into our home and rebuke the devil for us (Zechariah 3:2, Jude 9). It takes the power of the Almighty to drive the devil away. We shall have absolutely no success trying to cast out devils on our own. We shall be like the seven sons of Sceva running naked in the streets (Acts 19:14), or like the faithless disciples who could not quite get the devil out (Matthew 17:14-21). Jesus rebuked them for their unbelief and reminded them that this sort of devil comes out through prayer and fasting. Faithful prayer and fasting calls on the Lord to do for us what we cannot do for ourselves.

We may encounter a devil that has become embedded in our home. The only way to get that stubborn spirit out—whether it be a spirit of worldly entertainment, a spirit of lust and covetousness, a spirit of bitterness and division, or any other evil spirit—is by prayer and fasting, by calling on the Lord and getting self out of the way. We cannot cast out devils in the flesh. We need the Spirit of the Lord to rise up in the face of the serpent, to curse him and cast him out. While the Lord is in our garden confronting and correcting our sin, we must allow Him to take charge of the spirit *of* our home and every spirit *in* our home. When God speaks His Word against Satan, he falls "like lightning from heaven" (Luke 10:18).

Only God can speak a word against Satan and root him out of our house. And God has chosen to speak His Word through anointed preaching and teaching. We receive this preaching and teaching through weekly worship at church and daily in the home through family devotions offered each morning and evening. Men who fail to submit to the Word of God are destined to abandon their family to the wiles of the devil. The only answer to the devil is God's answer—the answer of God's curse upon sin and His gospel of grace to atone for sin.

The Far-reaching Effects of Sin

Because of the serpent's treachery and betrayal, he was cursed by the Lord "above all cattle, and above every beast of the field." This statement lends credence to the idea that the serpent was a literal snake that Satan indwelled for his diabolical purpose. Further, it indicates that God made the judgment upon the serpent greater than the judgment that God pronounced upon the rest of creation. Satan's curse is greater in that all creation is offered redemption, whereas Satan has no opportunity to be redeemed. The Bible declares that all of creation shall be liberated by the resurrection of the righteous (Romans 8:21), but Satan and his angels are destined without recourse for hell.

The curse upon the serpent also shows that all of creation—the cattle and the beasts of the field—shares in the curse that God placed upon Adam. We shall see in a moment how God cursed the ground for man's sake, but here, even the animals are described as being under the curse of sin. Paul spoke of creation as "groaning" and "travailing" under the curse of sin, longing for the resurrection and redemption that is coming (Romans 8). All creation was affected by Adam's fall.

The curse upon the serpent also affected the heavens. Satan was created, as were all angels, to be a "ministering [spirit] sent forth to minister for them who shall be heirs of salvation" (Hebrews 1:14; *cf.* Psalm 104:4). He was a guardian angel, and he fell from this office when he led man into sin rather than keeping him from it. The fall of Satan affected the entire order of the heavens, and the heavens came under the same curse as the earth. This is why we insist that the work of redemption is not complete until the physical heavens and earth are made eternally new.

When Satan fell, all principalities and powers under his command fell with him ("the devil and his angels"–Matthew 25:41). Satan has been falling since the garden and shall fall finally and eternally into everlasting fire. The ultimate destiny of the serpent is to be crushed by the work of Christ beneath the feet of redeemed humanity.

The curse upon the serpent ensures our victory over him and over all evil heavenly powers. Christ fulfilled the promise of the curse when He bruised the head of the serpent at Calvary. The fullness of this victory awaits the Second Coming, but it is "worked out" in the evangelistic task of the church. Satan is being defeated by the church here and now. This has tremendous implications for the life of the Christian family, as we shall see.

The widespread effect of the curse bears witness to the terrible fact that every man who sins in his home brings consequences that affect everything under his influence, even things that he influences indirectly. The "cattle and beasts" of man's life (his job, his friends and neighbors, his hobbies and interests) and the "heavens" of a man's world (the spiritual powers that influence his actions) are all affected tremendously by the man's decision to allow the serpent in the home. We cannot deny that sin distorts and perverts every relationship we have. When we are tempted to sin, we must remember that our decision to sin will have a far-reaching and long-lasting effect.

A Diet of Dust

God declared that the serpent would go upon his belly eating a diet of dust, which is a sign of his total humiliation. These two things—going on his belly and eating dust—are vivid metaphors of Satan's defeat by Christ through the church. The serpent being forced down upon his belly is a powerful sign that the church shall continue pressing Satan down so that he is unable to stand upright again with dominion and authority. His original dignity and prestige is stripped away, and he is made lower than all of the beasts of the field.

The serpent also must choke on dust for the rest of his days, which is a symbol of Satan's defeat by humanity, by those formed from dust. God promised the devil that he would be utterly defeated by lowly mortals, particularly through the man Christ Jesus, who shared in our mortality. This part of the curse must have driven Satan absolutely mad with rage. The promise of man's triumph over him was the ultimate disgrace. It is one thing for a fallen angel to be cursed by God or defeated by another angel. But to be defeated by man—that is absolutely intolerable! And yet, that is exactly what happened in Christ at the Cross and is still happening in the evangelistic mission of the church. The serpent is being crushed under the feet of man. "How art thou fallen from heaven, O Lucifer, son of the morning! How art thou cut down to the ground, which didst weaken the nations!" (Isaiah 14:12).

It is God's purpose and promise that godly Christian families shall defeat Satan completely. That slimy serpent has been forced onto his belly where he crawls choking on the clouds of dust kicked in his face by the dancing feet of victorious men. It is the promise of God that we should defeat the devil in our home and cast him out. If the devil has the upper hand in our home, it is because we have allowed it. We must claim the power of the Cross to give us the victory and destroy the works of the devil. Moreover, the family is central to the task of dominion. Christian families are ordained to be the training center for Christian dominion in the earth. Faithful fathers and mothers are called to rear up serpent-stomping, devil-defeating, dust-raising children of God who tread upon serpents in the name of the Lord.

Satan knows better than we do the power of the curse upon him, and he knows better than we do the power of the Christian family to make it a reality. Thus, Satan will stop at nothing to steal, kill and destroy the power of the family. We are at war with all of the powers of hell, but we have the assurance that the devil is cursed, that he is on his belly and choking on our dust.

The Enmity

The Lord promised to put enmity between the serpent and the seed of the woman. That promise has certainly been fulfilled. As the words of the curse echoed in the serpent's ears, and his glistening, upright body began to wither down into the dust, writhing in useless resistance against the Word of the Lord, Satan surely went down hissing foul and blasphemous oaths of vengeance against the man and the woman he had deceived. Certainly a burning hatred smoldered in his narrowed eyes as his legs became twisted and useless, and finally fell away like dry, shriveled leaves in winter.

The serpent collapsed onto his belly and then slowly twisted and slithered away into the forest, and the words of the Lord burned like the fires of hell in the devil's soul. From then until now Satan has never forgotten God's promise that the seed of the woman would crush his head. And from then until now Satan has sworn the total annihilation of mankind. The only way Satan can live is for man to die.

Satan is at war with the seed of the woman. This is primarily Christ and the body of Christ, the church. But in a larger sense, the seed of the woman is mankind. The devil hates the children of men. The devil sees every child, every teenager, every man and woman as a threat. We may look around us and see only children playing in a schoolyard, but Satan sees potential missionaries, evangelists, and preachers. He sees potential witnesses and prayer

147

warriors. Thus, he is on a desperate quest to promote abortion, euthanasia, infanticide, murder, nuclear war, terrorism, and any other means to destroy the human race. It is only by the mercy and forbearance of God that we are not destroyed already.

The Family and Christian Dominion

This has particular relevance to the family. Satan recognizes the value of the family. He knows that the family is the centerpiece of the plan God designed for attaining dominion in the earth. "Be fruitful and multiply," God says, and "have dominion." There is a direct connection between the growth of the family and the growth of the kingdom of God. God has determined to use people for His work, people who are born into families and reared in families, who leave home in order to build their own families. Those born and reared in godly families stand a much better chance of carrying on their parents' vision for life in their own families. Those who are born in a sinful family stand a good chance of reproducing and multiplying the sins of their parents. Thus, it is to the devil's advantage to undermine and destroy the family.

This is why the devil has worked so hard to destroy the roles of fathers and mothers, husbands and wives, parents and children. This is why the devil has worked so hard to promote ungodly views of dating and courtship, of engagement and betrothal, and of the marriage relationship itself. This is why Satan has worked so hard to promote divorce and remarriage, cohabitation and "open marriage." He has attempted to persuade our culture to accept homosexuality as an alternative lifestyle and legitimate form of "marriage." He has "pornographized" our society and promoted lust and covetousness as normal. He has mainstreamed adultery and fornication until our world has forgotten the beauty of exclusive, covenantal relationships.

Satan has successfully placed a stigma within Western culture on having children. The shame that was once attached to having children outside of wedlock is now attached to those within wedlock who choose to have many children. We now reserve the scorn that was once directed at the parents of illegitimate children for the parents of numerous children. It is okay in America to have children out of wedlock as long as you only have one or two and abort the rest.

We no longer believe the Word of God when it says, "Lo, children are an heritage of the LORD: and the fruit of the womb is his reward. As arrows are in the hand of a mighty man; so are children of the youth. Happy is the man that hath his quiver full of them: they shall not be ashamed, but they shall speak with the enemies in the gate" (Psalm 127:3-5). Satan largely has succeeded in distorting God's blessing into a curse.

Of course, the reason he is so desperate to do so is revealed in the verse quoted above: our children are like arrows in the hand of a mighty man. The devil knows that he is the target of well-aimed arrows, and he must strip the mighty men of their weapons. Therefore, he is out to discourage and prevent the birth of children. Satan is a firm believer in population control.

Of course, we know that the Word of God cannot fail. Satan is defeated by the Cross of Jesus Christ and the victory is already won. But the victory of the Cross shall be "played out" in our lives and made a reality by our faith. The defeat of Satan shall come through the seed of the woman, Jesus Christ and His church, the redeemed of the human race who shall inherit the earth. This is the work of evangelism.

And the very center of this evangelistic, redemptive force rests in the Christian home. Both the church and godly society are built upon the foundation of the Christian home. We shall crush the head of Satan under the feet of children who are sent out as arrows into the earth to pierce and destroy the works of the devil. Obviously, not all Christians come from godly families, but every Christian should be seeking to build a godly home that we might raise up countless family discipleship centers around the world. Building up our family is a matter of spiritual warfare and dominion. No wonder Satan is frantic.

12

The Curse upon the Woman

*Genesis 3:16. "Unto the woman he said, I will
greatly multiply thy sorrow and thy conception; in sorrow
thou shalt bring forth children; and thy desire shall be to
thy husband, and he shall rule over thee."*

The curse upon the woman followed the curse upon the
serpent. Her curse was two-fold: multiplied *sorrow* in
conception and imposed *subjugation* to her husband. This
marked a profound change in the woman's relationship to both
her children and her husband. It marked the beginning of pain.

Sorrow

When God declared that the woman's sorrow would be
multiplied in childbirth, He did not say that her conception itself
would be multiplied. This is often misunderstood. The English
Standard Version correctly renders the Lord's statement: "To the
woman he said, 'I will surely multiply your pain in childbearing; in
pain you shall bring forth children. Your desire shall be for your
husband, and he shall rule over you.'" The curse multiplies the
pain, not the rate of conception. Multiplied conception is never a
curse in Scripture. Fruitfulness always is considered a great
blessing. God commanded Adam and Eve to be fruitful and
multiply long before they sinned. God said that the sorrow itself
would be greatly multiplied during pregnancy and childbirth. This
was the beginning of travail and labor in childbirth.

The Lord's promise that the woman's sorrow would be
multiplied in "bring[ing] forth" children refers to her pain in
childrearing as well as childbearing. Mothers are cursed with a
unique sorrow in the rearing of children from infancy into

adulthood. It is in this sense that the pain of pregnancy and childbirth is but a physical emblem of the spiritual sorrow that prevails in the sin-marred relationship of a mother and her children throughout their lifetimes. As Jesus stated, the sorrow of birth is quickly forgotten in the joy that a child is born (John 16:21).

But every mother bearing and rearing children under the curse of sin can testify that the pain does not end in the delivery room. Rather, it soon becomes a different kind of pain, a deep emotional pain, as the mother watches her children growing up in a fallen world. The pain of mothering can be almost unbearable at times, particularly when the woman is forced by time and space to loosen loving arms and let her children grow and go.

The pain of childbearing and childrearing can be intensified through the vicarious suffering that a mother endures when she sees her children suffer. Mary, the mother of Jesus, felt this pain as she beheld her Son dying on the Cross, when, as the Bible describes it, "a sword [pierced] through [her] soul" (Luke 2:35). The greatest instinct of a mother is to protect her children from the suffering of life. And yet, that protection is never adequate and may even become harmful if not properly restrained and retrained. Many children are unwisely sheltered from the hurtful realities of life by an overanxious mother. Only God can give a mother the wisdom to know when and how to let her children go.

The pain of a mother can also be multiplied through the sin and disobedience of her children. Eve quickly discovered, as all mothers do, that the momentary pain of childbearing is but a fleeting discomfort compared to the ever-present sorrow of wayward children. Surely Eve's heart was broken in the loss of her first two sons, Cain and Abel, as one was banished as a murderer and the other buried as his victim. Sometimes the child is an Abel who suffers wrong at the hands of others, and the tenderhearted mother suffers with them through their pain. At other times, the mother's child is the wrongdoer like Cain, and her heart is broken with shame for the sin her child has committed and compassion for the sinner her child has become. Thus, the mother's sorrow is greatly multiplied.

Subjugation

The second part of the woman's curse was that her "desire shall be to [her] husband, and he shall rule over [her]." There are two elements of the curse described here:

Desire

The word "desire" here means "a longing, a craving, a stretching out after." It comes from a root word that literally means "to run after; to overflow." The woman will have an intense longing for her husband, a craving for the man she was created to serve as a helpmeet. But this part of the curse has both a positive and a negative sense. The words "your desire shall be *to* your husband" can also be understood as "your desire shall be *against* your husband." The woman shall be driven by an intense desire to overflow against her husband like a river floods out of its banks. Thus, the Scripture predicts one of the most fundamental conflicts known to man (or woman): the woman has an innate and inescapable desire for her husband, and yet she finds herself desiring nothing more than to overthrow his authority and rule in his place. She desperately longs to run *to* him and run *over* him at the same time.

Dominion

Due to the fact of a woman's desire for and against her husband, sinful man shall respond to the woman's desire by suppressing her into compliance and subjection. The word "rule" literally means "to have dominion." However—and this must be properly emphasized—this is never what God intended for the relationship of man and wife. The fact that man shall impose his dominion over the woman is a result of sin. Both Adam and Eve were created to share dominion over the earth as rulers together. God never intended for the man to rule over the woman as if she were a beast of the field or a servant to do his bidding. Certainly God intended for man to lead the family and for the wife to be his willing helpmeet. But there is a great difference between the relationship of co-workers with a designated leader and the relationship of an oppressive ruler and an unwilling subject.

Conflict of Desires

So, Eve, and all women after her, was cursed with a conflict of desires, the desire to cling to a husband and the desire to strangle him all at the same time. Women naturally want a husband "to have and to hold," but just *how* they choose to have and hold him is the question. Some have him so completely and hold him so tightly that they smother the life out of him. Every woman, no matter how godly, struggles against the urge to rise up against their husband's authority. No woman is exempt from this inclination. The sooner a godly woman recognizes this sinful urge and brings it under the power of the Cross through repentance, the sooner she will overcome her urge rather than overcoming her husband.

Any man who is truly a man at all will react with some sort of resistance to the woman's attempt to usurp his God-given authority and responsibility to lead. Sinful man will react just as the Lord said he would: he will rise up and take dominion over the woman and subdue her through brute force if necessary.

Civilized men stop short of actual violence, but only because they are taught to control their aggressive masculine urge by a cultural and moral code with a residue of Christian influence. Christian culture holds it to be fundamental that "boys do not hit girls!" Those cultures where Christianity has exercised little or no influence are often incredibly oppressive toward women. This is particularly true in Islamic societies. This highlights an amazing contradiction in the ideas of modern feminists who want an antichristian, relativistic society, but they want it very selectively. When it comes to violence against women, the weaker sex, they suddenly reject the Darwinian idea of "the survival of the fittest." If evolution is true, then men should simply follow their animal instinct to dominate anyone weaker than themselves. Of course, feminists abhor that result.

The only thing that prevents all-out everlasting war between the sexes is that men get tired of fighting and women learn to get their way through other, more subtle means. Women learn to get their way by patient *man*ipulation and *man*agement. Women learn to bide their time and wait for what they want. Women can be supreme opportunists, such as Herodias, the adulterous wife of Herod, who waited until the right moment and then connived to cut off the head of John the Baptist (Matthew 14:8). Herod was sorry that he had to kill John the Baptist, but the powerful king was a slave to his lusts. He was trapped by his cunning wife and was not man enough to refuse her. It was unfortunate for John, but Herod decided that he would do the practical thing. Even kings can be hen-pecked.

Men learn that dominion over a woman can be costly, and some decide it is not worth the trouble. As we have seen, one of the primary failings of men in the first place is the tendency to abdicate leadership to their wife, who often is very eager to assume it. Often, the woman agitates for control until the man abdicates control. Then, both learn to live in their unnatural arrangement until sin blows it apart.

So, the woman desires a man and then attempts to control that man. The man responds either by oppressing the woman or by deciding that he does not want the trouble of ruling her and lets her run the house so he can enjoy peace of mind. Either way, it is the man who decides the outcome. Sinful men will rule either by aggression or abdication, but they *shall* rule.

They will either force the women to submit to their will, or they will submit to the will of the woman because they *choose* to do so. Then they set back and let the women do the heavy lifting because she thinks she knows better how it should be done. This kind of man does not mind if the woman thinks she knows better how to do anything so long as she does not demand that he do it. He refuses to lead because he is too lazy to lead. No man is subject to any woman without choosing to be. It is inevitable that the man shall rule over the woman. Societies and cultures may seem to reverse the trend for a while, but it will never last. Sinful man will always dominate and oppress the sinful woman.

Even in feministic societies, where the women seem to dominate, the reality is simply nothing more than languid men abdicating their responsibilities until they are ready to rule again. Indeed, the men rule by *not* ruling. Feminism is promoted by effete men, men who acquiesce to bossy women because then *they* do not have to feel responsible for anything.

Look at what the modern man has accomplished by feeding the intellectual vanity of feminists: the men have "liberated" the home-bound wife and cordially invited her into his workplace. But guess who generally still does the dishes at home? The man might still take out the trash on occasion, but most women have been duped into doing the man's job *and* hers. She stupidly bears both her curse and his and proudly boasts of emancipation.

Modern woman was "liberated" by the male-engineered sexual revolution and deceived into surrendering the greatest power she ever had—the right to require the man to marry her and faithfully provide for her and her children before he could share her bed. And now the women give the male beasts what they wanted all along without an ounce of commitment. The modern enlightened man persuades the modern enlightened woman that she was shamefully repressed all these many years by Puritans and Victorians and should boldly strip off the restrictive garments of legalistic tradition and parade down the boulevard in naked freedom. Then, the generous-hearted men gladly crowd together along the parade route to ogle freely. So, who is really free? The only thing free about feminists is that they no longer charge for their harlotry.

Hurting and Helping

The woman was created to be a godly wife and mother. She was created to be a helpmeet to the man as he fulfilled his task of dominion through work and worship, and she was created to bear and rear his children for the worldwide extension of dominion through work and worship. She was created to find her fulfillment in helping her husband and training up her children. She was created to be the helper of her husband and the keeper (guardian) of the home. But when the woman sinned, the curse came upon the very essence of her role as a person. Sin completely altered the relationship of women to their children and to their husband. The joy of bearing and rearing children was mingled with terrible pain, and the willing submission to the man's headship and leadership became a reluctant and grudging subjection to be resisted and overthrown, marked by a desperate desire to be *with* and *against* her husband.

Sin, and the pain it brought with it, turned the woman's orientation away from serving others to preserving self. The woman struggles with a conflict of needs. She was created to serve and desperately needs to be fulfilled in helping her husband and nurturing her children. But the pain and passion of being a mother and wife makes the woman selfish in the very thing she was created to do selflessly. The pain of mothering, the sorrow of watching children grow into independent adults who no longer "need" to be mothered, can turn nurture into nagging, care into control and mothering into smothering. A mother reacts against her own pain and thoughtlessly hurts the ones that she loves the most. She does not mean to hurt anyone, particularly not her children, but the sorrow she feels makes her blind with pain.

The wife reacts selfishly against the desire she feels for her husband. The woman knows instinctively that the man needs help; the Lord said it was so. However, the woman sometimes forgets that the Lord declared that man needed a "helpmeet," a "helper that is fitting." The woman just knows he needs *help*! She then selfishly focuses more on giving him the help she thinks he needs than the help that he really *does* need. She needs to help and he needs to be helped, so she determines to help more in the sense of satisfying her own need to help than in discovering what kind of help the man needs. Since the man often does not agree with the woman on the kind of help he needs, her desire to help and his refusal to be helped creates a tremendous struggle for control, a perfect storm. Thus, her selfish help becomes a hindrance and hurts much more than it helps.

The curse of sin can destroy the relationship of a woman to her husband and her children. The children begin to withdraw, and the grieving mother cannot understand why they seem to be shrinking ever smaller in the distance. She does not see that her need to help has made her unbearable. She is satisfying an urge to feed without considering who has the urge to eat, and her babies, who have become adults without her noticing, are choking on her nourishment. Therefore, the only recourse left to mother-smothered children is to flee the hand that rocks the cradle so that it cannot rule their world.

The curse of sin affects the relationship of the wife and husband as the husband refuses to be less than a man and surrender control. Because he is a sinner, he does not respond properly to her usurpation of authority. He overreacts with anger and resentment. This is why the apostle warns men not to become "bitter" against their wives (Colossians 3:19). The woman feels frustrated because she is just doing what she was created to do—she's just trying to *help*! And the man is crying out for help, but it is not the kind of help the woman is giving.

So, either the man berates the woman into a moody silence, or he withdraws into complete isolation. He works extra hours, goes fishing with the boys (they never try to *help* him!), or he spends time with another woman who is not sworn to be his helpmeet and thus feels no passion to help him (she just uses him for her guilty pleasure). The man is running from help because he is not receiving the kind of help God ordained the woman to give. She is giving a self-centered help that simply uses the man as a convenient object to satisfy her own need to help somebody. She is driven by her pain and passion, and she drives her children away and her husband crazy.

The Chastening of the Curse

God created the woman to be fulfilled as a wife and mother. Because of sin, the curse came upon these fundamental roles of womanhood, and the woman lives with terrible pain as a result. As we noted, the physical pain and passion of being a mother and wife is but an emblem of the spiritual pain that goes far deeper and hurts far worse. But the curse upon the serpent precedes the curse upon the woman and contains a promise that that the seed of the woman shall crush the serpent's head. This was a powerful promise of victory made to the woman just before she heard the terrible news of the curse. The curse upon the woman (and later, upon the man) should always be considered, then, in light of the promise of redemption. God gave no hope of redemption to the serpent. His sin is irremediable and final. But the curse upon the woman follows close upon and flows out of the first promise of redemption in the Bible. This is important, for the curse upon Adam and Eve must be viewed as being an extension of the promise made to them. Thus, as we shall see, God intended to accomplish the promise by the means of the curse.

God's curse upon the woman was administered as a chastening for her sin. And, as we noted earlier, God's chastening is never mere punishment. God always chastens remedially, to bring about repentance and restoration. The purpose of the curse upon mankind is not to destroy mankind, but rather to save him. The sorrow of sin should always bring the sinner to repentance.

The only hope for redemption a man has is his dissatisfaction with sin. As long as sin is more pleasure than pain, more fun than frustration, the sinner will never seek to be free. Remember Israel: they did not cry for deliverance from Pharaoh until his hand became cruel and oppressive. As long as things were easy, Egypt was a nice place to live, even if you were a slave. However, God hardened Pharaoh's heart until he oppressed the people of God so severely that they cried out for deliverance. The same is true of fallen men and women: God put the curse upon us that we might never be content to remain in our sins, estranged from God and righteousness. Therefore, the pain and passion of being a wife and mother should cause the sinful woman to look to the Lord for mercy and deliverance.

So, there is a redemptive aspect to the curse upon the woman. In spite of her pain—in fact, *through* her pain—God has promised to bring salvation. Indeed, it is only by accepting the curse that the woman can truly find salvation. It is the tendency of sinful woman to struggle against the curse, to remove the pain of childbearing and childrearing, and to subdue by any means possible the passion of desiring a man. This has been the objective of radical feminists. They desperately want to cast off the curse and rid sin of its power. They think they can "choose" whether or not to live under the curse. They choose abortion; they choose a career; they choose to live without a husband; they choose "alternative lifestyles." And yet, with all of their choices they cannot avoid the unavoidable: they are under the curse of sin and cannot find peace and contentment outside of the purpose of God.

13

The Curse and Childbearing

Paul's teaching in I Timothy 2:8-15 is a powerful explanation and application of the curse pronounced upon Eve in the garden. Paul spoke about the transgression of the woman and how she may overcome the curse: "I will therefore that men pray every where, lifting up holy hands, without wrath and doubting. In like manner also, that women adorn themselves in modest apparel, with shamefacedness and sobriety; not with braided hair, or gold, or pearls, or costly array. But (which becometh women professing godliness) with good works. Let the woman learn in silence with all subjection. But I suffer not a woman to teach, nor to usurp authority over the man, but to be in silence. For Adam was first formed, then Eve. And Adam was not deceived, but the woman being deceived was in the transgression. Notwithstanding she shall be saved in childbearing, if they continue in faith and charity and holiness with sobriety."

Paul spoke here of a woman's subjection to her husband, the modesty and meekness that should characterize the good works of a Christian woman and how she should "learn in silence with all subjection." Paul gave two reasons for this subjection: (1) Adam was first formed, which speaks of the creation order and Adam's priority as man and leader; and (2) Adam was not deceived, which speaks of the fact that the woman was never intended from the beginning to be the spiritual leader. When the wife does lead, she becomes vulnerable to deception by stepping outside of God's ordained headship. It is not a matter of intelligence; it is a matter of authority and spiritual covering. The woman is exposed to spiritual forces beyond her power to resist when she steps away from the protective covering of her husband's authority. And this was true prior to Eve's disobedience. The woman's willing submission to her husband's leadership is a fact of creation. "Adam was first formed then Eve." The woman should recognize the authority of her husband and remain under it.

Paul also stated that the woman "being deceived was in the transgression." The woman's sin involved a component of deception that Adam's sin did not. Then Paul declared that the woman shall be "saved in childbearing, if they continue in faith and charity and holiness with sobriety." This statement has produced a variety of interpretations, including the idea that women are saved from sin by having children. However, this interpretation is unacceptable seeing that it is obvious that scripture nowhere teaches that the biological fact of motherhood is God's plan of salvation. We are all saved by the work of Christ at Calvary, not our work in a delivery room having babies. Moreover, if women are saved in childbearing, in the sense of eternal salvation, then this opens up the question of whether barren women can be saved without bearing children. Of course, nowhere in scripture is barrenness viewed as damnable. Barrenness was considered a reproach upon the woman, but barren women were never shut out from the presence of God. It seems evident that Paul's statement is not referring to eternal salvation.

Some have interpreted this statement to mean that God will protect all Christian women from dying in childbirth, but the precedent of scripture as well as practical experience refutes that idea. Others have connected the idea of childbirth here with the promise made to Eve that the Messiah would come through her seed and that all mankind would be saved by the seed of the woman, Christ Jesus. Of course, there is a sense in which this is true, but that is probably not what Paul had in mind since he referred to "they" (mothers) who must continue in righteousness to be saved. The saving life and work of Messiah was not dependent upon the continuing righteousness of believing mothers.

The best sense of this statement is that Paul, by connecting the transgression of Eve to the childbearing of believing women, was hearkening back to the curse that God pronounced upon the woman for her transgression and showing how the woman can be "saved" from the transgression, "saved" from the curse. The word "saved" here includes the meaning "to be made whole." Therefore, the wife is made whole by bearing and rearing children as she continues in the faith. She becomes a "complete" woman through childbearing.

Transforming the Curse

Now, we must recall here that the curse upon the woman was not childbirth itself, but rather the pain and travail that now accompanies childbirth due to sin. Transgression created travail. So, when Paul speaks of overcoming the curse through childbirth, he is promising that the sorrow of bearing children can be transformed into joy. He does not mean, of course, that the physical pain of labor and travail will be taken away for Christian mothers. Rather, he means that Christian mothers, as they "continue in faith and charity and holiness with sobriety," shall overturn the power of the curse and transform the pain of motherhood into joy. Mothers can be confident that if they "train up a child in the way that he should go," then when he is old he will not depart from it. This is how the curse upon the woman is overcome and she is "saved" through childbearing.

John declared that we have "no greater joy" than to know that our children walk in truth (III John 4). When our children are faithful to the Lord, then the terrible pain that pierces the soul of a mother is transformed into indescribable joy. Mary, the mother of Jesus, suffered terrible pain as she watched her Son die upon the Cross, the emblem of suffering and shame. Even though she knew that He was God in a way that no one else could know, she could not help but feel the grief of a mother as He died a horrible death and was sealed away later in the borrowed tomb. Then on resurrection morning, Mary must have been overwhelmed with unspeakable joy as the suffering of the Cross was transformed into the glory of the resurrection, and the power of sin's curse was broken in her Son, Jesus Christ. This is the perfect example of how the gospel of Christ can break the power of the curse upon women and transform their transgression into triumph. They simply must accept the responsibility of bearing and rearing children and continue, as they do so, in faith, charity and holiness with sobriety.

Accepting the Curse

Here is the key: the woman must accept the pain of motherhood in order to overcome it. The only way to overcome the curse is to submit to it. We can only get past the curse by going through it, not by trying to go around it. The curse cannot be avoided. In fact, those who seek to avoid the curse only prolong their misery. But those who recognize the mercy of God in His judgment upon the woman learn that God always hides the promise in the pain, the answers in the question, the joy in the sorrow. The blessing is *in* the curse.

And here is how. We are forced over time to learn in every part of our walk with God that it is impossible to share in the glory of the Lord without sharing in His suffering. There is something about God's glory that cannot be known by man until he has gone through the process of testing. Deification (in the biblical sense of sharing in His glory as we are made partakers of His divine nature—II Peter 1:4) only comes through purification. Mortal flesh cannot share in the fullness of God's indwelling presence—which is the only thing that permanently prevents sin—without going through the process of perfection through testing.

Christ accepted the curse of sin and endured the Cross. The Cross is comparable to giving birth, for Christ gave birth to a new creation through His resurrection. Christ manifested that He was filled with the fullness of God the Father by His perfect obedience. Even though Jesus despised the shame of the Cross and groaned under the curse, yet He knew that the blessing lay in the curse. "Cursed is everyone that hangeth on a tree" (Galatians 3:13). Christ accepted the curse and transformed it into a blessing through obedience.

This is very relevant and very important to the godly woman who wants to overcome the power of the curse and transform the curse into a blessing. No godly mother wants to go to her grave in sorrow over the sin of her children. No mother wants to bring children into the world and then see them lost forever. The sorrow of losing children to hell is almost unbearable. And yet, the Word of the Lord gives hope to the mother. If she will understand that the power to overcome the curse lies within accepting the curse itself, then she will overcome it by her faithful life. The woman must humbly submit to *being* a mother with all of its pain trusting that God will turn the sorrow into joy.

The tendency of unbelieving women is to resent the pain and rebel against the curse. Some even reject the role of being a mother and a wife altogether because they are seeking to avoid the pain. They loathe the curse that is upon motherhood, thus they come to loathe motherhood itself. They are like Christ in Gethsemane considering the unbelievable shame of crucifixion and struggling with the will to obey. And yet, so many fail to follow Christ's perfect example and totally surrender their will to the will of the Father. The mothers that resist the pain and reject the role that God created them to fulfill are destined to prolong and increase their pain. They are postponing the inevitable. If they refuse to share in the Cross of Christ, then they will fail to share in His glorious resurrection. And in refusing to accept the curse they ensure that they shall never escape it.

The Power of Pain

We must consider Paul's teaching further. Remember, we are considering how the woman can be made whole through childbearing. The pain of the curse is a symptom of sin. If we had no pain, then we might never recognize the presence of sin. The pain of the spirit is like the nerve endings of the soul. Just as bodily pain prevents us from being wounded terribly and possibly even killed, the pain of the soul can prevent us from destroying our lives and possibly even being damned. Pain in the hand saves the hand. Pain in the soul saves the soul.

Of course, we are not saved by the pain itself. There is no redemptive power in the pain. People who misunderstand this end up doing penance and believe they can earn salvation through self-inflicted punishment. But, though the pain does not save us, it does turn our hearts toward the Savior. Just as pain in the body makes us aware that we are sick and compels us to call for a physician, so the pain of the heart should make us know that we are sinners and compel us to call for the Great Physician.

The pain of the body keeps us out of the fire. The pain of the soul keeps us out of hell. Unbelievers deny the pain and refuse to be led by their hurt to their Healer. To accept the pain is to bring up the question of why the pain is there, which brings up the question of seeing the Doctor. Unbelievers are reluctant to see the Doctor because they know what He will say and they do not want to hear it. So, they attempt to mask the pain and pretend it is not there. But if they refuse to acknowledge the pain now, then they are condemned to acknowledge it for eternity.

Moreover, when unbelievers do acknowledge that they are in pain, they will generally deny the real reason why. They offer any explanation other than the right one, that they are under the curse of sin and need to repent. They seek relief through the narcotics of pleasure and entertainment, of money and materialism, of business and busyness. Sinners spend a lifetime looking for quick and easy solutions, for pain management, a sort of morphine for the soul. But they are looking for the wrong answers in all the wrong places because they are trying to escape the pain without dealing with the real problem. The pain points to a problem, a problem they refuse to confront.

Others who acknowledge that they *are* in pain go to quack doctors, to the fraudulent practitioners of a deadly medicine. The so-called experts—the psychiatrists, psychologists and counselors of our world—confidently write out prescriptions for treatments and therapies that simply dull the pain for a while but never treat the root of the problem. The medicine never gets to the heart of the matter, to the matter of the heart. It never gets in the bloodstream of the soul where the sickness flows. The sin-sick sinner can never get well, for he is being injected again and again with even more potent strains of the very disease of which he is dying—humanistic pride and unbelief. The hapless victims of humanism are injected with a lie that contains just enough truth to inoculate them against the gospel. The patients are dying because of their sins, and by turning for help to doctors who are themselves the slaves of sin, both the patient and the doctor assure their mutual destruction. So, the dying treat the dying and they both fall down together.

Sinners cannot solve the pain because they cannot solve the problem. They cannot remove the suffering because they do not recognize the source of the suffering. The source of the suffering

166

is sin; the problem producing the pain is sin. Therefore, we must gratefully acknowledge that God gave us the pain to save us from the problem. God knows our pain is terrible but our problem is fatal. So, He made the burden of our sins just heavy enough to make us stumble under its weight without crushing us completely.

So, the pain points to the problem, but the pain is not the problem. Indeed, the pain can lead to a solution for the problem. We might never confront our problem if it were not for the pain. However, we must learn to distinguish between the pain and the problem. In every relationship, pain is but a sign of deeper problems, whether they be marriage problems, parenting problems, problems at work or problems at school. We must allow the pain to lead us to the problem. When we try to alleviate the pain without fixing the problem, we simply prolong the pain.

The Problem of Pride

Now, we have taken this brief excursus on pain for a reason. This all has a very practical consequence upon the woman and her role as wife and mother. We must understand the purpose of the pain as it relates to women so that we do not ignore the pain and perpetuate the problem. In other words, the pain of being a mother and wife indicates a deeper problem that is fatal if left untreated. The pain should lead godly women to consider the fundamental problem that sin introduced to the role of being a wife and mother. There is a deeper problem that the God-given pain seeks to reveal.

So, what is the sin of the woman that brings the curse upon her? What is the problem that brings such pain? What is the problem to which the pain is pointing? We have said that the problem is sin, and that is so. But what form does this root of sin take? What specific sin is the root of the problem? The answer is *pride*. Eve was tempted to sin and deceived through pride. Just as Satan (who came to the woman as the serpent) was lifted up through pride and fell into condemnation, the woman was persuaded to sin and fell into transgression through pride. Simply put, *pride is the attempt to promote and preserve self*. Satan sought to exalt himself above God, and he tempted Eve to do the same. Of course, both Satan and Eve failed to attain divinity. We can only partake in the divine by "humbling ourselves under the mighty hand of God that He may exalt [us] in due season" (I Peter 5:6). However, this is how pride became the problem.

Now, we have already discussed the nature of the fall at length, but we need to recall it for just a moment. The sin of Eve was that she sought godlikeness apart from God. She trusted in the flesh. She was deceived by the serpent into believing that she could find maturity and perfection through intellectual knowledge apart from the indwelling fullness of the Spirit of God. Eve was deceived by pride into believing that she could become all she needed to be alone, without God or man. Pride made her believe that she could be independent and fulfilled without a submitted relationship toward God and man. She made the decision to sin apart and alone. Eve was the first "independent" woman.

Eve was tempted to believe that she could be a fulfilled woman apart from the purpose and plan of God. She thought she could stuff her head full of intellectual knowledge and be fulfilled as a woman. She thought she could be like God through the strength of her own mind, will and emotions. In other words, Eve thought she could be a wife and a mother in her own strength. And this is still the problem of sinful women today. The problem is pride: the idea that a woman can achieve success as a wife and mother without the help of Almighty God.

The idea that we can survive and thrive without the help of the Almighty is the lie of humanism, and it was the first lie that the serpent told Eve. Eve believed that she could be a wife and mother through the power of human strength. This is still what women are tempted to believe through pride. Though most Christians are rightly horrified by the idea of secular humanism, most of us live at times like *practical* humanists. We live as if we can make it without God. Christian men and women do this everyday when they fail to search the Word of the Lord and pray for spiritual guidance for the day. Christian women do this when they attempt to succeed as wives and mothers without a humble recognition of their desperate, daily need for God.

This is the sin of pride that the pain exposes. This is why God placed pain upon the woman in her fundamental roles as a person. The Lord wanted her to be constantly reminded that all creation is utterly dependent upon Him. A woman cannot be a truly successful wife and mother (as God defines success) without the grace of God. Her problem and her pain will not permit it.

Thus, the woman's pain is boiled down to this essence: God cursed the work of the woman as wife and mother with pain so that she could never know proud and selfish satisfaction apart from Him and so persist in her sin and death until her spiritual separation from God ends in the eternal isolation of hell. God created the woman to serve Him as she served her husband and children, and when she sinned, God cursed the very essence of her existence. Thus, He made it impossible for the woman to be satisfied merely serving the man and child without ultimately serving the Lord. He also made it impossible for her to be satisfied serving only her self.

The pain of the curse brings the woman to her knees in desperate agony. She can see no remedy for her pain. Then, God in His mercy sends her a preacher and she hears the good news of Jesus Christ. She learns by faith that Christ died to take the curse in her place and that through Him the curse can be transformed into a blessing, that the pain can be healed in the promise of redemption. She learns that Christ will transform her life as a wife and mother as she glorifies God daily in her work. The broken and repentant woman responds in faith and places her trust in the Cross for her salvation, for her wholeness and wellness as a woman, as a wife and mother. Now the power of a curse begins to be transformed into the power of a blessing as the woman repudiates the pride that made her trust in the flesh and places her confidence in Christ for her success as a wife and mother. The woman, who bears the curse of Eve, breaks through tragedy into triumph as she repents of the pride of Eve and seeks to be saved in humble submission to the will of God. This is how God uses the pain upon womanhood to teach the woman that she cannot be saved—and her family cannot be saved—apart from the grace of God.

By Grace through Faith

We are saved by grace through faith, not by works lest any man (or woman) should boast (Ephesians 2:8-10). The man or woman who seeks to be justified apart from faith on the basis of their good works can only be damned. Thus, everything we do that is done apart from the grace of God through human works produces condemnation. This is also true in the work of a wife and mother. When a woman seeks to be "saved" by works rather than by grace, she is condemned to a lifetime of frustrated and fruitless effort and an eternity of regret. No amount of human effort can save a man, a woman, a marriage or children. Therefore, there is good news in the bad news, a blessing in the curse. The curse upon the woman reminds her of the futility of fleshly works and brings her humbly before the throne of grace to "obtain mercy and find grace to help in the time of need" (Hebrews 4:16).

We generally acknowledge that this idea of being saved by grace through faith is fundamental to the Christian experience, but we often fail to understand its practical implications in the daily life of a Christian and, relevant to our discussion, the life of a wife and mother. It is true that we cannot be saved by works in our relationship with God, but neither can we be saved (fulfilled) by works in our relationship with anyone else. This idea underlies everything we shall discuss in our study on the family. Our marriages are saved by grace through faith. We rear our children in the fear of the Lord by grace through faith. We learn good stewardship and manage our finances wisely by grace through faith. Everything we shall study on the family is just a list of useless techniques if we do not learn that the works must flow out of God's grace. We must learn that we *cannot* be saved by works.

Success through Humility

The woman is thus "saved" in childbearing. By accepting the pain of childbearing and by understanding the purpose of the curse, the woman utilizes her pain to isolate and identify her problem and to be reminded of her ever-present need for God. The godly woman embraces the pain she feels as God's way of showing her daily the areas where she most desperately needs help. She learns to let the pain reveal the problem: *her pride*. She hurts the most where she is trying to help the most, where she is trying the most to stay in control. Her proud manipulation of her children and husband makes her heart ache, and the only remedy is humble surrender to the grace of God.

Therefore, the godly woman turns daily to the Lord for help and healing. She confesses daily to the Lord her frustrated and fleshly attempts to take control of her children and her husband.

She repents of her manipulation and prays for God to give her sufficient grace to rear her children and help her husband with a meek and quiet spirit, rather than with the controlling, manipulative spirit of proud flesh. In other words, she humbly repudiates the idea of being an "independent" woman. She recognizes her dependence upon God and man—*the* man, her husband.

Hence, the woman's role of wife and mother is delivered from the pain of the curse and made joyful through the power of the Cross. She beholds her sorrow turned to joy as she is loosed from the chains of pride and lives every day by the grace of God. Then, God does through her by His grace what she could never have done alone in the flesh. Pride guarantees failure, for "pride goes before destruction and a haughty spirit before a fall" (Proverbs 16:18). But humble submission guarantees success, even if it hurts for a while.

14

The Curse and Childbearing (Continued)

In I Timothy 2, Paul oriented the woman toward obedience and godliness by summing up her "salvation" (being made whole) in the work of childbirth. The work of bearing children is what should begin to fulfill the woman. This does not mean that all a woman does is birth babies. Rather, Paul *centered* the woman's fulfillment in the act of bearing children. Then, her fulfillment moves out either direction from the *central* act of childbirth to her prior act of submission to her husband that caused conception and to the consequent work of rearing children. Childbirth requires two necessary relationships for the woman: husband and children. Thus, childbirth is preceded by submission and followed by sorrow. So, when the godly wife is "saved" (made whole) in childbirth, she is "saved" (made whole) in her relation to her husband and to her children. Submitting to the curse breaks the power of the curse through the cross of Christ. In other words, when a woman truly seeks godly fulfillment in bearing children, she will find fulfillment in her relationship toward her husband and children in her role as a wife and mother. For a woman, childbirth is the fulcrum of a balanced life.

The woman's submission as a wife precedes her conceiving and bearing children. Her work in training children naturally follows their birth. Thus, her service to her husband and her service to her children is "briefly comprehended" (as Paul said elsewhere), or summed up, in the act of bearing a child. This means then that when a woman begins to revolt against the pain of the curse, she will rebel at first against childbirth, which is the gravitational center of her roles and relationships as a woman. She will cultivate a deepening resentment against the idea of having children, which finds its initial expression in a flat refusal to bear *many* children. She becomes unable to see the blessedness of having children because of the curse of pain.

Then, after the resentment against bearing children has invaded and pervaded her heart, the sinful woman wrests away from the man altogether the decision of when to have children and how many children to have. She declares that childbirth is her pain and thus her prerogative. She usurps authority from the father and makes him an incidental "impregnating apparatus" when and if she gets ready to have a baby. This rebellion against the authority of the father perverts sexual relations into a form of artificial insemination without ever visiting a clinic. The submission and relationship is removed.

In this sort of arrangement, the children are no longer seen as belonging to the man, but the kids are *hers* because she bore them. This, of course, denies the obvious fact that no woman has ever borne a child without yielding her body to the desire of a man. Modern science may have removed the intimacy, but they have not removed the necessity. Much to feminists' chagrin, a man is still required for a woman to have a baby. God intended this to be a metaphor of the submission inherent within childbearing. The physical act of copulation and conception should also be a symbol of the woman's willing and joyful submission to her husband in all of life. However, when the woman seizes the sole rights to reproduce, then her submission becomes *impossible* in all of life.

Childbearing is the central fact of godly submission and faithful childrearing. Hence, when radical feminists mount their assault against the idea of marriage and homemaking, they will always make "reproductive rights" the central theme of their resistance. They begin their agitation for a feminine uprising by exploiting the pain of women and persuading them that they alone hold the right to control their body and the fruit of their womb. Feminists first seek to make childbirth itself an act of feminine defiance by asserting that the woman alone holds the rights to her body. Then, the "right to choose" when to bear children and how many children to have becomes the "right to choose" life or death for her own offspring through abortion. The right to choose is the foundation of the woman's resistance to the authority of her husband and the inconvenience of unwanted children.

Struggling Against the Curse

To the radical feminist, men are oppressive and children are a nuisance, as both impede the progress of the feminine "self." And yet, in the quest to promote the feminine self, they end up destroying it. Sinful women who rebel against the law of God come to hate womanhood and true femininity and end up trying frantically to "masculinize" the female creature. And the best they can achieve is the worst sort of pathetic androgyny. And this disorder can be traced back to a woman's unwillingness to submit to God's command for the woman to bear the curse of pain in childbearing.

Strangely enough, the woman's resistance to childbearing is often welcomed and encouraged by sinful men. Men (as we address below) are also fleeing their own curse. So long as the woman is submitted to biblical childbearing and looks to the man for leadership in bearing and rearing children, the man feels terribly responsible. This produces unwelcome beads of sweat on his brow. Sinful man is a selfish sluggard and loathes the restrictions of responsibility. He wants his freedom. Fallen man wants to roam the earth at will gratifying his lusts whenever and with whomever he wishes. Sinful man resents the idea that he should have any responsibility for the children he fathered. He was just having fun.

So, when the women begin to agitate for masculine authority in childbearing, the dissipated men gladly surrender it, just as long as they can shirk masculine responsibility as well. Of course, these men are already emasculated by their own lusts, by their own lack of self-control. They gladly allow the women to take charge of their reproductive rights because they like the idea of satisfying an indiscriminate sexual desire without being held responsible for the everlasting consequences. Then, they console themselves on their lost manhood through the feeble masculinity of sexual conquest, only to find that *they* have become the victims of the conquest and slaves to their own urge. They may be male, but they are no longer men.

When the men become profligate and degenerate, they encourage their women to be degraded and debased before them. The men encourage the women to indulge their selfish desires so the men may do the same without the women nagging them

175

about it. Thus, when the women rule over the men and the children, the men feel justified to fornicate with other women and abandon their children. If the women want the rule, the men say, then let them have it and we shall be free to do as we please. But, alas for the philandering men, while the women will gladly usurp the authority over the men, they will *never* cease berating them and hating them for refusing to lead. The abdicating man cannot escape the nagging woman no matter how hard he tries! And God will make certain that it is so.

Women who seize the "sole-proprietorship" of children, beginning with the decision of how many children to have and when to have them, are developing a wholly selfish view of childbearing. The decision for children (when and how many) should be decided by *both* the man and his wife under the husband's godly leadership. Paul taught in I Corinthians 7:4, "The wife hath not power of her own body, but the husband: and likewise also the husband hath not power of his own body, but the wife." The idea of a woman holding exclusive "rights" to her own body is antichristian nonsense.

The godly wife is a lovely garden where the husband sows his seed, and the children that the woman bears are the fruit of the husband's garden. The Song of Solomon uses this metaphor extensively to describe the lovely relationship of a man and his bride. This image is also used of Christ and the church. The seed of the Word is sown in the hearts of believers, which is compared to the ground of a fruitful garden. In marriage, the man is responsible to lovingly tend to his wife as he would a garden that he might cultivate a fruitful place of peace and beauty. Ground that is either barren or producing fruitless weeds desperately needs a gardener. The husband is the *husbandman*, and he assumes authority and responsibility for the fruit that the ground bears. This includes many fruits of godly womanhood, but it specifically includes bearing and rearing children.

The woman that refuses to submit to her husband's authority in childbearing is like a garden that refuses to bear fruit under the hand of the gardener. In this sense Jesus' parable about the sower and the seed is a powerful lesson to the godly woman (Matthew 13). She can choose what sort of ground she will be. Some may be like the wayside, producing nothing at all. Other may be like the stony ground, producing only for a while. Some will even become like the ground that bears thorns and briers, producing fruit that is choked out by the world. This sort of ground brings forth "no fruit to perfection" (Luke 8:14). However, the godly woman is like the good ground that "bring[s] forth fruit with patience" (Luke 8:15). The godly wife yields to her husbandman and brings forth the fruit of a Christian family. Her children grow to perfection (maturity) through patience (endurance). This is the goal of godly childbearing and childrearing. The "garden idea" radically reorients the idea of Mother Earth.

When the woman rejects the father's role and relationship toward their children by making childbearing a purely female task, she succumbs to the sin of Eve. She steps away from the authority and responsibility of her husband to make family decisions on her own. If she allows the pain that she suffers alone to force her to make the decisions alone, then she has guaranteed that she will continue to become even more alone—and lonely— in her relationship with her husband and children. God intended for childbearing to be a team effort as so plainly demonstrated by the act of conception. The woman allows the pain to make her *selfish*, and this selfishness corrupts every part of her life and love.

Remember, all sin is rooted in selfishness. So, when the wife seizes control of the decision to have children, she cannot prevent her selfish usurpation from becoming a corrosive acid that dissolves her relationship with her husband and later with her children. Thus, the woman's resentment will never remain focused just on the idea of bearing children. Her cancerous resentment will start eating at her relationship with her husband. She will come to resent the intrinsic submission of marriage and the man who represents it. This does not mean necessarily that she wants to be unmarried, but she will do her best to learn how to be married without submitting. Of course, this does not work, and the marriage relationship is severely damaged as a result.

Then, the woman turns in anger upon her role as a mother. The woman who develops resentment and rebellion against her husband's authority will soon begin to resent her children as they grow up to resist *her* authority. She grows ever more frustrated at the loss of control. Her anger becomes a suffocating pressure she cannot escape. She may feel she has wasted her best years on people who scorn her effort. She may rail against the objects of her frustration, or she may learn to brood silently with an intense bitterness as she allows self-obsession to drive her crazy with pain. She sees her children as an additional reason for her unbearable pain, and she strikes out in blind defiance. But the pain never goes away. She is losing her life because she sought to save it (Matthew 16:25).

The answer is surrender. The woman must quit struggling against the curse. She must accept the pain of childbearing and the inherent submission that defines it. Otherwise, her resistance to the pain will erode her selfless service to both her husband and children. The good and blessed relationship of a woman with her husband and her children is rooted in the selfless act of having children. When the woman submits cheerfully to the God-given task of bearing children (even many children), she has the basis for transforming the curse into a blessing. Paul said she will be saved, or made whole, in childbearing.

Of course, this certainly does not mean that every woman who bears children automatically breaks the curse. Nothing works automatically apart from faith in God and His Word. However, the woman's willing submission to childbearing does mean that she has accepted the fundamental basis for transforming the curse into a blessing. *"She shall be saved in childbearing."*

Modesty and Submission

In I Timothy 2 Paul also spoke to the wives about modesty and submission. He summed it all up in the fact of childbearing. Childbearing becomes the paradigm in Paul's thought for all that the Christian woman should become. She should be submitted to her husband in loving surrender. She should give her life to bear the fruit of their relationship. She should give her life to rear a godly family for the glory of God. Childbearing is the emblem of all she was created to be.

This does not mean that Paul's teaching reduces women to mere baby machines. But he did see childbirth as the supreme example of fulfilled womanhood. The wife is "saved" (made whole, complete) through childbearing. Thus, two things are lost when the woman revolts against the idea of bearing children for her husband's posterity. First, submission to her husband is lost. Second, her faithfulness to her children is lost. Her attitude toward *having* children controls her attitude toward her husband and her children. This fact cannot be avoided.

When a woman rebels against God's purpose for her life, her rebellion is manifest in several ways. Paul shows the type of behavior we can expect of ungodly women by describing what the behavior of a godly woman should be. The positive side of the command implicitly reveals the negative side. For example, Paul commands godly women to dress modestly, without a "bold face," with dignity, and without undue ornamentation. In contrast, therefore, we can expect ungodly women to dress immodestly, with a sensual and impudent face, without decorum and dignity, and with unacceptable ornamentation.

Modern feminists despise motherhood and its unique femininity. Therefore, they have persuaded the world that the perfect model of feminine beauty is the maiden rather than the mother. And of course, the feminist's maiden is no maiden at all, but rather a young strumpet who perpetually celebrates sex and sensuality without a hint of motherhood and encroaching old age. Modern women vainly attempt to preserve this youthful ideal through artificial means, but death is inevitable and it shows.

The world, in its revolt against maturity, has chosen to prize youth and disdain old age. This is exactly opposite of the Word of God, where the beauty of an old man is his wisdom proclaimed by his head of gray hair (Proverbs 20:29), and the true beauty of a woman is her meek and quiet spirit displayed in the maturity of a serene and lovely countenance (Proverbs 31:30; I Peter 3:4). This kind of beauty never fades, but rather grows with age. A godly woman grows lovelier as she grows older. Of course, we must not deny that youth has its own beauty. The Word of God prizes the pristine beauty of maidens and the unbroken strength of young men. But the Word of God presents the beauty of young men and women as a childish beauty that should mature into the fruitful beauty of the aged. To the master of the orchard, a sapling apple tree is exceedingly beautiful from the first day it is planted. Yet, it is not nearly as beautiful to him as it shall become as a mature fruit-bearing tree producing gorgeous apples. The farmer loves the virgin soil, but he loves the fruitful field even more. His appreciation for the soil lies in his knowledge of its potential. His objective is a mature crop ready for the harvest. The same is true of a godly husband—the *husbandman*—who marries the girl of his dreams and then gently leads her into a fruitful and blessed old age with his harvest of children and grandchildren gathered around his table. This is true beauty.

The world's standard for beauty is cheap and shallow. They idolize youth because they despise the pain of growing old. They despise maternal beauty because they despise the curse of bearing children. Thus, they manifest their revolt against God and His command to bear children by changing out of maternity clothes into nearly nothing at all. Immodesty is a sign of rebellion. Immodesty is a refusal to accept the curse.

Paul commanded godly women to display good works and to learn in silence with all subjection. They are forbidden to teach their husbands at home or other men in public worship. Paul taught the Christian woman to embrace quietude. Conversely, ungodly women will display evil works and refuse to accept instruction from their husband in silence and subjection. They will rather attempt to wrest control of the family "pulpit" from their husband either by open command or subtle suggestion. Some will even take their conflict public by voicing their concerns and opinions loudly enough for all to hear.

Paul directly connected all of this to the woman's willingness or unwillingness to submit to the curse of childbearing. When godly wives submit themselves to God's purpose in childbearing, then they are satisfied to be modest and moral serving their husband and children faithfully. When women resist the idea of bearing children, they soon will resist the idea of serving their husband and children. Moreover, this resistance will sooner or later find its expression in immodesty and immorality.

Again, some women may protest that this extreme picture does not resemble them at all, that it is an absurd caricature at best. And for now they are perfectly correct. And yet, the fruit of sin is not always harvested in one or two generations. However, "be not deceived: God is not mocked" (Galatians 6:7). If we sow this sort of rebellion against the creation mandate of fruitfulness through childbearing, then we cannot hope to escape the consequences of our sin. The harvest of family destruction is often sown in the seeds of resentment against childbearing

Conclusion

Finally, Paul teaches that being saved from the curse takes time. The woman must *continue* faithful as a mother. "She shall be saved in childbearing if she continues...." Just delivering a baby does not overcome the curse. The curse is overcome through time. The promises of God do not work automatically apart from faith. The promises of God are "yea and amen" (II Corinthians 1:10). God speaks the "yes" to our need, and we respond with the "amen" to His promise. The work of salvation is by grace through faith. The woman breaks the power of the curse according to the promise of God. And the promise must be received by faith. Then, the godly woman lives every day expecting the healing of the pain to come through her willing and joyful surrender to the chastening of the Lord in the curse. This is a process, and it takes time.

The godly wife must accept the curse as a chastening from the Lord, and understand that God chastens those He loves in order to save them (Hebrews 12:5-13). She must resist the urge to flee from the pain of being a mother by refusing to bear children and guide the house. She must overcome the urge to usurp her husband's authority by any means. She must willingly submit to the pain of childbearing and the authority of her husband. When she does so, and continues in doing so by grace through faith, then she will "be saved in childbearing." She will be fulfilled and made whole in submitting to God's will for her life.

181

15

The Curse upon the Man

Genesis 3:17-20. "And unto Adam he said, Because thou hast hearkened unto the voice of thy wife, and hast eaten of the tree, of which I commanded thee, saying, Thou shalt not eat of it: cursed is the ground for thy sake; in sorrow shalt thou eat of it all the days of thy life; thorns also and thistles shall it bring forth to thee; and thou shalt eat the herb of the field; in the sweat of thy face shalt thou eat bread, till thou return unto the ground; for out of it wast thou taken: for dust thou art, and unto dust shalt thou return. And Adam called his wife's name Eve; because she was the mother of all living."

After the Lord God judged the woman, He turned to the man and pronounced the curse upon him. The curse upon man was two-fold, just as it was upon the woman. God cursed the ground, which became the field of man's labor after the fall, and pronounced the sentence of death upon man and his family. The curse upon man was a lifetime of frustrated labor ending in death. Man was cursed with dual sorrow of *futility* and *fatality*. The curse upon man is more comprehensive than that upon the woman in that it affects everything under the sun, including all people, places and things.

Man's curse is rooted in a curse upon the ground. Man came from the ground and his food comes from the ground. His work is in the ground and his grave shall be in the ground. Thus, every aspect of man's essence and existence was cursed when God cursed the ground. God promised that man would eat of the ground only through sorrow (painful toil) and the sweat of the brow (hard work). And to further complicate matters, the cursed ground would bring forth thorns and thistles. Man would never be able to escape the curse, for his food would come from the cursed ground, and man would make bread from the fruit of the ground harvested by the sweat of his brow. The curse would extend to all the days of man's life. And then, ultimately, the cursed ground would be man's final resting place in the restless toil of death, as the cursed ground becomes man's grave. The curse upon man is the futility of labor and the fatality of death. A man is cursed to work in frustration until he dies. That is the summary of man's curse.

The curse upon man, just as the curse upon the woman, is a remedial curse. It is a chastening upon man to bring him to salvation. God placed within the curse the promise of redemption. Man shall be saved by confronting the curse head on and accepting it with all its sorrow. Man shall be liberated from the curse by going through it and triumphing over it. Indeed, Christ has already done so on our behalf, and our final triumph shall be the triumph that we share with Him by grace through faith. The curse is upon the ground, and after being buried in the ground, we shall arise in the power of the resurrection to overcome the curse forever. The ground is the place of our curse, and the ground shall become the place of our blessing. We shall plunge in death into the heart of the earth and arise in the resurrection to ascend the heights of the heavens. The curse shall become the means of our blessing. Let's look closer at the particulars of the curse.

God Addresses Adam

First of all, *God spoke to Adam.* Adam, as the man of the house, is finally and ultimately the one responsible for sins in the family. God addressed the serpent and the woman and cursed them for their sins, but then the crescendo of judgment came. The man's judgment affects much more than just himself. His judgment affects the entire human race, the entire human family. The man of the house must remember this when he is tempted to sin or to allow sin to enter into his home. Each one in the home who sins will face the judgment of God for his own sins, but eventually God will summon the man before the judgment bar for the sins of the entire house. Every man shall hear the voice of the Judge call his name. "And unto Adam He said...."

This point was raised above, but it must be stated again for emphasis. Godly men must expect to be called into account for their family. The man is the federal head of the family and will answer to God for all that occurs on his watch. The man must assume daily responsibility for his family before God. As we noted earlier, if godly men would come willingly and confess the sins of the family, then redemption would be received for the family. Adam fled from accountability and responsibility when God came into the garden, but it is impossible to escape judgment forever. The judgment of God upon man is certain and sure. The Christian husband must remember this and approach God in confession and repentance for sin.

Hearkening to the Woman

Second, God said to Adam, "Because you have listened to the voice of your wife...." God's rebuke begins by recalling Adam's decision to hearken to Eve. Adam was not excused for listening to his wife's suggestion to disobey the Lord's command. Indeed, Adam was condemned for listening to Eve's voice. He may have expected to be exonerated by pointing the finger at his wife, but the very fact that he listened to her was of itself evidence of sin. It was not only wrong to eat of the tree, as the Lord shall say next, but it was also wrong to listen to the woman's voice in the first place. Of course, listening to her voice means more than simply engaging in a good conversation with his wife, or accepting her advice and input. It means that Adam hearkened unto Eve's voice. He gave in to what she had to say. He allowed her to have *the* say in their decision. The man's sin began when he allowed the woman to take the initiative in making decisions.

Listening Correctly and Speaking Correctly

Godly men should learn how to listen to their wives correctly. And godly women should learn how to speak to their husbands correctly. The husband should invite his wife to offer input, advice and encouragement in making daily decisions for the family. But the man should never allow the woman to assume a leadership role in making final decisions. He should not make the

185

decisions alone. If he does, he is a fool. God gave him a wife to help him. But *he* should make the final decisions, for *he* shall answer to God finally and ultimately.

The man should encourage his wife to speak, and he should listen when she does. But he should reserve the right to make the final decision. And the woman must learn how to speak when asked and how to be silent when finished speaking. The wife must remember that the final decision belongs to the man. She should humbly seek the Lord to grant her husband wisdom in making the right decisions.

The Sinful Husband

If the husband is involved in gross error, the woman may be compelled to appeal to the elders of the church for judgment over her husband. And this right to appeal must be respected by both the husband and the elders of the church. But the woman should never wrest the authority away from her husband arbitrarily. And the man should never silence his wife's godly counsel when it is offered in the right spirit with due respect.

We must also remember that a godly woman is never expected to go along with her husband in a sinful decision. The story of Ananias and Sapphira perfectly illustrates the trouble that a wife can get herself into when she goes along with a disobedient husband (Acts 5:1-11). Ananias concocted a scheme to sell a piece of property for a certain price and then present a lesser amount to the apostles pretending it was the full amount. This would make it appear that he and his wife were as generous as the others who were giving all. The Bible says that Sapphira was aware of Ananias's decision to try and deceive the church. Indeed, she participated in the deception when she arrived at the church later than her husband and told Peter, when he asked, that the price her husband gave was indeed the full amount. Peter condemned her for agreeing together with her husband to lie to the Holy Ghost. Both Ananias and Sapphira died that day for agreeing together to sin against the Lord.

Reporting Sin to the Elders of the Church

So, a godly wife must never agree to partake of her husband's sins. She may not be able to stop what he is doing, but she can certainly refuse to cooperate. And she is expected to answer the elders honestly when asked about his disobedience. Indeed, the wife may even be expected to make the elders aware of her husband's sin when it is an egregious sin against the congregation. Under the law of Moses family members were expected to report instances of gross immorality and idolatry to the authorities, and the next of kin were required by God to cast the first stone. God never intended for the family to cover up sin within their house. If we truly love our loved ones, then we must do everything in our power to see their sin confronted and forgiveness obtained.

Of course, we do not report every minor infraction in the home. This would keep the elders of the church on the phone constantly. We must allow love to cover a multitude of sins whenever we can. But we must not allow un-confessed and un-repented sin to continue in the life of a loved one. We must sincerely judge whether or not the sin will cause our loved one to be separated from fellowship with God and ultimately be lost. We must seek to remedy every sin privately; then, with witnesses; and then, finally, to the authorities of the church. We must follow Jesus' teaching about confronting sin even among those of our own household (Matthew 5:21-26; 18:15-22).

This actually works out in a very practical way. When the wife observes that her husband is unrepentant in his sin, she should entreat him privately at first with a humble spirit. Then, if he does not heed her entreaty, she should appeal for outside help, possibly her husband's father (if he is a godly man), a trusted family friend or a faithful brother in the church. As a last resort, she, along with the witnesses she has called so far, should appeal to the officers of the church, the pastor and the elders.

A godly woman should try to resolve every issue at home. But when her husband will not listen to her humble entreaty (and the right attitude is essential), the wife should refuse to participate in her husband's sin and answer the elders truthfully about the matter. The elders, then, exercise their authority to rebuke the husband and discipline him for his sin. The wife has handled the matter correctly when she refuses to usurp authority and refers the matter to those who hold authority over her husband. The wife who seeks to rebuke and correct her husband is herself guilty of sin and in need of a stern rebuke.

The Role of the Family in Confronting Sin

It does not matter who initiates the sin, the other members of the family must not go along. No one has the authority to require anyone to sin. And the family should encourage one another daily *not* to sin. This commitment to mutual accountability by itself would prevent so much backsliding and sin in the family. Sin cannot reign in a home where each member of the family is careful to please the Lord and seeks to persuade others to do so as well. We provide great strength to one another when we stand together in a quest for righteousness. A three-fold cord is not quickly broken (Ecclesiastes 4:12).

The family is a natural source of strength and encouragement, if we allow it to be so. We can become a well-organized team that helps one another stand when one starts to fall. When a soldier is injured on the battlefield, his own comrades are the first to rush to his assistance. The family must do the same. We must be sensitive to one another's weaknesses and strengths and help one another up when we begin to stumble. If we participate in another's sin, we are helping destroy our brother "for whom Christ died" (Romans 14:15). The husband must refuse to acquiesce to his wife's suggestion to sin, and the wife must refuse to go along with the husband's decision to sin. We must help each other stand strong for righteousness.

The Sin of Disobedience

After God rebuked Adam for hearkening to the voice of his wife and agreeing with her to sin, He charged Adam with the second part of his sin: eating the forbidden fruit. Adam's sin was both hearkening to his wife and eating the fruit. The voice of the woman drowned out the voice of God. Adam *listened* and *disobeyed*. God exposed and identified the two sins separately.

God's rebuke highlights the fact that sin has become inevitable, just a matter of time, when the man starts allowing his wife to wrest control of the initiative in the home. Adam listened, which was his first sin. But then Adam ate of the fruit, which was the inevitable second sin. One sin will always lead to the other. The husband must not abdicate his responsibility to be the leader in the home. This abdication always leads to other more egregious sins.

This also brings us back to what we discussed earlier. Every problem in the home is actually a matter of sin against God and man. When disobedience is viewed as a clear transgression of God's law, then we not only learn where we went wrong, but we learn by the Word of God how to get it right. The only remedy for sin is repentance. But we will not repent if we do not see our problems as *sin*.

When a family member sins, we must boldly preach the gospel to their sin. We must preach the Cross of Christ to every sinner in our home. We must take the Word of God and confront the error with the law of God. Then, as the law of God brings conviction of sin, we must demand repentance and restoration. We must point the sinner toward the Cross of Christ for hope and healing. The gracious promise of salvation and restoration by grace through faith always follows the demand for repentance. This is the only remedy for sin. This kind of gospel confrontation must be done for every member of the family regardless of age or position. The husband must come under the authority of the Word as he is taught by the elders of the church. The woman must come under the Word as she is taught by her husband. The children must come under the Word as they are taught by their parents. And maybe the kids can practice teaching the dog and cat.

16

The Curse upon the Ground

After detailing man's transgression, the Lord God moved on to the details of the curse upon the man. The curse is first pronounced upon the ground. When God pronounced the curse upon the earth for Adam's sake, the earth itself was "subjected to futility." The entire earth came under the curse upon man and began to groan under the weight of man's transgression. Paul spoke of God's curse upon the ground in this manner:

> For I reckon that the sufferings of this present time are not worthy to be compared with the glory which shall be revealed in us. For the earnest expectation of the creature waiteth for the manifestation of the sons of God. For the creature was made subject to vanity, not willingly, but by reason of him who hath subjected the same in hope, Because the creature itself also shall be delivered from the bondage of corruption into the glorious liberty of the children of God. For we know that the whole creation groaneth and travaileth in pain together until now. And not only they, but ourselves also, which have the firstfruits of the Spirit, even we ourselves groan within ourselves, waiting for the adoption, to wit, the redemption of our body (Romans 8:18-23).

Quite literally, all of the natural order of creation came under the power of corruption because of Adam's sin. Only the earth is specified in the Genesis account as being under the curse of Adam, but, as we noted earlier, the heavens also came under the power of corruption due to the curse upon the serpent. So all of creation, including the heaven and the earth, must be redeemed from the curse by the work of Christ. And when Christ cried, "It is finished!" it was done. We now live in the dawning of the new creation, awaiting the finishing of the finished work in the resurrection of the dead when Jesus comes again.

Later on, the Lord God mitigated somewhat the effects of the curse upon the ground. "And the LORD smelled a sweet savor; and the LORD said in his heart, I will not again curse the ground any more for man's sake; for the imagination of man's heart is evil from his youth; neither will I again smite any more every thing living, as I have done. While the earth remaineth, seedtime and harvest, and cold and heat, and summer and winter, and day and night shall not cease" (Genesis 8:21, 22). And yet, though God in His mercy did lessen the effect of the curse somewhat, Paul stated that the full lifting of the curse awaits the resurrection of the dead at Christ's return.

The ground is the material from which man was taken. The ground produces the fruit that man eats. The ground is the *terra firma* that man walks upon and builds upon. His walk and his work are connected to the ground. And the ground becomes the grave in which man is buried. These are the several aspects of the curse we must consider. We must also consider how each aspect of the curse affects the man and his family.

The Curse upon the Body and Mind

First of all, man was taken from the ground. Thus, the ground is the basis of man's material essence and existence. Of course, man is much more than material (matter). He became a living soul when God breathed His Spirit into him. But man cannot be disconnected from the material ground from whence he came. He is organically connected to the earth, for he is made from it. Thus, when the curse was pronounced upon the soil, it affected the soul. We cannot separate the effects of sin upon the ground from the man who was formed from the ground.

Our bodies, which were made from earth, are affected by the curse upon the earth. In the fall of Adam, the bodies of men became subject to mortal agony, to sickness and injury. The body is now decaying due to the curse upon the ground. God shall speak later of the "sorrow" (pain) that shall frustrate man's work.

This sorrow flows out of the very being of the man. He cannot escape it. Man is formed from the dust of the ground, and when the ground was cursed his body was cursed with it. The curse upon the ground extends to the human body formed from the ground.

Man was created with a perfect body, with great strength and ability. Adam knew neither weakness nor sickness. His body was unbelievably strong, without a hint of corruption. His physical prowess was far beyond our present ability. The story of Samson may give us an indication of the kind of natural strength that Adam possessed before sin weakened his body. Adam would have never suffered so much as the common cold if he had remained faithful to God. Man may have been created with the physical ability to travel at the speed of thought much like the angels apparently do as they move throughout the universe. God created the entire universe to display His glory to man, and it seems likely, in order for that display to be possible, that the farthest reaches of our galaxy and beyond must have been within man's scope of exploration. At least, this was surely God's intended destiny for man as he grew in maturity and ability.

Regardless of all that, it seems likely that man was created with mental and physical powers far beyond what we possess today. Scientists say that the average person uses two to five percent of his brain. Of course, many seem to use much less. But if even the most intelligent ones among us use only five percent of their brain, then the mind of man must be an incredibly powerful machine with untapped capabilities we have never seen or experienced. Adam surely possessed powers that now exist only as occasional flickers of former intelligence. Instances of telepathic or kinetic abilities, examples of psychic powers and other mind-phenomena that occur now and then may be indications of lost mental powers that Adam possessed before the fall.

Certainly, much paranormal activity is demonic, and those who covet such power often are involved in witchcraft. Satan definitely exploits every opportunity he can to lead people away from seeking the power of God in their life. And for many, this sort of power is a form of open rebellion against the limits God has placed upon the mind of man in the fall. But this is not always the case. It seems that some people experience these phenomena apart from any involvement with occultist or spiritualist experimentation. Whatever may be the case, it seems likely that Adam possessed much greater mental power than we have today.

However, the fall brought weakness and sickness upon man. His body was afflicted with disease and decay. His mind was affected and the great mental powers of man were severely diminished. Man was reduced to a pathetic shadow of his former self. This occurred when God cursed the ground from which man was taken. God, in His mercy, refused to allow man to continue on in his sin without any restraint upon his ability to satisfy his evil intentions and desires. This is another example of how the curse becomes a blessing.

After the fall, man became exceedingly wicked and filled the earth with violence. God destroyed the earth with the Flood, and then reduced man's capacity for evil even more by limiting the number of days he could live. Some men had lived nearly a thousand years before the Flood, but now man gradually began to be limited to a seventy year lifespan (Psalm 90:10). It is now highly unusual for a man to live even one hundred years. This is God's way of accelerating the curse of death and shortening man's potential for corruption. We see again God's mercy in judgment.

Struggling Against the Curse

However, sinful man can never accept the curse without a fight. Unbelievers think they can overcome the power of the curse through the strength of their body and mind, through physical and mental powers. Man has made a religion out of physical and intellectual prowess. Man worships at the altar of physical strength and intellectual ability. Athletes are elevated to the level of gods and goddesses. The academic elites, the "thinkers" of our age, have set themselves up as authorities on every subject under the sun.

Man has abandoned all pretense of humility before the vast expanse of creation and its Creator. The stars have lost their power to make mere mortals feel small and insignificant. Now we feel we have charted the universe, its origins and destiny, through the tiny end of a telescope. We learn a thing or two about the planets and think we hold the answers to the mysteries of the cosmos. Men, who once bowed before the stars of the heavens, have now learned to kneel before the stars of evolutionary science, charting their course by the twinkling lights of astronomical hubris.

Man thinks he can save himself by the strength of his body and the power of his mind. The unbelieving man, faced with challenges and difficulties in life, will turn within himself for help. He will train his body and develop his mind that he may become strong enough and smart enough to save himself apart from any help from God. This was Adam's sin: the mistaken belief that man could attain godlikeness in his body and mind. The serpent encouraged them to eat of the tree, which was a physical action. Then, he promised, their mind would be filled with knowledge and they would be like gods. Man still falls for this lie today.

The world is dominated by the considerable power of human strength and ingenuity. But man is still dying, and his strength and ingenuity cannot prevent the inevitable. His best efforts and most creative inventions perish in decay. Man seeks for immortality by building monuments to his genius, impressive feats of architecture and engineering. But no matter how beautiful and enduring his works may seem, all that man is building crumbles into dust. The greatest wonders of the world are destined in time to lie in ruins. Archeological digs and museum exhibits display some of the greatest proofs of God's curse upon man. Whatever man builds falls under the power of inescapable corruption.

Further, unbelieving man's inventions are devoid of any meaning or purpose beyond immediate personal gratification. The materialistic worldview has fiercely denied the existence of God and aggressively seeks to force God out of public and private life. Man is self-consciously seeking to bring heaven on earth by his might and mind. Even many Christians have become practical humanists, *de facto* materialists and atheists, living by the power of body and mind without a daily appeal to God for strength and wisdom. But this rebellious quest for glory is bound to fail, for the curse has made death inevitable. Humans are a dying race. Ironically, the death of the human race is the only basis for its hope.

The humanist believes that man can be redeemed from the curse of sin by man's strength and knowledge. The last century saw some of the most horrendous experiments with human existence in the name of humanistic progress. Countless millions were slaughtered in the quest for an earthly utopia. The strength and knowledge of man seemed limitless in those first, heady days of scientific advance and discovery. But man's arrogance has only heightened the power of the curse. The strength of man cannot break it and the knowledge of man cannot outsmart it. The curse is stronger than ever. Of course, sinners are continually deluded by their own unbelief, and they flatly refuse to submit to the curse that God pronounced. And in their refusal to accept it, they sentence themselves to a lifetime of slavery to it. The only way to overcome the curse is to accept it and find deliverance from it in the power of the Cross.

Sinful man must confront his failure of strength and knowledge. The body and the mind are under the power of the curse. And when man accepts that fact and acknowledges before God that he desperately needs the strength and knowledge of the Spirit, then, *and only then*, can he truly break the power of the curse upon the body and mind. The curse is given to constantly remind us that we cannot make it without God. Our body is decaying and our mind is failing. All flesh is as grass and the glory of man is destined to fade away. Admit it, accept it, and we can find deliverance from it. Deny it and defy it, and we are destined to live under it forever.

The Blessing of the Curse

As we noted in our discussion on the curse upon the woman, the curse is actually God's way of refusing to abandon man to his sinful condition. God cursed man in his fall and made it impossible for man to live peacefully and comfortably without His Holy Spirit. The curse draws men back to the Creator, desperately seeking repentance and restoration. The curse is God's chastening upon man. This point cannot be overemphasized.

The curse upon the body and mind of man brings pain and sorrow upon man's most fundamental everyday functions as a man. Man cannot attempt to live by his own strength and intellect without being confronted daily by the ever-increasing frustration of weakness and disease. He may deny it and try to avoid the inevitable, but the fact of his fall keeps pressing upon him. Man's physical frailty constantly reminds him of the need for a higher power much stronger than himself. Man intellectual weakness constantly reminds him of his need for the ultimate mind, the mind of Christ. Man's body and mind were created to be dependent upon the infilling of the Spirit of God. Thus, to attempt to live apart from God is to deny our own created nature.

Man is often tempted to trust in the flesh, in the strength of his own ability. The curse upon his body and mind, the physical and emotional pain he suffers, reminds the man of his need for the strength of the Spirit. As the body begins to fail, the man is reminded of his impending demise. As the mind begins to lose its keen edge, the man is increasingly aware of his fading glory. As the man gets older, and the shadow of death lengthens over his life, his thoughts are turned toward the hereafter and the preparations that he has made for eternity. The weakness of the body is designed to do just that. The curse increases man's awareness of his own weakness and his need for God's strength. This is the blessing of the curse.

The Cursed Body and Mind and Its Effect upon the Family

The curse of God upon the body and the mind of man has tremendous implications for the family. Men are tempted to think that they can rear up a healthy family just through the power of a strong body and mind. This is a particular temptation to us when we are young and just starting out in life. If we are physically and mentally strong, then we think that we can conquer any challenge. The man who sees himself as a self-sufficient husband and father and without need for God will lead his family into futility and frustration. But the wise man, who confronts the fact of the curse and the pain that the curse brings upon his body and mind, accepts the curse as an emblem of his own inability to save himself apart from God. He turns to God for help and healing and thereby leads his family into blessing and salvation.

Materialistic presuppositions have paralyzed the spiritual growth of many families. We sometimes tend to view the world from a purely carnal, secular perspective and ignore the spiritual dimension of life. As a result, we too often push our children toward the secular disciplines of education and exercise and neglect the most important discipline of all, the discipline of being a Christian. Our culture is totally secular and carnal. America is a pagan nation. The world around us judges success purely on physical and intellectual criteria. But this falls far short of the way we were created to live and the goals we were created to attain. The body may be strong for now, and the mind may perform great feats of intellectual skill, but the soul that is neglected is dying a little every day. And when the mirage of physical strength and mental ability has vanished, then we are left with only an undernourished and impoverished soul that will live forever somewhere.

We must be ever aware of our physical and mental weakness and reach out for strength and wisdom that comes from above. We must learn that "the race is not to the swift, nor the battle to the strong" (Ecclesiastes 9:11). The family is not built up by the strength of man. The family is not built up by the intellectual power of man. Our sufficiency is not in our own body and mind. We cannot build up our family with humanistic schemes for self-help and carnal success. We need the power of the Spirit of God. God has promised us that salvation is "'not by might nor by power, but by my Spirit,' sayeth the Lord of Hosts" (Zechariah 4:6). We must allow the curse upon the body and mind to turn our hearts toward the Lord in a humble appeal for spiritual strength and godly wisdom.

The Fall of the Flesh and Spirit

Man was created both spirit and body. God formed Adam's body from the dust of the earth and then breathed into him the breath of life. By the union of spirit and body man was made a living soul. Man's essence and existence was both spiritual and physical. And yet, though man was created both flesh and spirit, man was made alive by the Spirit of God. The spiritual being of man was formed to be subject to the Spirit of God. Thus, the spirit of man was primary and in control of the flesh before the fall. But when man sinned, his soul came under the curse of the soil, and the body took precedence over the spirit. Thus, the body, made from the ground that was now cursed, was itself under the curse.

The flesh became the seat and source of human disobedience. Adam and Eve yielded to the desires of the flesh rather than to the voice of the spirit. The flesh is now so thoroughly corrupt that the phrase "the flesh" is used sometimes in the Word of God as a synonym for corruption. Another phrase for "the flesh" in Scripture is "carnal man," and both refer to the fallen nature within man with emphasis on his material part. The *carnal man* is opposed to the *spiritual man* in the Word of God. The fallen-ness of man proceeds from the body of man. When the ground was cursed, man's essence and existence were cursed. The curse upon the ground was a curse upon the body taken from the ground. Man's sin was a sin of the flesh, and the curse upon the ground went to the very root of sin. The flesh of man was cursed, and thus, the flesh can never produce anything other than corruption. This is why we must be born again. "That which is born of the flesh is flesh, and that which is born of the Spirit is spirit" (John 3:6).

Now, this does not mean that all matter is inherently evil, as in some sort of twisted Gnostic dualism. Rather, matter was created by God to be pure and holy. Matter is now evil because matter is cursed. And, as we noted, the curse itself is a means of salvation. God cursed the flesh that He might bless it. He subjected the creature to vanity that He might exalt it to glory (Romans 8:20). But the curse shall be lifted in the resurrection. Our fleshly body shall be glorified and become incorruptible. This corrupt "flesh and blood cannot inherit the kingdom of God" (I Corinthians 15:50), but God shall "change our vile body, that it may be fashioned like unto his glorious body, according to the working whereby he is able even to subdue all things unto himself" (Philippians 3:21). The material world shall be redeemed and creation shall be restored.

The Struggle between Flesh and Spirit

When God pronounced the curse upon man, Adam experienced an immediate spiritual death. Then, the spirit of man became subject to the body of man. The passions and desires of the body became primary, and the desires of the spirit were cruelly suppressed. Man's spiritual being fell under the control of man's fleshly being. A great war commenced between the spirit and the flesh that is still being waged today. When we receive the gift of the Holy Spirit, we are given power by the Spirit in our spirit to overcome the flesh. But the fact that we struggle in the first place

199

is a result of the curse upon the ground and upon the product of the ground, the flesh.

Paul described this war between the flesh and spirit of man in Romans 7. He spoke of the painful struggle of the man under the law.

> For we know that the law is spiritual, but I am of the flesh, sold under sin. I do not understand my own actions. For I do not do what I want, but I do the very thing I hate. Now if I do what I do not want, I agree with the law, that it is good. So now it is no longer I who do it, but sin that dwells within me. For I know that nothing good dwells in me, that is, in my flesh. For I have the desire to do what is right, but not the ability to carry it out. For I do not do the good I want, but the evil I do not want is what I keep on doing. Now if I do what I do not want, it is no longer I who do it, but sin that dwells within me.
>
> So I find it to be a law that when I want to do right, evil lies close at hand. For I delight in the law of God, in my inner being, but I see in my members another law waging war against the law of my mind and making me captive to the law of sin that dwells in my members. Wretched man that I am! Who will deliver me from this body of death? Thanks be to God through Jesus Christ our Lord! So then, I myself serve the law of God with my mind, but with my flesh I serve the law of sin (Rom 7:14-25 ESV).

The law of God is spiritual, but we are flesh, and the flesh was sold under sin by Adam in the garden. This creates a tension between the desires of the fallen flesh and the conscience of the spirit that God breathed into man. The law is righteous and demands righteous conduct. We recognize in our spirit that the law is right and we must obey it. Indeed, we desire to obey the law, but we do not have the power to do so. The corruption of the flesh has brought the body under the control of sin, so that we cannot do the things we know we should do. We desire to do right in our mind, but the desires of the flesh war against the desires of the mind. We know what to do, but we do not know how to do it. This is why Paul led us to the gospel of Christ as the only solution for this dilemma. "Wretched man that I am! Who will deliver me from this body of death? Thanks be to God through Jesus Christ our Lord!" The victory is won over the flesh in the body of Christ at Calvary.

The man that Paul described here was a man suffering the pain of the curse. The curse of sin creates the conflict between flesh and spirit so that man may never be content to remain in his sins. God intends to save us, and the curse is an instrument of salvation. It is the pain of the curse that leads men to the gospel.

Paul spoke further of the struggle between flesh and spirit in his epistle to the churches of Galatia: "This I say then, Walk in the Spirit, and ye shall not fulfill the lust of the flesh. For the flesh lusteth against the Spirit, and the Spirit against the flesh: and these are contrary the one to the other: so that ye cannot do the things that ye would" (Galatians 5:16,17). He goes on to list the works of the flesh and boldly contrasts them with the fruit of the Spirit, which are produced by the Spirit of God in the spirit of man and manifested in the flesh (Galatians 5:19-23). He concludes his letter with this stark warning, "Be not deceived; God is not mocked: for whatsoever a man soweth, that shall he also reap. For he that soweth to his flesh shall of the flesh reap corruption; but he that soweth to the Spirit shall of the Spirit reap life everlasting" (Galatians 6:7, 8). The flesh is corrupt, and everything fleshly that is sown into our lives will produce fruit after its kind. Corrupt flesh will always produce corruption.

The Struggle between Flesh and Spirit in the Family

The flesh and the spirit are also at war in the family. What is true in the heart of man is true in the house of man. "For the flesh lusteth against the Spirit, and the Spirit against the flesh: and these are contrary the one to the other: so that ye cannot do the things that ye would." A tremendous battle rages in every Christian home between the impulse of the flesh and the demands of the Spirit. The force that wins becomes evident in the fruit that we produce. If we sow to the flesh in our house, then we shall produce the works of the flesh. But if we sow to the Spirit in our house, then we shall reap the fruit of the Spirit.

The spiritual home will produce "love, joy, peace, longsuffering, gentleness, goodness, faith, meekness, temperance." (Galatians 5:22, 23). The fleshly home will produce "adultery, fornication, uncleanness, lasciviousness, idolatry, witchcraft, hatred, variance, emulations, wrath, strife, seditions, heresies, envying, murders, drunkenness, reveling, and such like." (Galatians 5:19-21). Not every fleshly house will produce all of these evil works, but some of these works will be present in varying degrees in every fleshly home. And, of course, this is not an exhaustive list of the terrible works that accompany sin and disobedience. Other forms of evil fruit crop up as well. We must "walk in the Spirit" so that we do not "fulfill the lusts of the flesh."

This is so *very* important to our study on the family. These are not peripheral issues. The family *cannot* produce spiritual fruit from fleshly roots. If we build our house in the flesh, then our house will be corrupt. There are no exceptions. We need a spiritual mind to build a spiritual house so that we may reap life everlasting in our homes.

It is the specific responsibility of the man to see to it that his house is a spiritual house built up by the Spirit of God. This can only be done by faith. The gospel is the only answer for the sins of the flesh. Paul declared that the fleshly man has been crucified with Christ, and that the life that we now live we live by the faith of Christ (Galatians 2:20). This means that our family must live by the faith of Christ. We must reckon the fleshly nature of the sinful home to be crucified with Christ by faith. We must choose by grace through faith to walk in the Spirit in our home. This will produce an abundant crop of spiritual fruit in our family that shall lead to perseverance in salvation. This happy outcome cannot be accomplished through the flesh. We must be filled with the Holy Ghost.

Most Christians recognize that we are saved by the indwelling Spirit of God in our soul. Certainly, no Christian would assert that anyone can be saved in the flesh apart from the Spirit of God. And yet, we so often seek to "save" our families in just this way, in the flesh apart from the Spirit of God. Too often we build our homes only in the carnal realm of work and education, recreation and relationships. And all of these are extremely important. In fact, they are so important that we must insist on building them *in the Spirit* and not in the flesh. Whatever is built in the flesh is sure to perish. But all that is built by the hand of the Lord shall last forever. The war between the flesh and Spirit that is waged in the Christian household must be won decisively in favor of the Spirit.

We must walk in the Spirit in the rooms of our house. We must walk in the Spirit in our conversation and in the correction of our children. We must discuss finances and pursue godly stewardship in the Spirit. We must plan for the future in the Spirit. We must seek education and career choices in the Spirit. We must pursue family recreation and entertainment in the Spirit. Everything we do must be done in the Spirit. We must search the scriptures for direction in everything we do every day. And then, having read the promises of God for all of life, we must "pray in" the promises for our family. Moreover, we must confidently persevere in the promises of God for us and our children. If we walk in the Spirit, then we shall not fulfill the lusts of the flesh, and we shall reap the harvest of spiritual fruit. The flesh of man is cursed, and everything man does in the flesh is sure to be cursed as well.

A Diet of Curse and Corruption

The curse upon the ground caused corruption to flow out of the soil. Man's food comes out of the soil. We live of the fruit of cursed soil, and thus, we live on a daily diet of corruption that ends inevitably in death. The very produce created to sustain life for man has become the source of man's corruption and death. We partake of the curse every day that we eat of the fruit of the soil. The ground is cursed, the food is cursed, and we are cursed. We cannot escape the curse. God made certain that it is so.

After the Flood, God gave man meat for food (Genesis 9:3). But here again, man ingests the curse of death when he eats what has been slain. This is not to say that sin is a biological agent like a form of bacteria or viral infection that man contracts from plants and animals. Rather, the curse is a spiritual, covenantal curse upon the ground and all that the ground produces. However, the power of death that holds the earth in its grip has "contaminated" in some spiritual and covenantal sense the very material universe that we occupy. We become what we eat.

The Diet of Doctrine

Of course, eating in scripture is a metaphor of ingesting doctrine. We are what we eat in a spiritual sense, as well. We are warned to be careful what we eat. The poison of sin and death is in the food and drink of false doctrine. The family should be a safe place for eating and drinking together. Every child safely trusts in his parents to provide a wholesome meal at the family table. The same must be said of the doctrine that we allow our children to be taught, whether the doctrine is being taught by a preacher in a three-piece suit or an entertainer from Hollywood. We must carefully guard our family's doctrinal diet.

17

The Covenantal Curse

God told Adam that the ground was cursed for his sake. This brings us back to the idea of Adam's federal headship and the legal imputation of sin upon all creation because of Adam's dominion. Just as an entire team loses the game when one member drops the ball, or just as a corporation is penalized for the illegal activities of its directors, so the earth that had been placed under Adam's headship and dominion was cursed for his sin. The imputation of sin is a covenantal, corporate and legal act. God placed the curse upon the ground for Adam's transgression. God cursed the ground for Adam's sake.

It is here that we immediately begin to see the universal nature of Adam's sin and the curse upon him. The entire earth is affected by Adam's sin, and every generation that follows shall be affected by Adam's sin. This includes both men and women, though men, as laborers in the field, shall feel the effects more directly. The curse upon the woman was limited in a sense to the woman herself. No man can truly share in the woman's pain in childbearing and childrearing, except as he voluntarily lays down his life for his wife and shares in her sorrow on the cross of his loving self-denial. But, even then, the man's experience of sharing the woman's pain is vicarious.

However, the curse upon the man has direct consequences upon the wife and children. "Cursed is the ground *for thy sake.*" Something entirely outside the man—the ground and those who eat of it—has been cursed for the man's sake. The consequences of the man's sin extend far beyond the man. The sin of the father has a far deeper effect upon the human family than does the sin of the wife and children. Every godly man should be greatly sobered by this reality. Our sins affect far more than ourselves. Others are affected *for our sake*. We affect the very ground that our family walks on and eats from. The soil of our souls is affected by the sinful decisions that men make in the home.

The father has the power to affect everyone in the home in a way that no one else can. Certainly, mom can make everybody miserable, and one child can make the entire family ponder the relative merits of infanticide. But dad affects the family in a decidedly different way. Dad does more than just affect the mood of the home. Dad decides whether or not sin shall reign in the home or be defeated. Dad decides whether the family as a whole shall follow the Lord Jesus Christ. Dad decides whether or not the family shall "seek first the kingdom of heaven." Dad decides whether or not the family shall dress modestly and forsake the entertainments and pleasures of the world. It is dad who will ultimately determine the spiritual direction and attitude of the home.

Furthermore, God actively pronounces either a curse or a blessing on the home based on dad's covenantal faithfulness in Christ. Of course, the faithfulness of the father is by grace through faith. The husband and father lives in faithful obedience by grace through faith, and the blessing of God is pronounced upon his home as a result. "Blessed is the man that endures temptation" (James 1:12). When the father is tested and proves to be obedient through the power of the Holy Spirit, he releases into his home the covenantal blessing of Christ's obedience.

Both women and children can be faithful in the home of an unfaithful man. Peter spent a good bit of time telling them how to do so (I Peter 3). Entire families can be saved while the father is lost, but it is a rare occurrence indeed. Usually one or two members of a family may be faithful without dad leading the way, but rarely will the majority of the household do so. And the mothers and children that are saved in spite of the father will make it with tremendous difficulty. It is like the near-impossibility of rich men being saved of which Jesus spoke. Of course, "all things are possible with God" (Matthew 19:26), yet the father brings a curse upon the home that only a miracle can overcome. It can be done, and it *must* be done, if your circumstances are such. But it should never *have* to be done. Fathers should realize the far-reaching effects of their obedience or disobedience and live faithfully.

Adam disobeyed and brought the curse upon all men. Christ obeyed and brought the blessing upon all men (Romans 5). Just so, the man, as head of the house, can choose either to stand in the faithlessness of Adam or the faithfulness of Christ, and he will bring either a blessing or a curse upon his home as a result. Just as the ground is cursed for Adam's sake, the ground is redeemed for Christ's sake in the resurrection. The Christian father has the great privilege in Christ of living out the cross of Christ in his daily life thereby breaking the power of the curse and bringing the blessing of salvation upon his home. The man must be ever mindful that the ground is either blessed or cursed *for his sake.*

The man is called to imitate the love of Christ for the church in his love for his wife (Ephesians 5:25). The man must accept that he alone bears the responsibility for the entire household. Everyone in the house bears their own individual responsibility for their particular role in the family, but the man alone is responsible for them all. "The buck stops here." When sin runs rampant through the house, the godly man refuses to point fingers and humbly accepts the blame. He accepts that sin should have never been tolerated, and the fact that it was is due to his oversight—in both senses of the word. The man alone has the power to redeem the family. He can stand before God as the imitator of Christ and offer himself to God as the man of the house. He can accept responsibility for sin and then trust for forgiveness offered in Christ. He can pray for the family and intercede for the fallen souls in his household. The father can appeal to God to keep the promise He has made toward men in Christ. The man can *be* Christ in a sense for his family. Certainly the man can never actually be the Lord Jesus, but he can stand in the power of Christ's loving sacrifice at the Cross and trust that the power of Christ will flow through him to redeem every situation in the home.

The Christian husband and father must imitate Christ. Jesus bore the sins of the entire "family" of God. The husband and father must bear the sins of his entire family. He must imitate the example of Job and pray every day for his family that their sins might be forgiven and that salvation might come to his house (Job 1:5). He must see the sins of everyone in his family as his own and bear them before God in the imitation of Christ. Of course, only the blood of Christ is efficacious to remit sins. And yet, the father is playing out (realizing, *actualizing*, as it were) the redemptive work of the Cross when he takes up the cross of Christ and "bear[s] about in the body the dying of the Lord Jesus, that the life also of Jesus might be made manifest in our body" (II Corinthians 4:10). The man is standing before God on behalf of his family and reckons the work of salvation done by faith in Christ. The father has been given the "ministry of reconciliation" (II Corinthians 5:18) on the behalf of his family. He lays down his life for his wife and children just as Christ did for the church. And just as Christ broke the curse for us, the father breaks it for his family. The ground is cursed or blessed *for his sake*.

A Lifetime of Eating In Sorrow

God tells Adam that he shall eat of the fruit of the ground "in sorrow...all the days of [his] life." The word "sorrow" used here is the same word "sorrow" in God's curse upon the woman. The man is promised sorrow in working the ground just as the woman is promised sorrow in childbearing. The woman shall bring forth the fruit of her womb with sorrow, and the man shall bring forth the fruit of the ground with corresponding sorrow. Both man and woman shall endure great travail.

There are three things to note here. First, man shall eat of the ground that has been cursed. The simple fact is man cannot escape the curse because man cannot live without eating. He must eat to survive, and yet he must eat food grown in cursed soil. Second, man shall eat in sorrow. Eating was given to man for the purpose of sustenance, but it was also given to be a delight. It was God who gave us the more than ten thousand taste buds that do so much to enliven our simple supper. God intended our meals to be a rousing feast of joyous fellowship, but sin has turned it into the lonely last meal of a man condemned to die. Third, this tragic state of affairs shall continue until the end of the sinner's life. There is no escape from this sentence. Sinful man cannot escape the pain no matter how much he tries. Every meal he eats, every bite he takes, is just another pungent reminder of his mortality.

Sorrow is toil and labor, pain and suffering. The man shall work and he shall eat, but he shall never be satisfied. And his sorrow shall extend to the end of his days. The man shall be forced to work the ground in order to survive, but the pleasure of productivity shall be lost in the sorrow of futility and frustration. The curse remains upon man for all of his life. Men seek escape, but they cannot find it. They cannot find it by going on vacation to the mountains or the sea. They cannot find it by taking an early retirement. Just like the feminist who seeks to escape the curse of motherhood by fleeing femininity in the refuge of wannabe manliness, men often seek to escape the curse of frustration and futility by running from work. But they cannot get away. For even when they eat, they are living under the curse. And it becomes very difficult to go very long eating without working.

The Apostle Paul declared that the man who does not work should not eat (II Thessalonians 3:10). And a man that does not eat cannot live. So, we are caught in an inevitable quandary: we must accept the curse in order to overcome it. As we noted above, God has blessed us with a curse so that we might look toward Him for salvation from our sin.

And this also has an application to the family. The family meal is a tremendous indicator of the health of a family. The family that is overcoming the curse by the power of the Cross is a family that finds the blessing of Christ increasing around their table. The family who is living under the power of the curse is a family that has escalating discord and bitterness around the table. When the Lord speaks of His blessing upon the faithful house He says, "Blessed is every one that feareth the LORD; that walketh in his ways. For thou shalt eat the labor of thine hands: happy shalt thou be, and it shall be well with thee. Thy wife shall be as a fruitful vine by the sides of thine house: thy children like olive plants round about thy table. Behold, that thus shall the man be blessed that feareth the LORD. The LORD shall bless thee out of Zion: and thou shalt see the good of Jerusalem all the days of thy life. Yea, thou shalt see thy children's children, and peace upon Israel" (Psalm 128:1-6).

What a beautiful picture of a blessed family! God gave us the blessing of eating together from the beginning of creation. Feasting is one of the primary metaphors of fellowship with Him in the kingdom of God. The call of salvation is compared to being invited to a feast. The Lord's Supper, where once again Jesus eats with sinners, is the primary reminder of His death, His presence and His imminent return. God gave food and feasting for rejoicing in His creation. Sadly, sin crashed the party, and now, the curse is upon our meal.

The Christian family must reclaim the blessedness of feasting together in the household of faith. The table must become again the center of the home where father and mother, sisters and brothers gather to fellowship, to be instructed in the Word of God and to enjoy the bounty of God's green earth. The curse is broken in Christ, and we receive that increasing blessing when we reclaim the right to "eat the labor of [our] hands" in happiness and joy.

God declares that man will work the ground, but it will bring forth thorns and thistles. The ground is cursed, and it will bring forth fruitless plants that are useless to man as food. The ground that once brought forth only good things will now bring forth weeds that serve only to make sowing and reaping a difficult task. Adam is promised a lifetime of frustrated labor where the amount of effort put in never matches the amount of produce taken out. Where he sows and reaps he shall constantly be on guard against the encroachment of wild and uncultivated plants that seek to take over and choke out his domestic labor. There will be fruit of the ground, for man shall eat of it. But it shall be a harvest eked out from an unwilling and reluctant soil. The work of man will be an exercise of futility and frustration. Never will he be able to truly rest from his labors, for the demands of another day keep calling "all the days of [his] life." Man's tiring work *will never end* until the end of his days.

Then, God told Adam that he would eat of the herb of the field, which is a radical departure from God's plan for man to cultivate the garden and eat of its abundant and ready fruitfulness. The field, as we noted earlier, was the wilderness outside the orderly rows of the garden. Man soon would be thrust out of the garden into the outlying fields where he would be required to eat whatever he could grow out of the weed-choked soil. He would be required to clear fields for planting and coax out a meager harvest. This was a terrible blow to the man who was given the privilege of bringing the earth under his dominion with the eager cooperation of all of nature. But now, the natural world would be man's first and foremost enemy, resisting his best attempts to be fruitful and productive. Whatever man would accomplish from now on would be the result of unceasing and unrelenting toil.

Adam was sentenced to a lifetime of hard labor, producing bread for food by the sweat of his brow. The sweat on his face was a daily reminder of the unceasing toil that was now required because he sought salvation by works rather than by faith. It is neither the work nor the making of bread that is the curse. Work was God's purpose and bread was intended for food before the fall. Rather, the curse is the difficulty of making the bread. It is the fact that he must do so against God, in his own strength rather than cultivating the earth with God's blessing and spiritual cooperation. The sweat of the brow is a sign of man's attempt to save himself.

We are taught to pray, "Give us this day our daily bread" (Matthew 6:11). Thus, we are instructed to recognize that bread comes from the hand of God. God sometimes gives us bread from heaven, like manna in the wilderness, while we are in the infancy of our faith. But God will always seek to lead us into the promised land of mature, Christian experience where He teaches us to sow and reap and produce bread as He gives the sun and rain to make it possible. Man tried in the garden to live without God, apart from the grace of God, and the curse is a stark reminder that we cannot pull it off. We depend on the Creator for every breath we breathe, for every bite we eat. This is why we offer thanks before every meal. We thank Him for His grace when we say grace.

God solemnly informed Adam that he would be under the curse of futility and frustration until he returned to the dust through the corruption of the grave. Adam was taken out of the ground, and he returned to the ground. But we see elsewhere that the ground becomes the scene of a new creation when the power of Christ's resurrection transforms man from shame to glory. This is the only way that the curse can be broken. Mortality brings futility, and there is no escape other than to face the curse squarely and accept it in Christ. The man of the house must accept the futility and frustration of life and surrender it to Christ in humble resignation. Then, Christ will nail our works to the cross, accepting the curse on our behalf, and plunge the curse into the heart of the earth from which we were taken. Then, our works will arise with Christ by grace through faith into the newness of life and be transformed into works of eternal meaning and purpose. This breaks the curse of futility and frustration and makes life eternally rewarding. The man is cursed until he dies. However, when he dies with Christ by faith, then he lives again and lives forever, and his works will follow him.

18

Ecclesiastes and the Curse upon Man

The book of Ecclesiastes is a powerful example of a man dealing with the effects of the curse. The preacher said,

> Vanity of vanities, says the Preacher, vanity of vanities! All is vanity. What does man gain by all the toil at which he toils under the sun? A generation goes, and a generation comes, but the earth remains forever. The sun rises, and the sun goes down, and hastens to the place where it rises. The wind blows to the south and goes around to the north; around and around goes the wind, and on its circuits the wind returns. All streams run to the sea, but the sea is not full; to the place where the streams flow, there they flow again. All things are full of weariness; a man cannot utter it; the eye is not satisfied with seeing, nor the ear filled with hearing. What has been is what will be, and what has been done is what will be done, and there is nothing new under the sun. Is there a thing of which it is said, "See, this is new"? It has been already in the ages before us. There is no remembrance of former things, nor will there be any remembrance of later things yet to be among those who come after (Ecclesiastes 1:2-11 ESV).

The preacher went on to sound a theme that echoes throughout the book, that all is "vanity and vexation of spirit." Vanity and vexation of spirit are *futility* and *frustration*. And the root of futility and frustration is the fact that men work a lifetime of ceaseless toil and then die leaving nothing to show for it. Work is not the problem. Death is the problem. Death makes work rather senseless. The next generation will occupy the houses that we build, spend the money that we earned and eat of the gardens that we planted. But then they, too, will die and cannot take with them anything accumulated by hard work. This is the source of futility and frustration. Why work?

Of course, if we do not work then we do not eat, and if we do not eat then we die. But we are going to die anyway, right? So why not just quit working, quit eating and go ahead and die? If it is inevitable, let's just go ahead and get it over with. And yet, every man, though he is cursed with futility and frustration, feels the pull of something beyond the grave, a power far beyond the curse of sin and death, the draw of another world. The preacher spoke of this other-worldly impulse when he said, "[God] has made everything beautiful in its time. Also, he has put eternity into man's heart, yet so that he cannot find out what God has done from the beginning to the end" (Ecclesiastes 3:11 ESV).

God has put "eternity into man's heart." Man is overwhelmed by the futility and frustration of life, and yet, he cannot escape the desperate will to live. Even under the power of the curse man is compelled to break through its power and live forever. But this quest for immortality only produces even deeper futility and frustration until a man truly discovers the only means of breaking the power of the curse. And the power to break the curse lies only in accepting it in humility and surrender, by placing our trust in the death, burial and resurrection of Christ, who bore the curse on our behalf and destroyed it at the Cross.

The Conclusion of the Whole Matter

After the preacher described his futile and frustrated attempts to overcome the curse, he finally gave us the conclusion of the whole matter: "Let us hear the conclusion of the whole matter: Fear God, and keep his commandments: for this is the whole duty of man. For God shall bring every work into judgment, with every secret thing, whether it be good, or whether it be evil" (Ecclesiastes 12:13,14).

The preacher declared that the only meaning in life is serving God. He tried to break the power of the curse in every way possible. He tried money, women, pleasure, parties, feasting, architecture, education, asceticism, self-denial, philosophy, human wisdom, on and on. He tried everything he could think of. But nothing worked. Sweat still poured down his furrowed brow. He was still working in the shadow of a tombstone digging his own grave. All was futility and frustration.

This lesson needs to be learned by every godly man who seeks to be a good husband and father. We cannot break the power of the curse through human effort, through the power of good works. We can only break the curse by realizing that we *cannot* break it and that it has already been broken in Christ. Therefore, the power of the curse is broken when we accept that salvation is by grace through faith and allow the obedience of Christ to transform our frantic works into the easy effort of true grace. Then, the futility and frustration are gone, the sweat evaporates, the brow clears, and we rest in the finished work of Christ. When we live in this grace, our work on earth is done with an eternal purpose and the real meaning of life is restored. This is how Christ "saves" our life's work and rescues us from the power of the curse. Fearing God is the conclusion of the whole matter, the end of the curse in Christ.

The Redemption of Work

Christ's redemption of the earth brings the redemption of work. Sin came when man shirked his responsibility and allowed his wife to lead the family and the serpent to lead her astray. So, the curse drags man kicking and screaming back to the role he is forced to play as head of the home. Man tries to flee the responsibility God gave him in work and worship, but the curse forces man to reckon with the inevitable. Further, it does not allow him to remain in rebellion against responsibility. Therefore, in this sense, the curse is evidence of God's grace upon the man just as it is upon the woman.

Christ took the curse upon Him in the sweat of His bloody brow. He shared in the agony of the woman and the man. He broke the curse for us, and we, by trusting in Him, share in His triumph over it. But trusting in Christ is the only means of breaking the curse. Work and worship was God's purpose before the fall, and it has not changed after the fall. The curse makes this purpose inescapable, and the pain makes the curse unbearable without looking to Christ for salvation. Those who insist on bearing the curse alone will be damned to an eternity of bearing the curse alone. But it would be ultimate folly to suffer this needless fate. Christ has made it possible that we can be saved from the curse, not by fleeing from it, but by accepting it in His acceptance.

Man must accept the curse of work and death, finding redemption therein, rather than trying to escape the inevitable through an insolent slothfulness and a vain quest for immortality. Man was created to rest and to live forever, but neither can be attained apart from work and worship. Man was created to achieve perfection through sanctified labor and to live forever through the gift of eternal life received in worship. This is how godly men will break the curse and be restored to the original purpose for which Adam was created.

19

Marriage after the Fall

Genesis 3:20-24. "And Adam called his wife's name Eve; because she was the mother of all living. Unto Adam also and to his wife did the LORD God make coats of skins, and clothed them. And the LORD God said, Behold, the man is become as one of us, to know good and evil: and now, lest he put forth his hand, and take also of the tree of life, and eat, and live for ever: Therefore the LORD God sent him forth from the garden of Eden, to till the ground from whence he was taken. So he drove out the man; and he placed at the east of the garden of Eden Cherubim, and a flaming sword which turned every way, to keep the way of the tree of life."

After the Lord God pronounced the curse upon the fallen trio of serpent, woman and man, it was Adam's turn to speak. And it is very interesting what he said. In fact, his next statement illustrates perfectly what begins happening within the family when the curse of God is pronounced upon our sin.

Surely when the last echoes of God's thundering judgment died away, an eerie silence settled over the garden. The serpent was slithering his way through the dust out of the garden back to the field from whence he came. The man turned slowly toward the woman with the slow-dawning realization of what had happened breaking upon him. His eyes narrowed as he looked in bitterness upon the woman who had "caused" him to eat of the fruit. She was created to be his helpmeet, but now she had become his adversary. She had offered him the fruit in the first place, and now, according to the Word of the Lord, she would be ever contending against him for preeminence in the family. Her desire would be both *for* him and *against* him, putting him in the frustrating position of constantly asserting his rule and authority by pressing her down. God did not create them for this sort of competition.

The man and the woman were first divided before God came into the garden when they realized they were naked and ran into the bushes to hide from one another. Then, they were divided further when God stood them apart from one another and cursed them individually for their sin. But the division went even further as Adam glared at the woman with utter contempt, slowly pointed a trembling finger at her and hoarsely whispered that her name would no longer be called "Woman," she who came out of the man, but now she would be called "Eve," the mother of all living. The man was announcing a new identity for the woman, for sin had estranged her from her beloved. From then on her orientation and focus would be toward her children rather than toward the man she was created to help in the task of dominion.

When God created Adam and his wife, they stood before God as a family united together in the purpose of God. The man stood facing God with the woman looking toward the man and the children (who would later be born) looking toward the mother. This family orientation flowed smoothly toward the Creator with all eyes turned toward those immediately ahead of them and ultimately toward God, the final authority in the family. But now man would look toward his daily work of futility and frustration, and the woman would turn her back upon the man and focus upon *her* children, as they would now be seen (*See* 4:1, 25). The man and woman would focus most where it hurts most. And, as chapter 4 clearly shows, the children would turn their focus upon one another in a violent rage. This is the tragic familial breakdown that begins when sin enters the home. The family is divided, and confusion disrupts the harmony of the home.

Two things were happening in verse 20. First of all, Adam's attitude toward his wife was changed. The fact that he re-named her was an indication of his rejection of her. He had lovingly called her "Woman" because she came out of him, but now he shoved her away from him toward a reduction of identity. To the man she was now "Eve," the mother of all living. Sinful man bitterly pushes the wife away from her connection to him and reduces her to just the mother of his children, much less than the partner she was created to be. So, first, Adam rejected his wife.

The second thing happening in verse 20 was that the woman also turned away from her husband and accepted his reduction of her purpose as only "the mother of all living" rather than the "fitting helper" taken out of man's side. The man pushed the woman away, and the woman angrily recoiled from the man. She turned her attention toward the kids (as we see in chapter 4) and brooded in resentful anger against the oppression and disrespect of the man. Adam and Eve were effectively and completely sundered now, and the family was pulled apart by their divided focus.

This is the sort of division that sin brings into the Christian home. This tragedy is played out before us again and again. The man becomes bitter with the woman that God gave him because he thinks she has let him down. The man pushes the woman away and refuses to allow her to be his helpmeet. He labels her as "mother" rather than "wife" and withdraws into his isolated existence. The woman feels the man shove her away, and she recoils with hot resentment against him for rejecting her. She deliberately turns her focus away from the man and seeks her fulfillment in their children. She becomes just "mom" in the household and grudgingly accepts the reduction of purpose, though it is much less than the helpmeet and confidant she was intended to be.

The man goes his way alone and refuses to allow his wife into his private world. The woman, who is desperate to be near her husband and yet struggles at the same time with the urge to control him, is hurt deeply by his rejection and withdraws further into her own world. She tries again to reach out to him occasionally, but he is untouchable. She recoils even further at the cruelty of his callous rebuff. They drift ever farther apart, until the only thing they have in common is the kids. This is how, when the kids are grown and gone, mom and dad end up in divorce court. Sin has driven them apart, and when the kids are gone, they have nothing left holding them together. Of course, in these amazingly self-centered times, many couples will not even allow the well-being of the children to hold them together.

The godly Christian couple must recognize the centrifugal force of sin and disobedience that seeks to pull them apart and resist it with all of their power. Indeed, they must resist it with the power of the Holy Spirit within them. Sin and bitterness will compel fallen man to re-name his wife and force her out of the office of "wife" into only the office of "mother." But the godly man recognizes this sin for what it is and insists that, by grace through faith, the woman God has given him must fill *both* the offices of wife *and* mother. She must remain his helpmeet while she bears and rears his children. He must not shove her away and live alone in his bitter isolation. He must draw her into his everyday life through careful and considerate conversation and consultation. He must make her a part of every decision and deliberation about his work and worship. He must see her as the most important part of his team. He should never allow a division and dichotomy to develop between home and work. He must insist that his wife occupy the office of wife as well as mother.

The woman is more than a nanny for the man's children. She is his closest ally and confidant. She is his lover and his best friend. She must be the light of his eye and the strength of his life. This sort of esteem requires constant fellowship and communion. It requires deliberate effort on the part of the man. It requires a steady suppression of the urge to become bitter toward the woman for her failures, a steadfast refusal to become an accuser by bringing her sins into judgment and condemnation in the courtroom of his mind. The man must not change his wife's name.

Coats of Skin

After Adam had re-named his wife, Eve, the Lord God covered their nakedness with coats of skin. As we noted earlier, God never intended for them to remain naked. They would have been clothed later as they grew in grace and the knowledge of the truth. They were created naked as a sign of their innocence and spiritual immaturity. They would have been clothed in righteousness when God led them graciously into an understanding of their need. Their covering would have been a product of God's gracious instruction. But Adam and Eve sought a covering by works rather than grace when they ate of the tree of law, and their eyes were opened to the truth of their nakedness. They covered themselves with the inadequate covering of fig leaves, which, as we noted, represents the insufficient covering of fleshly righteousness.

However, God refused to leave them in their uncovered state. He slew one or more animals and used the skin of the animal to make coats for them. And yet, it is apparent that God was doing more than just obtaining the necessary material to provide coats. God also was teaching Adam and Eve about the provisional covering of an animal sacrifice to provide atonement for sin and to bring them into fellowship with God even though they were now sinners under the curse of His judgment. This is surely where God taught them how to offer animal sacrifice as worship to the Lord.

This animal sacrifice represents the sacrifice of Christ at Calvary. It anticipates the blood that was shed for sinners at the Cross. Just as God covered the first sinful family in the blood of an innocent sacrifice, so the sins of the family must be covered today with the blood of Christ. We have emphasized this theme throughout our study. The fallen family needs the salvation that only comes through the work of Christ at Calvary. The family will remain naked and exposed to God's judgment as they attempt to cover their sin with inadequate human righteousness. We must turn to the Cross for redemption and forgiveness. This is the only way that the fallen family can find its way back into the presence of God. We must be clothed in the righteousness of Christ.

Driven Out of the Garden

After God clothed Adam and Eve, He drove them out of the garden into the field to till the ground for food. The Lord God observed that man had become like Him "to know good and evil." Adam had attained unto a twisted sort of god-likeness, but this god-likeness was rooted in the flesh and not the Spirit. It was a humanistic awareness of right and wrong that could only lead to corruption. God had cursed man for his sin, but He did not take away his newly acquired awareness of right and wrong. Man was aware of right and wrong, but he was powerless to overcome the wrong and achieve the right. This would lead to tremendous guilt and condemnation as man attempted to reach righteousness and continually fell short. Thankfully, it was not the will of God to leave man forever in this miserable state. So, God determined that

He would not allow fallen man to remain in the garden near the tree of life lest he should eat of the tree of life and live forever in his fallen and sinful state. Therefore, God's decision to expel man from the garden so he could not eat of the tree of life was actually a show of mercy.

So, God sent Adam and Eve out of the garden into the field surrounding the garden where man would till the ground and live out his cursed existence. God "drove out the man" and placed guardian angels at the east of the garden to keep Adam from returning. The angels wielded a flaming sword that turned every way "to keep the way of the tree of life" (v. 24). There was no way back into the garden to eat of the tree of life. And this remained so until Jesus came and opened the way back into the presence of God by His perfect obedience. Now, the Christian family can return to the garden that God created and eat freely of the ultimate tree of life, the cross of Calvary.

The sinful family will be cast out of the garden of perfect communion with God. It is impossible to allow sin to reign in the home without a breakdown in spiritual relationship with God and one another. So many families are living outside the blessings of God and are not even aware of it. They have become accustomed to the field where they eke out a meager living. But the way back into the garden has been opened by Christ. When we repent of our sins and turn in faith to Christ, then our family is taken with Him safely through the sword of judgment into the cool, leafy glades of divine fellowship. There is no longer any reason to camp out in the field of cursed existence. Let us return to the garden where we walk again with the Lord God in the cool of the day.

20

Children after the Fall

Genesis 4:1,2. "And Adam knew Eve his wife; and she conceived, and bore Cain, and said, I have gotten a man from the LORD. And she again bore his brother Abel. And Abel was a keeper of sheep, but Cain was a tiller of the ground."

The next part of the Genesis story shows the ongoing and on-growing results of sin. Possibly no part of the story is more heart wrenching than the account of what sin did to Adam's children. Adam was created in the image and likeness of God and destined to be crowned with glory and honor. Instead, the image of God was marred in him, and he was shackled with the chains of sin and death. Adam was promised that his children would be the holy seed that would fill the earth and take dominion over all creation. Instead, his children became a fallen race of evil men groaning under the dominion of malicious principalities and powers. The world was filled with violence, and finally, the Lord God destroyed man from the face of the earth, leaving only Noah and his family to rebuild human civilization. There is no way that Adam could have envisioned all the pain and suffering that one small decision would entail. As one minister preached, Adam's sin was "a moment of weakness and a life of regret."

The story of Genesis is in many ways the story of all history. All of man's failures and successes are prefigured there. The outlines of redemption are drawn there, and everything that occurs in history flows out of the initial experiences of Adam and

Eve. Adam was the father of all people, and his sin came upon them all. He could not have anticipated the future, for he was in the grip of unbelief. Only faith can see the future. We must consider this carefully as we make daily decisions that seem so small and insignificant. We must see through the eyes of faith that the future is being written by the decisions we make now. We cannot forsake the future and abandon our children to the whim of fate. We are determining their fate now. We are casting their future upon them. They cannot escape our mistakes. They may overcome them by the mercy of God, but they cannot escape them. Our sins will affect our children. This is an incredibly sobering thought.

There is no more poignant example in Scripture concerning the effects of sin on our children than the story of Cain and Abel. It is a worst case scenario that portrays the many potential pitfalls of rearing sinners. These things are "written for our learning" (Romans 15:4), and the lessons observed here are possibly more relevant to the family now than ever before.

Sexual Love as Knowledge

The story began with Adam "knowing" his wife. It is noteworthy that here and elsewhere the sexual union of man and wife is described as "knowledge." The intimacy of relationship is based on knowing one another. Thus, sexual union is a supreme physical example of the spiritual union of the marriage relationship. A good relationship is based on knowing one another. Marriage is relationship. Indeed, it is the ultimate human relationship. The husband must seek to get to know his wife better every day, and the wife must seek to know him as well. Physical union apart from knowledge is destined to become a selfish exercise of fakery and hypocrisy.

God created the sexual relationship while Adam and Eve were still living in the state of innocence in the garden. Sexual union was created to be the means of covenantal consummation and natural propagation. This is implicit in the command to be fruitful and multiply. We must never accept the idea that sexual union was either a part of the fall or a result of it. Sexual union is God-ordained and God-blessed. It was the Lord who first taught

Adam how to make love to his wife. We must not blush at the idea, for sexual union was God's idea and God's gifts are good. As the Lord said, "It is very good!" It is a wise man who learns from Scripture to be "ravished" with the wife of his youth (Proverbs 5:19). Just because sin has perverted sexuality does not mean that the church should act embarrassed and ashamed about godly love. "Marriage is honorable in all and the bed undefiled" (Hebrews 13:4). Christians should boldly proclaim that only those who "glorify God with [their] body" (I Corinthians 6:20) really know what love is all about.

Even in his fallen state, Adam's sexual union with his wife was one of loving intimacy. He "knew" his wife. What a beautiful way to describe the marriage bed. This is where so many go astray today when they seek to reduce sexual relationship to just "sex"— physical union without relationship. Sex without relationship, which the Bible calls fornication, is union without "knowledge." We could say, then, that fornication is ignorant sex. Fools miss the larger spiritual point of sexual union and pervert it into mere entertainment. The lofty purpose of procreation is reduced to recreation. That *is* truly ignorant.

The world has disconnected sexual union from its primary spiritual and physical meaning of *relationship* and *reproduction*. Sexual union is a matter of relationship as man and wife are joined together and represent physically what God declared covenantally when they made their vows to be married. God joins a couple together in marriage, and their physical union celebrates and consummates that fact. Their pleasure together signifies the enduring beauty of oneness of relationship as they are made one together in daily life. They are fulfilled in each other and learn to live for the other's delight and satisfaction. Selfless love in the bedroom should be a perfect emblem of the sort of selfless relationship being cultivated every day in every other room of the house. The ecstasy of sexual love should express physically the deep, continual joy that characterizes Christian marriage.

Therefore, fornication is a mockery of sexual love, for it symbolizes nothing but selfish gratification. There is no commitment, no covenant, and thus no relationship. Fornicators partake of sexual love without marriage and thus without meaning. They cannot love for the benefit of the relationship, for there is no relationship. Relationship does not exist without commitment. The only love expressed in fornication is a narcissistic love for self. These self-lovers offer commitments to no one other than themselves, and yet they are driven to gratify their biological urge. They reduce the beautiful sacrament of marital love to the lowest sort of animal instinct. The wonder of spiritual relationship is lost in mere biological coupling. This is the tragedy of fornication. They can never understand true love. They do it all in the name of love, but it is love in name only. In fact, the love of the world is more *lust* than love.

The world also emptied sexuality of its greater meaning when they set out to eliminate reproduction as the ultimate purpose of sexual union. Under the guise of family planning they have produced countless methods of preventing fruitfulness. And they take their obsession with barren pleasure even to the point of outright murder if one "accident" happens to slip by. And they call this murder "abortion," as if giving murder a clinical name makes it somehow alright. They set out with remarkable determination to make sex nothing more than just a physical act for the fun of it. And they smartly congratulate each other on having obtained this enlightened goal. It has always been this way with fools. They end up sacrificing their future for a moment of fun and never realize what they lost.

Ironically, love that has fun as its object is not really fun at all. This is why they must keep seeking for weirder and more perverted thrills. Just plain sex will not satisfy fornicators for long. Something within keeps reaching for greater satisfaction. They do not understand that they are looking for spiritual satisfaction. Man was made body, soul and spirit, and when sexuality is viewed only in terms of body it is profoundly dissatisfying. It is sex without soul. They travel far and wide, becoming more enlightened and more sophisticated by the moment. They sail to far away, exotic lands, loving and leaving countless broken hearts. And still, they are empty. And what troubles them the most is that they are getting older every day. They become frantic and more desperate with every encounter. They have gained the whole world and lost their souls.

Of course, God did create the sexual union for pleasure. And yet, it is such a revealing emblem of our age that the larger meaning of love is lost and the wonder disappears in the cheap, tawdry action of soulless bodies exploiting one another for selfish gratification. And the world ignorantly believes that they are wild and free. They have no idea that they have become slaves to their own lust and are missing out on the true pleasure altogether. It is the godly who understand the greater spiritual and physical realities of relationship and reproduction that truly find the deepest meaning in loving one another.

Fornicators are craving the satisfaction that is only attained when more than bodies are joined together. Their spirit longs to be joined when their body is joined. However, this sort of union only occurs when man and wife are joined together by God in covenantal relationship for the purpose of reproduction and family-building. The world will never learn the truth about all of this. Therefore, the church must never give into the pressure of learning from fools how to make love. They do not know *how* to make love. They cannot make what they have never known. We must boldly reclaim the Christian doctrine of marital fidelity and godly love. And while fools search the world over "looking for love in all the wrong places," let us turn toward the loved one that God gave us and be ravished in the wife of our youth.

Christian couples should get to know one another in both physical and spiritual ways. Our materialistic, image-driven world today has terribly overemphasized the physical component of sexual love. As Christians, we must avoid such extremes and strive for balance in our homes. We cannot overreact to the world and eschew the physical in some sort of gnostic repudiation of the flesh as unholy. Paul addressed this problem very explicitly in I Corinthians 7. He expressly taught Christian couples to satisfy one another sexually to prevent Satan from exploiting their lack of self-control. But we must understand that sexual union is a spiritual/physical emblem of the overall marriage relationship. Therefore, couples—men in particular—must spend adequate time cultivating deep and true relationship outside the bedroom.

Too many modern couples think that they can build a great marriage on great sex. This is *so* wrong. Often, good sex (as the world defines it) can mask or even intensify the problem. The world's idea of great loving is nothing more than great lusting. And this selfish approach to lovemaking exemplifies the root of the problem in every other area of the relationship: *selfishness!* So, more selfish loving will not correct the problem. The problem will only be corrected when we truly learn how to love, and that sort of right loving can only be learned in the example of Christ and the church. We do not need to look to the world for lessons on how to spice up our love life. Their solutions will only worsen the problem. The answer is to see love-making as an expression of everyday love-giving. A good love life flows out of a good life of love.

Evaluating Children

When Adam "knew" his wife, she conceived and bore him a son. She named this child "Cain," which means, as her statement implies, "procured" or "achieved." Clearly Eve saw Cain's birth as a great achievement. However, she also knew that his birth was a miracle, and she rightly offered thanks to God for giving the child to her. Cain was "gotten...from the Lord." The miracle of birth is still the same today. Giving birth is quite an accomplishment for every mother, and yet, we must all recognize that every child is a gift from God.

Furthermore, it seems that Eve's name for Cain indicated a great hope for him. She remembered very well that God had promised that her seed would crush the head of the serpent. Perhaps she felt that this child would be the promised one. She believed that he was given by the Lord. However, if this is the case, Eve missed an important aspect of the promise of redemption given to her in the garden. The Lord God specified that the victory over the serpent would be from the woman, but He did not say that the deliverer would be from the man. The woman would bear the redeemer, but he would not be of the seed of fallen Adam. Adam's seed would be a race of sinners born "in his own likeness, after his image" (5:3). Only the Righteous One, born of a righteous seed, could defeat the adversary and redeem mankind. God had in mind the incarnation of Christ when He promised the woman deliverance. Eve must have missed this point if indeed she placed her hope in Cain. And yet we cannot fault her for hoping.

However, Eve's misplaced hope may have affected Cain in a very negative way. It may have been a mistaken sense of destiny that caused Cain to become the presumptuous man that he was. He may have been favored and feted. Eve failed to see that Cain was a sinner and not a deliverer. He was made in the image of his father, and he needed salvation as much as anyone else. He was a worker in the field like his father. Possibly, he felt that his labor was superior to others'. Who knows? But this much is clear: Cain became a presumptuous man who felt he did not need atonement, a man who believed that the works of his hands were sufficient to save.

Cain's problems become much more evident further on in the story. However, the point about presumptuousness must be raised now. Eve's mistake (if our assumption about her assumption is correct) about Cain's destiny may have been the very thing that destroyed him. She had lofty expectations for her firstborn son. She overlooked the fact that he was born in sin. All she could see was that God had given her a son, and it seemed like this was the beginning of redemption. She failed to understand the need for Cain to be saved before he could save anyone else. He was Adam's seed, and Adam's seed is condemned to die. Eve's favored son needed salvation.

Modern parents tend to do the same for their children. We imitate Eve's bad example and "think more highly than we ought to think" about our children (Romans 12:3). We often end up spoiling and indulging our children rather than giving them the discipline that they demand and deserve. Our society has compounded the error with "guilt-complex" driven childrearing. Modern parents have abandoned their children to others while they seek the careerist and consumerist "American dream." Then they feel terribly guilty (as they should) for abandoning their children. So, they try to compensate for their absence by indulging their children and giving them whatever they want. This is disastrous for everyone involved. The parents are never truly free of their guilt and the children do not receive the discipline needed for their proper development and maturity.

Many parents defend the little amount of time they spend with their children by explaining that children do not need much time, only "quality time." This is a complete myth. The idea of "quality time" is a false idea propounded to excuse parental neglect, to make those who spend a lifetime investing in the pursuit of wealth and pleasure feel better about their disastrous parenting. The first problem with quality time is that it is poor quality. Quality time is by definition time spent catering to the child, *which is exactly the opposite of what children need!* Children need time spent with mom and dad when they are *not* the focus. They need to learn that they are not the center of the universe. They need to spend time learning to be silent when they wish to speak, to sit still when they wish to run free, to be respectful when they are tempted to complain about how bored they are. These things can only be learned when they spend time, and a great deal of time, that is not focused on them.

Children do not need *quality* time; they need *quantity* time. They simply need to spend as much time as possible just being with mom and dad. They need the broad range of daily interaction and experience that inspires parental instruction. The Lord commanded Israel in Deuteronomy 6 to speak with their children "by the way" (Deuteronomy 6:7). Some of the most effective instruction offered to a child is "by the way" instruction: "Oh, by the way, let me tell you about…." But we cannot instruct our children on this daily, personal level if we do not spend daily, personal time with them. Our children simply need to be with us. It is as they are with us regularly that we get to know them. As we spend hours together every day, all that is working in their hearts becomes manifest to us. The issues of life come out of their spirit as we walk, work and worship together. Then we can focus on training them in the areas most needed. We must learn our children before we can teach them.

It is impossible to really get to know a child in just a few moments in an artificially contrived family experience at the playground. Certainly there is no problem with taking the children down to the playground for an hour or two of family fun. But when that is all the time we spend with them, when all we do is try to give them this sort of "quality time" to make up for the lack of ordinary time spent together, then we are missing the point of parenting. And yet, this is what guilt-complex parenting does. It tries feebly to compensate for neglect. We must get back to the biblical model of teaching our children in the morning, in the evening and all day long in between (Deuteronomy 6).

The myth of quality time is just another manifestation of the modern tendency to think more highly of our children than we should. We are imitating Eve's presumptuousness when we do so. We must understand that our children are born in sin. They come into the world needing a savior. The innocence of a newborn can deceive us as to the latent power of corruption lying within their breast. When our children are first born, we can never picture them being anything but precious little angels. How quickly they can become fallen angels! We must understand from the Word of God that no child of Adam is the hope of mankind. Our precious little one may be a genuine child prodigy, a gift from above; but that precious little one needs a new birth, a new father, a new name and a new lineage. The sons of Adam are all sinners, every last one. We must never presume upon the destiny of our child. Certainly we can trust the promises that God has made to us concerning the salvation of our children. But that is not presumption; that is faith. When we believe the promises of God concerning our children we are placing our trust in God, not in our little bundle of joy. Yet we must never presume that everything is okay with our child because they are such a wonderful gift from heaven. They are sinners, and their life will soon prove it. We must watch and pray for our children from the moment they are born so that they may be born again. We must believe God to save our children.

Unbelievers place their hopes for redemption within the children of men. They look to their sons and daughters for deliverance. This is the hope of humanism. Humanists look toward education and economics for the salvation of the ignorant, impoverished masses. They look toward technology and medicine, and a thousand other things, for help and hope. Of course, many of these things are perfectly fine in their place, as long as we understand that everything good comes from above as a gift from God and that God's material blessings cannot save us from our sins. We can only be saved by the gospel of Jesus Christ. However, unbelievers keep on eating from the tree of knowledge expecting to become like gods.

It seems these days that everything is done "for the children." The world looks to their children as the bright hope of the future. They seem to believe that a perfect world can be attained if only we can teach the children to see and grasp their own potential. Humanists have a naïve faith in the perpetual climb of human progress. Their vision is utopian and idolatrous. It is also rather ridiculous when considered in the light of history. Our hope is not in our children, the sons of Adam. This must be emphasized. No matter how good things get for our kids, they will never get good enough to lift humanity out of the slough of despair. Eve placed her hope in Cain and ended up with a murderer. She was presumptuous about Cain and his potential. She ended up projecting this presumptuousness upon him until he felt emboldened to bring before the Lord any offering he chose. This is what happens today when our silly world exaggerates the self-worth of their children and places the hope of their future upon them. They become presumptuous. We tell our children how great they are and the only greatness they achieve is great evil. We must point our children toward the only hope we really have: Jesus Christ. Surely, we must encourage our children; but we must encourage them to have faith in God, not in themselves.

Preparing Children

Cain and Abel followed different paths in life. Cain worked as a farmer, plowing the field as did his father. Abel worked as the first shepherd in history. Though there is nothing intrinsically nobler about one job or the other, it may have at least indicated a difference in their priorities. It is seen later that animal sacrifices were required by God for atonement offerings, and it may be that Abel worked in a pastoral/priestly role of herding sheep for sacrifice in worship. Certainly, man would have eaten of the milk of the flock, and wool was probably already being used for clothing. But it is surely safe to say that there was more to Abel's shepherding than merely tending sheep. Cain's work was focused on the cursed ground that he plowed every day; Abel's work was focused on things sanctified for worship. This seems to be some sort of spiritual type. At least, it is probably not coincidental that their work is reflected later in the sacrifices they brought.

Whatever the case may be, Cain and Abel demonstrated from the beginning how that two children reared in the same home can diverge widely in their individual directions for life. Parents discover immediately after having their second child how different each child really is. God blesses each child with their own distinct personality, and this is a good thing, if cultivated properly. This presents a challenge to godly parents to judge each child individually and develop within each one his own particular and unique gifts. We must carefully guide and guard each one's personal potential.

There probably is no area in childrearing where Christians have erred more than here. We have surrendered the task of guiding our child's destiny to everyone but the ones responsible before God—the parents. We have surrendered the task of cultivating our children to educators, to doctors and medical professionals, to guidance counselors and career coaches, even to Sunday school teachers and church leaders. Certainly all of these can play a supporting role of augmenting the parents' leadership. But we must never allow others to replace parental guidance. We must insist that others supplement but never supplant our influence. It is the parents who will give the final account to God for the training of their children. We cannot excuse ourselves by saying that we are "only their parents" and leave their future to the direction of so-called experts.

We must begin helping our children prepare for their life's work from infancy. We must discipline them to serve the Lord in work and worship. Our sons must be cultivated for their occupation and our daughters must be prepared as helpmeets for godly men. Scripture describes our children as arrows sent out into the earth (Psalm 127). We must whittle the shaft of the arrow into shape, attach the fins, and sharpen the arrowhead razor sharp. Childhood is a time of preparation for war. And when it is time to send them out into the earth to do battle for the kingdom of God, we must find the bulls-eye and aim for it. We must spend their childhood preparing them to hit the mark. Certainly we do not know from infancy what a child's particular vocation shall be, but we can know generally the characteristics and traits needed for success in life. We can teach them diligence and responsibility from the time they are old enough to learn anything at all. We must begin with the basics and develop more specific skills as they grow.

We must not wait until our children are nearly grown to start inquiring what they want to be. It is a little too late when they are eighteen and preparing to leave our home to start showing an interest in their future. By that time, the vacuum of parental oversight and influence will have been filled by others, and the parents will find it near impossible to guide their child into his destiny. Once a sapling has grown into a full-grown tree it is pretty well impossible to change its shape. It will spend a lifetime growing according to its established pattern with very little capacity for change. We must begin early and often to prayerfully consider the question of direction for our children.

Moreover, we must never simply leave the question of destiny and purpose up to our children alone. They are not capable of figuring out what they want to do with their lives. This is one of the predominant themes of the Book of Proverbs: children must be taught and trained by their parents. "My son, hear the instruction of thy father, and forsake not the law of thy mother" and "My son, keep thy father's commandment, and forsake not the law of thy mother" (Proverbs 1:8; 6:20). It is foolish parents indeed who hearken to the wisdom of the world and think that they must humor their child in his ever-vacillating dreams about his future. Children do not know what they want—they *cannot* know it. Children are double-minded and unstable by nature. It is the parents' task to firmly stake the young oak and shape the way it grows. Parents must play an active role from the start in helping the child determine his or her particular gifts and developing them. This is a daily task. We are taught to train our children everyday (Deuteronomy 6). We must look to the future to see, at least in vague outlines, the person they should become and start working toward this goal from the beginning. Our sons and daughters are men and women waiting to happen. We cannot stop the clock. But we can prepare for the future. And we must do so.

Of course, parents must not be overbearing about this. We must humbly seek the Lord for direction for our child's life and refuse to impress our own hopes and dreams upon them. We cannot live our lives vicariously through our children. Our children are different from one another, and they are different from us. We cannot force them into our idea of destiny. We must be wise enough to study each child and discover daily the gifts that God has placed within them. It is God who formed them in the womb and presented them to us for cultivation. It is our task to train them according to the will of the Lord for their lives. We cannot impose our own will here. The teaching of the Word of God on the necessity of parents to train up their children is not an excuse for the overbearing control freak who demands that everyone submit to his or her will.

Parents who demand that their children submit to their own will are demanding that their children be conformed to their own image. This is idolatry. Our children, just like Cain, are born in the image and likeness of their father. This image is a defaced and marred image of God. Indeed, sinful man is a lying image of God. Thus, when we demand that our children conform to our image, we are guaranteeing their corruption and condemnation. Our children must be born again and conformed to the true image of God revealed in the Son of God, Jesus Christ.

Therefore, the ultimate standard for our child's destiny should be the example of Jesus Christ. We must turn to the Word of God and see how the nature of Christ can sanctify and indwell our child and transform him or her by the Spirit into a reflection of Jesus Christ. Of course, everyone reflects Christ in his own unique way, which is the beauty of incarnational sanctification. The Spirit of the Lord fills up unique individuals, and when all of the individuals are filled with the Spirit of God and reflecting Him in their own unique way, the family shines like the brilliant rays of the sun glistening through a prism. Each one contributes his own special display of the image of Christ. Then, as it is said, the whole is greater than the sum of its parts. The Spirit of Christ shines through each family member, and everyone's gifts are displayed to the glory of God. This result is so much more glorious than when everyone is suppressed into one dominant parent's mold. So much is lost, so little is gained in such circumstances. The will of God and the image of Christ should be our model for shaping and sculpting each child. Let Jesus be revealed in each unique personality. This is the biblical way.

It is also important to learn from Cain and Abel that the sins that destroy our children in adulthood are always evident long before they leave the house. If only Adam and Eve would have possessed the wisdom to discern where Cain was headed, they could have prevented a murder. They should have perceived that Cain's unchecked anger would lead to violence. We must learn from Adam and Eve's failure. We must look down the road and project biblically where our children are headed. We must rear our children with wisdom. Not the wisdom of the earth, but the wisdom from above. Wisdom learns from past experience how to predict future outcomes with accuracy. Wisdom combines hindsight with foresight and obtains insight. Wisdom sees the end from the beginning. Wisdom perceives the stress fractures that shall someday topple the building. Wisdom takes the time to study the children and learn from their daily actions and attitudes the people they will become if their sins are not corrected.

This takes us back to the point raised above. Our children's problems (as well as ours) must be viewed correctly as *sin*. We cannot minimize the problem by labeling our disobedience as anything other than sin. When our children are "angry without cause," rude to their brothers and sisters, envious and competitive—or any one of a thousand other problems confronted in the home—we must address their problems as sin. If we treat sin as a minor problem, as a personality conflict, or just hormonal disturbances; if we write their foul moods off as just being tired and grumpy, then we shall tolerate behavior that can no longer be changed as they grow older. Their souls will be "hardened through the deceitfulness of sin" (Hebrews 3:13), and they will grow into adulthood as warped arrows that will not fly straight.

We must recognize that sin will destroy the souls of our children. If we love them, then we must chasten them biblically and confront the sin in their lives. God has promised us that "foolishness is bound in the heart of a child, but the rod of correction will drive it far from him" (Proverbs 22:15). This is both an accurate assessment of the state of our sinful children and a powerful promise of salvation for them. They are born becoming fools, but Christian doctrine and discipline will drive the folly out of their heart. This means that we must evaluate our children honestly. We must recognize their problem as *sin*. Then, we must place our trust in the promises of God and boldly drive sin out of their heart with loving discipline. We must identify each child's particular besetting sin and deal with it daily with firm discipline.

Of course, biblical discipline is much more than just a daily spanking. So many go wrong right here. The rod of correction is much more than just a belt or paddle used for punishment. Certainly physical discipline is needed. But the "rod of correction" is also the Word of God. We must correct our children daily with scripture as we teach them every morning and evening in family devotions. Correction must be positive and proactive. We must apply the scriptures to the problem. We must preach the gospel to sinners (our children) and resort to physical correction only when a little extra incentive is needed. Sometimes a good spanking can give children ears to hear what the Spirit is saying.

The differences in our children force us to rely on the Lord as we rear them to serve Him. We cannot create a legalistic sort of rulebook to build the family by. Each child has a unique personality and responds differently to instruction, discipline and chastening. We cannot form a rigid manner of treating each child the same and expect that they shall all turn out alright. Cain and Abel are not much alike. We must study each child carefully and prayerfully and entreat the Lord for wisdom to tailor our parenting to each child. Certainly there are bedrock principles that we build on, biblical precepts that are the same for everyone. But the manner of applying these principles varies from child to child. This is the wonderful thing about the wisdom of God as revealed in Scripture. It applies. It fits in myriad situations. We can learn the basic principles of the teaching of Christ and then allow the Holy Spirit to lead us to apply them to particular children.

This is why, as noted above, we must walk in the Spirit as we build our family. Successful childrearing is Spirit-led childrearing. Is our child a Cain or an Abel? Does he have gifts toward working the soil or tending sheep? Does he struggle with a presumptuous spirit? Does he tend toward faith or unbelief? We must consider each child carefully every day. We must pray every day over each one and teach them from the Word of the Lord the things that each one needs to hear. We must hold Christ up before them as the perfect example of what they should become. This is why we cannot farm out the task of training up our children. We must accept the responsibility of studying each child so we can teach them. The Lord has promised to work with us as we do so. His wisdom works, but it must be applied in the right way by the right people to the right children. This requires discernment. So, let us develop the ability to discern between our children. We must get to know the Cain's and Abel's in our home. Maybe then we can prevent the tragedy that occurred just east of Eden.

21

Worship after the Fall

Genesis 4:3-7. "And in process of time it came to pass, that Cain brought of the fruit of the ground an offering unto the LORD. And Abel, he also brought of the firstlings of his flock and of the fat thereof. And the LORD had respect unto Abel and to his offering: But unto Cain and to his offering he had not respect. And Cain was very wroth, and his countenance fell. And the LORD said unto Cain, Why art thou wroth? and why is thy countenance fallen? If thou doest well, shalt thou not be accepted? and if thou doest not well, sin lieth at the door. And unto thee shall be his desire, and thou shalt rule over him."

After Adam and Eve were expelled from the garden, God appointed a time and place for Adam and his children to return before Him to worship. The first family was cut off from daily fellowship with God in the garden, but the account shows they were not cut off entirely. Though they were cast out of the holy mountain into the valley of sin below, they were invited to ascend and worship. Here the first explicit account of blood sacrifice was introduced. Apparently, the Lord taught Adam and Eve how to offer animal sacrifices in the garden when He slew the animals and clothed them in coats of skin. Surely this is where they first learned that "without shedding of blood is no remission" (Hebrews 9:22). Admittedly, this is an assumption, but it is a good one. It certainly fits with the later patterns of redemptive history. Many things were offered to the Lord throughout the Old Covenant, but offerings of blood were necessary for remission if sins and made all the other offerings acceptable.

Cain and Abel brought their offerings "in the process of time." This indicates they were summoned to worship at a specific season, on a day appointed by God. Some think it was a weekly Sabbath worship, while others see parallels with the annual Day of Atonement instituted by the law of Moses. Whatever the timeframe involved, whether annual or weekly, it seems certain that it was a time specified by God. Moreover, the context indicates that it was a place specified by God. Cain later described this time of worship as coming before the face of the Lord (v. 14). Most likely, Adam's family offered sacrifices at the east entrance of the garden. This was where the Lord God placed the angels that whirled about with the flaming sword keeping the way to the tree of life (3:24). Regardless, God clearly specified the place as well as the time of worship. Furthermore, if God specified the time and place for worship, surely He specified the methods and manner of worship. We must assume from all that we know about God from the subsequent witness of scripture that He told them *when*, *where* and *how* to worship. Anything less flies in the face of the self-revelatory nature of God. This is relevant to our discussion of the judgment upon Cain that follows below.

Two Offerings

When the appointed time for sacrifice arrived, both Cain and Abel brought an offering unto the Lord. Cain brought an offering "of the fruit of the ground." Cain, as a tiller of the ground, brought a meal offering (produce and grains) unto the Lord. Abel, as a shepherd, brought a blood offering of his flocks. Scripture notes that Abel's offering was "of the firstlings." The Lord accepted Abel's offering but rejected Cain's. There is no clear indication how the Lord demonstrated His favor, but we may adduce from later scriptural witness that the fire of the Lord fell upon the accepted offering. As noted above, it seems likely that Cain and Abel offered their sacrifices at the east entrance of the garden where the angels stood with the flaming sword. Possibly the fire issued out from between the cherubim and consumed the sacrifice. No one knows for sure, but certainly God signified His favor in an obvious way. Cain and Abel were not left guessing about the matter.

The Genesis text does not explicitly state why God accepted Abel's offering and rejected Cain's. However, the writer of Hebrews made it plain: "By faith Abel offered unto God a more excellent sacrifice than Cain, by which he obtained witness that he was righteous, God testifying of his gifts: and by it he being dead yet speaketh" (Hebrews 11:4). "By faith" Abel offered a "more excellent sacrifice." This speaks both of the nature of the sacrifice itself and the manner in which it was offered. Thus, the reason for God's favor upon Abel's offering becomes obvious. First of all, Abel's offering was a blood sacrifice. It was an innocent substitute. Life is in the blood (Genesis 9:4; Leviticus 17:11, 14). Secondly, Abel's offering was of the firstlings of the flock. It was the first and the best he had. Thirdly, and most importantly, Abel offered his sacrifice in faith.

Cain's offering lacked each of these things. It was not a blood sacrifice, and even though meal offerings are acceptable in the proper time and place, a meal offering was unacceptable here. Surely Cain knew this. Cain's offering was just "an offering." It was not the firstfruits of the ground, and, apparently, it was not the best that he had to offer. It was not "more excellent." Further, it was not offered "by faith." Cain's offering was a presentation of self-righteous works, an offering of his own best effort to God rather than an offering that reached by faith through time to the ultimate offering of Jesus Christ. Cain's unbelief was the root of the problem.

A striking picture emerges here: Cain and Abel approach the face of the Lord and arrange their sacrifices carefully on separate altars. Both present their offerings to God and step back in eager anticipation of His response. The fire of God explodes with a blinding flash from between the whirling, flaming cherubim, and the altars disappear in billowing clouds of smoke. When the smoke of His glory-cloud drifts away, God's response to their separate offerings is obvious. Abel's offering lies smoldering upon the stones, consumed in the fire. But Cain's offering is untouched, still moist with dew. Cain stares in stunned disbelief at his rejected offering. He was so certain of divine acceptance. He simply knew that God would be pleased with his offering. And yet the Lord God turned his sacrifice away.

241

Cain's disbelief turned to shame and then anger, a flash of anger that ignited an inferno of seething rage. How could this be? He was the son of Adam, the *firstborn* son of Adam, the man-child gotten from the Lord. He was the heir of Adam, the favored child of Eve. He was the one who learned from his father the skills of farming, the backbreaking labor of eking out a meager harvest from reluctant soil. He was Abel's older brother, his superior, possibly the one who first told him about bringing an offering to the Lord. He was expecting today to be a display of his privileged status before his family. And yet, right in front of everybody, Cain was humiliated and rejected. No wonder the Bible says, "Cain was very wroth, and his countenance fell."

Did Cain know better? Did he know what sacrifice would please the Lord? Surely he did. And now that his offering was rejected, he should have known better how to respond to God's rebuke. Instead, he compounded his error by responding to God in anger. Cain was not willing to accept correction. He presumed upon God's favor by bringing just "an offering" from his garden rather than the firstfruits of the ground. And it was not offered in faith. And yet, when God rejected his presumptuous sacrifice, Cain was too proud to accept correction. He was wrong and surely he knew it; yet he would not admit it. This is where matters took a real turn for the worse.

God scolded Cain for his anger and said, "Why are you angry, and why has your face fallen? If you do well, will you not be accepted? And if you do not do well, sin is crouching at the door. Its desire is for you, but you must rule over it" (Genesis 4:6,7 ESV). Divine favor is within reach for those who do well. The Lord insisted that He was eager to accept Cain's offering if only he would bring the proper offering in faith. God's acceptance of Abel was not a matter of a respect of persons. Rather, it was a respect of faith and obedience.

God put the onus back on Cain. The outcome of blessing or cursing is determined by the worshipper. If any man will "do well," then he will be accepted. This should not be hard for anyone to grasp, and yet, Cain was too angry to think rationally or to accept constructive, critical advice. Finally, the Lord God warned him that sin is like a beast of prey crouching for the spring by the door. What a vivid image of sin's attack! The wild beast of anger had plunged its fangs into Cain's proud soul. Cain was the prey, and the only way to survive sin's brutal attack was to fight back with a desperate struggle to live. The Lord bluntly warned Cain that sin would destroy him if he did not destroy it first. As the story shows, Cain did not do so. He did not rise up and defeat the power of sin in his life. Rather, he was defeated and destroyed. Sin won.

Lessons for Our Children

There are several lessons here relevant to our children. First of all, we must teach our children how to approach God properly in worship. Second, we must recognize that God will bring our worship under His judgment and His favor will be upon those who believe and obey while He rejects those who refuse to do so. Third, we must teach our children how to accept correction from the Lord without anger and resentment.

Christian children must be taught that God expects us to appear before Him in worship "in the process of time," at the appointed time. We do not set our own terms and times for worship. God established a day for worship, the Lord's Day. The Lord's Day is "the day of the Lord," a day of worship, judgment and commission. The Old Covenant Sabbath on the seventh day has been born again, resurrected and transformed into the Lord's Day on the first day of the week, the eighth day of new beginnings. Worship on Sunday is God's decision. Each week we come before Him to offer the sacrifice of praise per His instructions. And there are additional times of worship that we choose to come before Him to worship and receive instruction. But we must not "forsake the assembling of ourselves together" (Hebrews 10:25) on the Lord's Day. Our children must be taught to be faithful to church.

Our children must be taught to appear before the Lord with "a sacrifice acceptable, well-pleasing to God" (Philippians 4:18). They must be taught to bring a sacrifice of blood, which is our trust in the cross of Christ. No offering is acceptable to God apart from the offering of Christ by blood. Our children must learn from us to approach the Lord with the firstlings of our flock, which means that we bring to God our *first and best*. Abel's offering of firstlings also foreshadows the later requirement of tithing. We must teach our children to give first to God the best that we have and the tenth of all our increase. Then, we after we have offered all that God expressly requires, we are privileged to bring free-will offerings of our own choosing. But we may not reduce our giving to only what we choose to bring. We must seek to please the Lord if we desire His favor.

Most of all, our children must be taught to worship the Lord in faith. Blood offerings and firstfruits are repugnant to God when offered in pretentious and hypocritical unbelief. Just one passage from Isaiah (among many others) illustrates God's attitude toward faithless sacrifices:

> Hear the word of the LORD, you rulers of Sodom! Give ear to the teaching of our God, you people of Gomorrah! What to me is the multitude of your sacrifices? says the LORD; I have had enough of burnt offerings of rams and the fat of well-fed beasts; I do not delight in the blood of bulls, or of lambs, or of goats. When you come to appear before me, who has required of you this trampling of my courts? Bring no more vain offerings; incense is an abomination to me. New moon and Sabbath and the calling of convocations—I cannot endure iniquity and solemn assembly. Your new moons and your appointed feasts my soul hates; they have become a burden to me; I am weary of bearing them. When you spread out your hands, I will hide my eyes from you; even though you make many prayers, I will not listen; your hands are full of blood. Wash yourselves; make yourselves clean; remove the evil of your deeds from before my eyes; cease to do evil, learn to do good; seek justice, correct oppression; bring justice to the fatherless, plead the widow's cause (Isaiah 1:10-17).

David spoke of the same matter thusly: "For you will not delight in sacrifice, or I would give it; you will not be pleased with a burnt offering. The sacrifices of God are a broken spirit; a broken and contrite heart, O God, you will not despise. Do good to Zion in your good pleasure; build up the walls of Jerusalem; then will you delight in right sacrifices, in burnt offerings and whole burnt offerings; then bulls will be offered on your altar" (Psalm 51:16-19 ESV). We must teach these things carefully to our children. We must demonstrate them in our daily lives and weekly worship.

The Judgment of Our Children

The story of Cain and Abel clearly demonstrates that God will judge our children. We must not presume that our children will be accepted before God just because they are covenant children. Certainly we trust in the promises of God toward them, but this trust must never degenerate into presumption. God will call our children into account, and His acceptance or rejection of their offering will become obvious over time. Our children must learn to expect judgment. They must not presume upon their Christian heritage, and they must not be surprised by God's evaluation of their gifts. This sort of expectation will produce carefulness in them. They will learn to serve the Lord with fear and trembling.

What a terrible thing to rear up children who approach the Lord without fear and trembling, children unprepared for God's judgment. We must determine that, by the grace of God, we shall rear our sons and daughters to be like Abel and not Cain. As true believers, we desperately desire the favor of God upon our children. This sort of favor will not be received by the casual worshipper. We must teach our children to approach the Lord with carefulness.

This raises a question: where were Adam and Eve when Cain and Abel came to worship? Did they come to worship with their children "in the process of time"? Surely they did. And if so, then why did they not teach Cain the protocol of worship? Why was their son allowed to go before the face of the Lord so ill-prepared to offer sacrifice? They could not know his heart, so they could not have discerned his lack of faith. But surely they could have observed his obvious lack of obedience. They could have noticed that something was seriously wrong. They could have instructed him better about bringing a blood sacrifice and offering the best to the Lord.

As noted above, Adam likely learned "without shedding is no remission" when the Lord God slew the animals to make them coats of skin. Could it have been that Adam and Eve simply were not paying attention to Cain's worship? They were not there when Cain needed them. Indeed, it seems that Adam was missing at the

245

most critical points of this story. He was missing when his wife was conversing with the serpent. He was hiding when God came to walk with them in the cool of the day. And then, he was missing when his sons approached the Lord to worship. Adam, where are you?

It seems that this failure is repeated often by Christian fathers today. We have already considered above the effects of a father's absence. But here the problem rears its ugly head again. Adam was missing when Cain needed him the most. We must rise up with outrage against this spirit of paternal absence and abdication. We must re-assert the authority and responsibility of fathers to lead their children in worship. It is a reproach upon all men that so many men laze around the house on Sunday while mom takes the kids to worship. Eve had already demonstrated that her evaluation of Cain was faulty. She needed her husband's leadership and discernment here. Cain needed a man, his father, to stand beside him and help him approach the Lord in reverence and godly fear. Adam, where are you?

Our Response to Judgment

Cain's response to God's rejection provides a powerful lesson for us. When he realized he was rejected, he was "very wroth, and his countenance fell." We must teach our children to receive correction from the Lord. This is the ultimate purpose of chastening in the home. We do not chasten our children to force them to conform to our will. We chasten our children to teach them to receive correction from the Word of the Lord. This is why we must confront the sins of our children with the Word of the Lord and demand their repentance and restoration. Spankings done correctly are repentance practice. We are teaching our children from an early age how to receive the rebuke of the Lord. As Hebrews says,

> And ye have forgotten the exhortation which speaketh unto you as unto children, My son, despise not thou the chastening of the Lord, nor faint when thou art rebuked of him: For whom the Lord loveth he chasteneth, and scourgeth every son whom he receiveth. If ye endure chastening, God dealeth with you as with

sons; for what son is he whom the father chasteneth not? But if ye be without chastisement, whereof all are partakers, then are ye bastards, and not sons. Furthermore we have had fathers of our flesh which corrected us, and we gave them reverence: shall we not much rather be in subjection unto the Father of spirits, and live? For they verily for a few days chastened us after their own pleasure; but he for our profit, that we might be partakers of his holiness. Now no chastening for the present seemeth to be joyous, but grievous: nevertheless afterward it yieldeth the peaceable fruit of righteousness unto them which are exercised thereby (Hebrews 12:5-11).

We must teach our children to "despise not thou the chastening of the Lord, nor faint when thou art rebuked of Him." Only by chastening can we "be partakers of His holiness" and "live." Our children are learning to receive correction when we chasten them. Thus, chastening is a means of grace that brings salvation to their souls. Those who refuse to chasten their children, for whatever reason, hate their children. "He that spareth his rod hateth his son: but he that loveth him chasteneth him quickly" (Proverbs 13:24). When we consider the outcome of Cain's unbelief, then we see clearly how parental neglect is a form of hatred. How can we stand by and watch our children plunge headlong into hell? If we really believe the Word of God concerning the fate of unbelievers, then we must intervene while there is still time to change their course. And then again, maybe that is our problem: maybe we do not really believe the Word of God.

The Lord queried Cain, "Why are you angry?" We must recognize the signs of resentment in our children against the judgment of the Word of God. If we chasten them correctly, we should be able to discern this problem long before it becomes a real problem. We should be able to recognize the signs of rebellion when they are still in diapers and start working on this early on. This is the entire point of childrearing: to teach children while they are still teachable. This is why babies are born twenty inches tall.

Cain had already gone too far. He could not be corrected. Correction only made him bitter. This is too often the case when parents wait until children are nearly grown to start clamping down on them. Our children must receive necessary correction long before they are old enough to rebel against it in any significant fashion. We must address the problem of rebellion long before our children are teenagers. It is assumed by our child-idolizing culture today that rebellion is a necessary growth stage for children. This is utter nonsense. Folly is not a precursor to maturity. The Bible calls rebellious children fools. "A fool despiseth his father's instruction: but he that regardeth reproof is prudent" (Proverbs 15:5). We must not accept the myth that our children must be rebels in order to lead healthy, "independent" lives. We should expect them to walk in the ways of their fathers. This presupposes, however, that their fathers will teach them their ways and that their ways are righteous. We must address this early and often.

God grants children the period of development we call "adolescence" for a specific reason. He grants them this period of time so that they may slowly grow into maturity under the watchful eye and careful hand of their parents. This is why they do not experience the first rush of desire only after they are grown and gone. This is why they are besieged by the onset of puberty while still at home with mom and dad. God allows them to undergo this transformation under the oversight of loving parents. We must not waste this opportunity. Our children's innate rebellious urge against authority must be carefully disciplined long before adolescence.

This is not mere wishful thinking or pie-in-the-sky theoretical optimism. This is the biblical approach. It is the approach of faith. For example, if we study the Books of Proverbs carefully, we find that God promises believers that He will drive folly out of the heart of our children (Proverbs 22:15). He teaches us to "train up a child in the way that he should go: and when he is old, he will not depart from it" (Proverbs 22:6). This is a promise of God. We must choose to believe it. Of course, the promises are reckoned by faith and unbelief causes the Word of God to be of "none effect" (Matthew 15:6; Mark 7:13; Romans 4:14; 9:6; I Corinthians 1:17; Galatians 3:17). However, God has promised the faithful that they can and must rear up their children to walk in the ways of their fathers. And, again, this assumes that the fathers are walking right.

Childhood is a time for correction. It is the right time for loving discipline. As noted earlier, this does not mean that parents can create their children in their own image. But it does mean that parents must boldly take the initiative in shaping their children to be Christians from birth. We must reject the manner of fools who allow their children to grow wild and untrained. We are teaching our sons and daughters to serve the Lord as adults when we correct them as children. We must not allow them to grow uncorrected only to discover to our horror that we, like Adam and Eve, have permitted our child to grow into a full-fledge fool, incapable of being corrected. Will our child be a Cain or an Abel?

22

The Way of Cain

Genesis 4:8. "And Cain talked with Abel his brother: and it came to pass, when they were in the field, that Cain rose up against Abel his brother, and slew him."

After Cain was rejected and rebuked by the Lord God, he "talked with Abel his brother." It is here that the root of sin bore its first bitter harvest of division between Adam's children. We do not know the details of their conversation, how long they spoke or what they spoke about. We also do not know how long it was between the time of their sacrifice and their conversation in the field. It may have been only a few hours, or it may have been days, even weeks. There is no way to be sure. But it seems certain that Cain left the scene of the sacrifice brooding deeply over his rejection. His anger at God began shifting toward his brother as envy rose like bile in his throat. It was bad enough that God had rejected his offering. That was humiliating enough. But to have his offering rejected and Abel's accepted? That was simply too much for Cain to take.

Perhaps Cain and Abel had grown up with the ever-increasing friction of sibling rivalry; many brothers do. However, the stakes were much higher now. This was more than just fraternal competition in everyday life. This was serious. This was a matter of acceptance before God and religious prestige in the family. This was a matter of patriarchal prerogative. If Cain was to be Adam's heir, then Cain needed God's approval. He needed more than daddy's blessing—he needed the blessing of God. And now, that blessing seemed to be stolen from him by that upstart, Abel. This was intolerable to Cain. His pride could not abide it.

If we are right in assuming that Cain had presumed that he was the chosen seed, then his bitterness at rejection becomes more understandable. If Abel's acceptance was a sign, at least in Cain's mind, that God had chosen the younger son to be the heir of promise, then no wonder Cain grew so terribly angry. Of course, all of this, if true, was a matter of presumption on Cain's part. And yet, it seems likely that this was the case and there was more spiritual significance to their offerings than just an occasional sacrifice. Thus, the rejection was a moment of high spiritual significance to Cain. As we see, it was important enough to him that he ultimately murdered his rival. For this is what Cain came to see: he came to see Abel as his rival for acceptance before God and prominence within the family. Abel became the focus of Cain's obsessive jealousy. There is no other logical explanation for the outcome of this tragic story. Cain came to hate Abel with intense passion because of all that the acceptance of his offering represented. Cain hated Abel because he had displaced him in worship as the leader of the family. Cain felt that the favor of God belonged to him by birthright. This is a common assumption by elder brothers throughout the rest of scriptural history. And it is always wrong.

This reminds us to teach our children that they cannot presume upon God's favor. This is particularly important among siblings. The precedence of birth can often be a stumbling block to older children. They can assume too much and come to resent younger siblings when it seems that God's favor rests upon them to a greater degree. We must teach our children to seek their own place before God and not allow God's approval upon others to become the measure of their own success or failure. And, of course, we must teach them to "do well." If they "do well" they shall be accepted. Our children must learn that every man and woman stands before God alone and for themselves. We must seek to be accepted before God on the basis of our own offering and refuse to cast sideward glances at those around us, especially our brothers and sisters in the Christian family. This sort of comparison always produces rivalry. Furthermore, Scripture declares that this sort of comparison is folly (II Corinthians 10:12).

Cain became a prey to this folly, and it drove him to kill his brother. He was angry first with God, then with his brother. And yet, it is striking that he never became angry with the one truly responsible for his rejection: himself. Cain blamed everyone but himself. Of course, this is not unusual among sinners. Indeed, it is characteristic of us all. Each one of us knows that this is the innate tendency of fallen man. Therefore, we should not be surprised when it crops up among our children. We must guard against this sort of finger-pointing, blame-passing in our home (beginning with dad and mom). Surely Cain's tendency to blame others for his failures did not crop up when he was a grown man. We can assume there were many instances where Cain demonstrated this failing before it became, literally, a matter of life and death. Adam and Eve probably observed this problem, and yet they failed to get it out of Cain's spirit. And finally, Cain's proud refusal to accept responsibility resulted in the first murder on earth.

We must wisely adjudicate disputes between our children. We must follow the Lord's example and dole out approval and disapproval for their actions before them all. Cain was corrected in the presence of his brother. As Paul said (addressing another subject), "Them that sin rebuke before all, that others also may fear" (I Timothy 5:20). Then, we must teach our children how to accept correction when it comes. We cannot permit our children to escape personal responsibility for their actions. If we overlook this tendency, we are hardening their hearts against repentance before God. They shall become like Cain, resenting the Word when it speaks to their failure and looking around for others to blame. There is probably nothing more important in child-rearing than this point. We absolutely must teach our children to accept the blame when they are wrong. It is a matter of life or death.

The Way of Cain

First, Cain "talked with Abel his brother." Then, he "rose up against Abel his brother." Finally, he "slew him." This shows the progression of sin. There were several points in the process at which Cain should have reined in his spirit. There were many opportunities for course correction, but Cain rushed furiously through them all. This is always the case when sin is permitted to work in the family. Our children will be tempted to anger and resentment that eventually deteriorates into bitterness and revenge. However, this sort of result does not occur in a moment. It takes time to make a murderer.

It is this process of time that allows us as parents to discern what is growing in our children and dig up the root of bitterness. This is why we *must* be led by the Spirit in our home. We must discern daily the spiritual condition of our children. We cannot allow sibling rivalries to be excused as mere child's play. We cannot allow division between our children to be tolerated. We must require our children to make things right between themselves, to repent to one another *sincerely* and often. The "way of Cain" (Jude 11) is a process that leads our children from angry speech to physical violence to murder, specifically the death of a relationship. We must prevent our children from walking in that way.

The process of Cain's sin against Abel—he *talked, rose up* and then, *slew him*—also shows how unresolved childhood conflicts can follow children into adulthood and mar later relationships with family members. Many childish problems may seem insignificant to adults, but often a minor disagreement can escalate into full-blown hostility later in life. Parents often are caught totally off guard when the slightest provocation triggers an unbelievable explosion of hatred within their grown children, only to discover to their dismay that their children have nursed deep grudges growing out of small insults and injustices long forgotten—at least, by everyone else. But the children do not forget, and the bitter memory erupts in hatred that causes the death of a relationship. This is the sort of murder that can be prevented by addressing division in childhood when it occurs and judging disputes between siblings fairly and biblically.

It is significant that Cain's sin against his brother had its beginning at the place of worship. Cain's worship was rejected, and his relationship with God was broken. This broken relationship with God produced a broken relationship with his brother. The Apostle John spoke of this same spiritual dynamic in his first epistle: "For this is the message that ye heard from the beginning, that we should love one another. Not as Cain, who was of that wicked one, and slew his brother. And wherefore slew he him? Because his own works were evil, and his brother's righteous. Marvel not, my brethren, if the world hate you. We know that we have passed from death unto life, because we love the brethren. He that loveth not his brother abideth in death. Whosoever hateth his brother is a murderer: and ye know that no murderer hath eternal life abiding in him" (I John 3:11-15).

John made it clear that we cannot separate our relationship with God from our relationship with one another. It works two ways: when we are out of fellowship with God, it affects our relationship with our brother; and when we are out of fellowship with our brother, it affects our relationship with God. The two relationships intersect. The vertical relationship with God crosses the horizontal relationship with our brother. When the proper intersection of relationship is lost, the spirit of murder begins to work. For I John says, "Whosoever hateth his brother is a murderer." What an incredible statement! All that is required to be a murderer is to hate your brother. Are we rearing murderers in our house?

John also stated, "If a man say, I love God, and hateth his brother, he is a liar: for he that loveth not his brother whom he hath seen, how can he love God whom he hath not seen?" (I John 4:20) We cannot separate our relationship with God from our relationship with our brother. We must recognize the spiritual component to our arguments and strife. If discord prevails in the home, it signals a broken relationship with God. We cannot be at peace with God and at war with one another. The Apostle James said it like this: "What causes quarrels and what causes fights among you? Is it not this, that your passions are at war within you? You desire and do not have, so you murder. You covet and cannot obtain, so you fight and quarrel. You do not have, because you do not ask. You ask and do not receive, because you ask wrongly, to spend it on your passions" (James 4:1-3 ESV). Cain's murderous passion went terribly wrong when he was rejected of God. If we are experiencing this sort of friction in the home, then we must prayerfully discover where either we or our children have failed in our relationship with God. Getting right with God means getting right with everyone else.

Therefore, our children must be taught to be at peace with one another. They will learn so much about loving others from their sibling relationships. We must not allow this tremendous opportunity for positive development to be swallowed up in fussing and fighting between them. We must refuse to allow our children to walk in the way of Cain.

Dwelling Together in Unity

As Scripture says, "Behold, how good and how pleasant it is for brethren to dwell together in unity! It is like the precious ointment upon the head, that ran down upon the beard, even Aaron's beard: that went down to the skirts of his garments; As the dew of Hermon, and as the dew that descended upon the mountains of Zion: for there the LORD commanded the blessing, even life forevermore" (Psalms 133:1-3). The blessings of God rest upon the family that insists on family unity by confronting sin and strife. It is like the anointing of God upon Aaron, the High Priest. Unity brings blessings like the abundant dew upon Mount Hermon. The blessing of the Lord, the favor of God, lays heavy upon the fertile soil of the unified Christian home. God makes us fruitful, both spiritually and physically, when we seek perfect peace between mom and dad, brothers and sisters, parents and children.

This peace arises out of righteousness and makes our home a place "good and pleasant." Does this describe our homes? Is our house a "good and pleasant" place where children can flourish under the Lord's "blessing, even life forevermore"? Our home can only be a "good and pleasant" place if we attain true unity of spirit. And this unity of spirit can only be attained through true righteousness, or *right-ness*. Things can only be right as we make them right. We must proactively seek open and honest reckoning with sin and strife. We cannot permit the bitter spirit of Cain to prevail in our home.

Division within the home is anything but pleasant. Ask Adam. It is quite impossible to imagine the dumb horror that struck Adam's heart as he learned of Abel's death. And Abel's death was no ordinary death. Of course, no death was "ordinary" yet, for Abel was the first person in history to die by any means. And yet, this death was doubly horrifying, for the first death was also the first murder. The only death Adam had witnessed was the killing of animals for sacrifice. But nothing could possibly have prepared him for the awful face of death disfiguring the countenance of his innocent second son.

Death is never pretty. And the death of a family is no better. It is horrifying to witness the slow agonizing death of brothers and sisters, mom and dads, parents and children. There are surely many who have felt that actual, physical death could have been easier to endure than the death of their family. No matter how grievous it may be to bury a child, nothing is more grievous than estrangement between family members. There is no escaping the everlasting sorrow of such division. Even Jacob's overwhelming grief for his beloved son, Joseph, cannot equal the pain of a broken home. God has promised "life forevermore" for those who dwell in unity. We must set out to avoid the heartbreak of Adam who discovered his son slain in the field. And then, Adam also suffered the loss of his firstborn, Cain, who driven out from the face of the Lord. Adam lost both sons in one day, all because he did not teach his sons how to work out their differences without resorting to violence. We must determine to prevent this sort of sibling rivalry from the beginning. We must insist on preserving unity in our home.

The children are the ultimate casualties of our indifference toward division. When we allow the seeds of strife to be sown within the home, we are guaranteeing that our children shall reap the harvest. Adam outlived both Cain and Abel. He died in old age still worshipping before the face of the Lord at each appointed time. But Abel lay in a restless grave, his blood crying out from the ground, and Cain wandered as an exile from the presence of the Lord. What a tragedy! This is the sort of fate that we are casting upon our children if we do not perform the unpleasant and difficult task of sorting out the differences and providing biblical judgment within our home.

Unity and Dominion

One of the greatest tragedies of familial division is the loss of familial dominion. As noted above, the kingdom of God grows through the growth of Christian families. And when the family is divided, evangelistic momentum is lost. The explosive power of spiritual unity that should be directed toward spiritual warfare in evangelism is misdirected toward one another in internecine warfare, a war within the family. We should not dismiss the discord in our home as just petty rivalries that normally occur between children. They *do* normally occur, but the fall made sin normal, which means that normal is sinful. So, we must demand that our children break the norm and rise to the level of God's righteous expectations. Paul spoke to the church of their need for "the unity of the spirit in the bond of peace." If this is the standard for the church, then it should be the standard for our homes. We must make peace our goal and reach for it through the Spirit. If we do so, then our children will take this sort of peaceful spirit with them into later life. Their families will reap the benefits of our present insistence on staying right with God and with one another. Ultimately, the momentum of familial Christian dominion will grow.

23

Judgment upon Cain

Genesis 4:9-16. "And the LORD said unto Cain, Where is Abel thy brother? And he said, I know not: Am I my brother's keeper? And he said, What hast thou done? the voice of thy brother's blood crieth unto me from the ground. And now art thou cursed from the earth, which hath opened her mouth to receive thy brother's blood from thy hand; When thou tillest the ground, it shall not henceforth yield unto thee her strength; a fugitive and a vagabond shalt thou be in the earth.

And Cain said unto the LORD, My punishment is greater than I can bear. Behold, thou hast driven me out this day from the face of the earth; and from thy face shall I be hid; and I shall be a fugitive and a vagabond in the earth; and it shall come to pass, that every one that findeth me shall slay me. And the LORD said unto him, Therefore whosoever slayeth Cain, vengeance shall be taken on him sevenfold. And the LORD set a mark upon Cain, lest any finding him should kill him. And Cain went out from the presence of the LORD, and dwelt in the land of Nod, on the east of Eden."

As Abel lay dead on the ground, Cain arose from where he knelt by his fallen brother and slipped furtively from the field. There is no way to know how long it was before the Lord challenged Cain with his sin. It may have been as he walked hurriedly back to his dwelling on the day of the murder. Or it may have been the next Sabbath worship when Adam and his family came before the face of the Lord. This seems most likely, for after Cain was judged the text says, "And Cain went out from the

259

presence of the LORD." This "presence of the Lord" seems more than just God speaking out of the blue sky. This seems to be a formal place of worship. There seems to be a pattern in Scripture of divine judgment being executed at the appointed times of worship. Adam was judged when the Lord God came into the garden in the cool of the day, which seems to have been the appointed time for man's fellowship with God. The same is true of Cain and Abel's sacrifice "in the process of time" when Cain was rejected and Abel accepted (4:3). And other examples could be multiplied from the rest of Scripture.

So, there is no reason to believe here that God rent the heavens and came down upon Cain immediately after the murder. Possibly a few days had elapsed between Cain's rejection and Abel's murder, and now a few more days had elapsed after the murder bringing Cain to the next day of worship when he and his family would come before the face of the Lord. Perhaps Abel, as a keeper of sheep, could be gone for days with his flocks. Maybe he was not missed until the day of worship. It certainly seems possible.

It this conjecture is correct, Abel was missing as Adam's family approached the Lord to offer sacrifice. This must have caused some consternation among the family. Possibly they questioned one another as to whether anyone knew where Abel was. No one seemed to have seen him for few days, but that was not unusual for a shepherd. Then, after they had waited as long as they could, they decided it would be best to carry on with worship. They began slowly approaching the altar to present their sacrifices. Just then, everyone stopped dead in their tracks, frozen in shock, as the voice of the Lord thundered out from between the flaming cherubim: "Cain, where is Abel your brother?" Adam and his family all turned in bewilderment toward Cain. What could he know about Abel? He had just told them that he had no idea where his younger brother was. And yet, God pressed the question: "Cain, where is your brother?" Cain knew something that he was not telling.

Surely Cain was startled at first by this direct question, and his guilty conscience reeled and stumbled about looking for an alibi. Then, somehow Cain assumed the forced nonchalance peculiar to the guilty and replied, "I do not know. Am I my brother's keeper?" Cain succeeded here in multiplying his transgression. He lied about knowing where Abel was—certainly he would never forget the broken body of his brother twisted in unnatural death on the ground—and further, he mocks the Lord by asking, "Am I my brother's keeper?" Cain's sarcastic arrogance before God is breathtaking. In addition to lying to His face, now Cain rudely declaims any responsibility for his younger brother. Cain's sarcasm was the inevitable overreaction of a guilty conscience. If he had done nothing wrong, then surely he could have replied very simply that he did not know Abel's whereabouts. But his sin forced him into saying much more than was necessary. Cain is the archetypal murderer, the wicked man that flees when no one is pursuing (Proverbs 28:1).

Cain was being disingenuous here. Of course, God was not implying that Cain was Abel's guardian. He simply asked where Abel was. And yet, there is a sense in which Cain should have been Abel's keeper. They were brothers, and brothers naturally feel a sense of fraternal affection and protection for one another. Cain revealed much more than he wished to show. He inadvertently displayed something bad wrong in his attitude toward Abel. His defiance against being his younger brother's guardian is unnatural. This is the spirit of Cain. It is the spirit of every murderer. Cain lost all sense of loyalty to his brother through pride and envy.

This happens in the Christian home when relationships between siblings are allowed to deteriorate. Brothers and sisters are born with a natural sense of loyalty to one another. However, prolonged division will destroy this natural affection. Children are normally predisposed to be "guardians" of one another. The older children are protective of the younger, and the boys instinctively defend the girls. And yet, this sort of sibling loyalty must be cultivated by resolving conflicts that threaten to destroy it. If family division is allowed to continue, then this sort of "Am I my brother's keeper?" attitude will choke out natural affection, and aggrieved children will mock their own family to God's face.

God's Judgment upon Cain

Just as God had confronted Adam with his sin, the Almighty intercepted Cain and demanded an answer for his sin. It is striking how God always seems to approach the sinner indirectly at first as if to give them a chance to confess the matter on their own. Certainly it is evident from later Scripture that God shows mercy to those who confess their sin before Him without being forced to do so by God's omniscient exposure of sin.

In the garden, God asked Adam where *he* was; but now, He asked Cain where *his brother* was. Cain did not have the shame to hide from God as his father had, and this had nothing to do with repentant and transparent honesty. And yet, in a sense, both Adam and Cain hid from God: Adam hid his nakedness, and Cain hid the body. However, Cain's hiding was a perversely perfected hypocrisy; he had learned how to stand before God as if nothing was wrong. Cain apparently was no amateur at this sort of pretense. No one learns this sort of thing overnight. Probably, Cain's problem stemmed from childhood.

Regardless, Cain's unrepentant and mocking response was intolerable to God. He wasted no further time asking about Abel. The Lord God immediately confronted Cain with his sin: "What hast thou done? The voice of thy brother's blood crieth unto me from the ground." God stripped away Cain's insolent pretense of innocence. Since Cain refused to confess what he had done, the Lord God "confessed" it for him. Abel was murdered, and now there was no hiding that fact. The cry of Abel's blood echoed through the heavens. Cain, who refused to offer innocent blood in worship, spilled innocent blood in wrath. The blood of the atonement would have cried out for mercy, but now the blood of his brother cried out for vengeance. And this vengeance was meted out instantly.

God said to Cain, "And now art thou cursed from the earth, which hath opened her mouth to receive thy brother's blood from thy hand; When thou tillest the ground, it shall not henceforth yield unto thee her strength; a fugitive and a vagabond shalt thou be in the earth." Cain was dumbfounded by the Lord's harsh judgment. It was unbelievable to him that the punishment could be so severe. All he did was kill his brother! And yet, Cain's response reveals in vivid detail the sort of attitude that sinners develop toward sin. It is characteristic of sinners that they cannot see the seriousness of their actions. Cain cries out to the Lord in petulant protest, "My punishment is greater than I can bear. Behold, thou hast driven me out this day from the face of the earth; and from thy face shall I be hid; and I shall be a fugitive and a vagabond in the earth; and it shall come to pass, that every one that findeth me shall slay me."

By considering the Lord's judgment together with Cain's response we see that his curse was fourfold: (1) the curse of Adam upon the ground was intensified, ruining Cain's occupation and making sustenance nearly impossible; (2) he was sent out of the presence of the Lord even further than Adam had already gone making worship practically impossible; (3) he was forced to become "a fugitive and a vagabond in the earth"; and (4) the inhabitants of the earth would seek to kill him for his crime against humanity.

The only part of this curse that God did not allow to stand was the fourth part. "And the LORD said unto him, Therefore whosoever slayeth Cain, vengeance shall be taken on him sevenfold. And the LORD set a mark upon Cain, lest any finding him should kill him." Cain was allowed to live, though it could be argued that death may have been a lighter sentence than life under such judgment.

"And Cain went out from the presence of the LORD, and dwelt in the land of Nod, on the east of Eden." The remaining verses of Genesis 4 conclude the tragic story. Cain fathered a son and named him Enoch (v. 17). He built a city and named it after his son. It seems Cain was trying to put down roots, but he apparently did not succeed, at least not for long. For his descendents became nomadic people "such as dwell in tents, and of such as have cattle" (v. 20). His children also became those who "handle the harp and organ" (v. 21), and "an instructor of every artificer in brass and iron" (v. 22). His children also imitated his murderous rage (v. 23) and the earth was filled with Cain's example of violence (6:11). What a terrible legacy! And all of this from the man "gotten from the Lord." This shows so clearly what the Christian family can become when sin is tolerated and permitted to grow unchecked.

Lessons Learned from Cain

Cain and his children represent the continuing fall of the family. The curse upon Adam was intensified in Cain and his descendents. The ground was cursed further. No longer did Cain's family attend worship. His children lived in continual violence. They multiplied wives and possessions. They were consumed with materialism. They became idolatrous artisans and artists. They became nomads and wanderers. Cain's children were vagabond children with no sense of their original origin and destiny. All of this because their father was faithless and disobedient.

What sort of destiny are we creating for our children? History proves that the mark of Cain still mars the children of men. Our children are no exception to the fall of the family. If we do not train them up in the way that they should go, then when they are old they are sure to walk in the ways of Cain and his children. This has been the tragic destiny of so many backsliding Christian children. We have observed it all around us. We must take lessons from the examples before our eyes. We must refuse the sins of Cain and bring our family to worship with faith and obedience.

We must teach our children to come before the Lord in faith and obedience. We must train them to accept rebuke when rejected. We must teach them to never blame others for their sins. We must root out the pride and envy that promotes division between brothers. We must recognize the spirit of hatred and murder that seeks to gain control in our home. We must teach our children that they *are* their brother's keeper. We must train our children to confess their sins before the Lord and trust in His mercy for forgiveness and restoration. We must convey to our children a sense of the hopelessness of life outside the presence of the Lord.

We must forbid our children to deflect attention away from their sins by responding to probing questions with evasive questions of their own. Sinful man, like Cain, thinks he can escape the heat of divine scrutiny by changing the subject. But God will not permit such equivocation. He asks direct questions and demands direct answers. Our children must learn this. And they shall learn it as we model it before them.

Our children must learn early on that nothing can be hidden from God for long. He will bring all of our works into judgment. And they should expect this judgment to come from the Word of the Lord in daily devotions and weekly worship. Our children should be taught to listen to the Word to be judged and corrected. If they will respond properly to the correction of the Word of the

Lord, then they shall be saved by the Word rather than be condemned by it.

The curse upon Cain was greater than the curse upon Adam. Both parents and children must understand that the effects of the curse never get better. They only get worse. Sin corrupts. Backslidden children will offer faithless sacrifices and be rejected of God. They will rise up in envy to destroy the righteous. They will try to cover up their sin by lying before God and changing the subject from their own sin. But, inevitably, they will be cursed in their labor and be driven out from the presence of the Lord. There is no escape for our children just because they are ours. Indeed, they *cannot* escape because they are ours. We must teach them this through careful, prayerful daily discipling. We are saving their soul when we teach them to receive correction properly. We must consider the consequences of sin and trust in the promises of God—both the good and bad promises. We must see far enough down the road to consider where our children are headed if they follow the trail we are blazing.

Cain was not sorry for his sin until he got caught. How often do we see this tendency within disobedient children? Cain did not cry out for mercy until he realized that God was serious about his punishment. "It is more than I can bear," Cain wailed pitifully. He could bear pride, anger and violence, he could bear murdering his own brother, and he could bear the hypocrisy of lying to God and mocking the omniscience of God. But he could not bear the burden of punishment for his sin. Poor Cain. And yet, this is exactly what we see in our own homes among our own children in a lesser form. Therefore, we must address this sin while it is still lesser, or we may follow the tragic pattern of Adam and Eve weeping over children lost to our family.

Cain was afraid of suffering the fate of Abel. He was a murderer who lived in mortal terror of being murdered. And yet, God was merciful. Indeed, the only aspect of Cain's curse that the Lord mitigated was this: He vowed to protect Cain from retribution and declared that anyone who harmed Cain would be judged seven-fold. This is the silver lining behind the dark clouds of backsliding. Though it is never pleasant to contemplate the lost condition of wayward children, at least we have the consolation that God does not withdraw His mercy completely.

The parents of prodigals must cling to this hope. We can only pray that our children do not sin "a sin unto death" (I John 5:16,17). We must heed the words of Paul and "deliver such a one unto Satan for the destruction of the flesh, that the spirit may be saved in the day of the Lord Jesus" (I Corinthians 5:5). It is here that so many parents of backslidden children err and prolong the disobedience of their children. They become what some have called "enablers." They provide the resources that make the continued backsliding of their children possible. They remain silent for the sake of peace when they should be speaking up. Certainly there is a time to remain silent and simply pray for lost children. But there is also a time to speak up and make it clear that the sin of backsliders is not excused. Furthermore, we must not do anything that assists them in their disobedience. We are simply ensuring their continued backsliding when we do so. We must commit our sons and daughters into the hand of God and allow Him to chasten and correct them for their eternal good.

The hope of Cain was that God refused to allow him to die in his sins. We do not know if Cain ever repented and served the Lord. The Scripture seems to indicate that he was forever expelled from the presence of the Lord and died in a castaway condition. Certainly his offspring perpetuated his faithless example. However, we do know that God is merciful, and we should rely on this for the hope of our children.

Cain never escaped the mark of God's protection. Surely the children of Christians can never escape the mark of their parent's faith. It is sad to watch a reprobate society try to escape its Christian roots. And yet, they can never quite achieve pure pagan secularity. The residue of Christianity prevents them from ever becoming fully atheistic. It is a tragic irony. And yet, for the children of believing parents, this irony is a thin shred of hope, hope that somehow the memory of the fullness of joy in the Lord's presence shall draw them back to the altar again. We can only pray that our backslidden children can never become quite comfortable in the world. We must pray that they never feel at home east of Eden in the land of Nod. We must pray that the garden keeps calling. If there is a hope for our "Cain," this is it.

Conclusion

Cain went out from the presence of the Lord and fathered a degenerate bloodline. His children established a posterity of apostasy, a reprobate generation. It is amazing how quickly a Christian family can lose its heritage and become an apostate generation. And this is the tragedy of parents who do not train up their children in the way that they should go. Their children very quickly lose any overt semblance of Christianity. They abandon the truth and forsake every obvious rudiment of righteousness. Cain's children were very successful in life, but their labors lost all eternal significance. They built cities, bred cattle, developed the arts and crafts, and played loud music to drown out the emptiness of it all. Life became an endless party. They sought to mask the dullness of life behind the façade of pleasure. Cain's children still walk the earth today. May God grant us the mercy that our children shall not be numbered among them. We must lead our family away from the way of Cain.

Cain named his city after his son, and thus glorified and deified his own progeny. The only thing Cain had to live for was mundane posterity. The eternal dimension of life drained away into the soil with the blood of Abel. When Cain lost his faithful family, he lost all sense of spiritual direction and became a wandering soul. Sinners do the same today. They rear up great cities in their own name and build monuments to their greatness. And yet the relics of their temporal achievements end up on display in a museum somewhere, conveniently arranged in glass cases for barely interested spectators at a dollar a head. Man's greatest works become rusting and decaying memorabilia of corruption, tangible proof of man's descent into sin and death. How are the mighty fallen!

In just a few generations the family of Cain was completely reprobate. They had no knowledge of God. Many feel that the lineage of Cain was "the daughters of men" that "the sons of God" married in Genesis 6. If so, then the seed of Cain was so corrupt that they corrupted the entire human race, with the exception of Noah, and brought total annihilation upon their race in the flood. It is terrifying to consider how quickly the descendents of believers can become a rival lineage to the seed of God. The children of backsliders are often the most corrupted and perverted of all sinners. It seems that there are no depths of depravity to which faithless Christian children will not go. They are running from the mark of Cain that is upon them, but they can never escape it. They have murdered their own identity by abandoning the wisdom of their fathers, and they live in mortal fear of suffering the same fate. May God grant us the grace to rear up faithful children! Just remember: if we follow the example of Adam and walk in disobedience, then we can be assured that our children will also follow. Moreover, they shall multiply and compound our sins a thousand times over and lead our heritage into total corruption.

24

The Promise of Redemption

Genesis 4:25-5:8. "And Adam knew his wife again; and she bore a son, and called his name Seth: For God, said she, hath appointed me another seed instead of Abel, whom Cain slew. And to Seth, to him also there was born a son; and he called his name Enos: then began men to call upon the name of the LORD.

This is the book of the generations of Adam. In the day that God created man, in the likeness of God made he him; Male and female created he them; and blessed them, and called their name Adam, in the day when they were created. And Adam lived a hundred and thirty years, and begot a son in his own likeness, after his image; and called his name Seth: And the days of Adam after he had begotten Seth were eight hundred years: and he begot sons and daughters: And all the days that Adam lived were nine hundred and thirty years: and he died.

And Seth lived a hundred and five years, and begot Enos: And Seth lived after he begot Enos eight hundred and seven years, and begot sons and daughters: And all the days of Seth were nine hundred and twelve years: and he died."

After the death of Abel and the exile of Cain, God gave Adam and Eve a new beginning in the birth of Seth. Surely Adam and Eve had many other children before Seth was born, for Cain departed into the land of Nod with his wife, who necessarily was a child of Adam and Eve. However, the birth of Seth marked a new day. Seth's name means "substitute." Eve was persuaded that God had given her "another seed instead of Abel, whom Cain slew." Adam and Eve were starting over with Seth after the unbelievable tragedy of Cain and Abel. What pain resounded in Eve's words, "...instead of Abel, whom Cain slew." What heartbreak! Eve had suffered as few mothers ever suffer. One son dead at the hands of a murderer, and the murderer was her other son, her firstborn. The agony here is completely beyond description. And yet, Eve's hope shone through: "For God, said she, hath appointed me another seed instead...."

It is noteworthy that Eve's hopes had shifted from Cain to Abel. Seth was the substitute for Abel, not Cain. This shift in Eve's thinking must have occurred when God accepted Abel and rejected Cain as we discussed above. So she felt sure that God had given another godly line through which the promised seed would come. And she was correct. The seed of the woman would arise through Seth to crush the head of the serpent. The promised seed, Jesus Christ, would be a son of Seth. This continued to be Eve's hope.

Eve never lost hope. This should provide a great example to all parents of wayward children. It also speaks of the redemptive power of God's mercy. So often the fall of the family seems irreparable, but redemptive history proves otherwise. As we have studied together the creation and fall of the family in Genesis 1-5 and applied the lessons to our own family situations, surely some have felt the dull throb of despair beginning to suffocate their hope. It is overwhelming at times to consider all that has gone wrong with the family and all that must be made right. We may be tempted to give up and forsake any attempt at family renewal. But the example of Eve's persistent faith should draw us up short just before we plunge over the cliff of abject failure. Stop at the edge and consider: God can raise up another, a substitute. And this does not mean necessarily that we must give up on our backsliding children and hope for new blood to replace them. No, this means that we can believe God for a new spiritual renewal in their lives that shall be a sort of "Seth moment." God can give our family grace to start over. We can be renewed in the promises of God. God is a God of restoration.

The objective of these studies is not to produce despair. We are looking to the Word of God for answers. We may have suffered the loss of our "Cain and Abel," as it were. Our families may have suffered tremendous division and strife. Marriages may have been broken and children scattered. But the "ministry of reconciliation" (II Corinthians 5:18) has been given to the church to bring repentance and restoration. God intends to put marriages back together and bring children back home. It is the will of God to "appoint us another," a new beginning of hope and promise.

Calling on the Name of the Lord

After Seth was born and fathered a son, Enos, "then began men to call upon the name of the Lord." There is considerable uncertainty about this text and how it should be rendered, but it seems that the KJV gives a good reading. It was at this time of renewal and restoration that men began to seek the Lord everywhere. This seems to indicate that private and public worship began to spread abroad throughout the earth among the children of Seth. Though mankind was thoroughly corrupted by the time of Noah, yet there was a period of considerable piety and devotion in the first generations following Seth.

Things can get better. If your situation seems hopeless, look back to Adam and Eve. Could anyone have a family situation worse than theirs? And yet, they believed that God would keep His promises. Eve insisted that Seth would be the replacement for Abel, that the promises of God could not fail. We must imitate this faithful attitude. Adam and Eve got a lot wrong, but they got this right. They believed in the power of starting over. They believed that God could replace all that Satan had stolen from them. We *must* do the same. Satan is still a liar, and the blessings of God still come to those who believe the promises of God against all odds. Cain may be exiled and Abel buried in an early grave, but Seth is here, and he shall be the hope of the family. His children shall start a lineage of faithfulness. The seed of Seth shall begin to call upon the name of the Lord.

Those who have suffered the fall of the family must believe God for a rebuilding of the family. God can raise up what has been cast down. If we can hear the Word of the Lord and believe that it is true, then we have not gone too far for family renewal. We must place our faith in the promises of God, not in the power of man. Seth is God's "appointment." God is appointing the restoration of our families. God is appointing a "Seth-spirit" in our home. The Lord is searching for those who will believe His

Word is true. We must turn our eyes and ears away from the father of lies and look toward the cross of Jesus Christ.

God has made all things new in Christ. He has formed a new creation. Therefore, the creation and fall of the family can be swallowed up in the victory of a new creation. We must earnestly look toward this new creation in Christ. As Peter said, "Nevertheless we, according to his promise, look for new heavens and a new earth, wherein dwelleth righteousness" (II Peter 3:13). Of course, the apostle was speaking of the ultimate consummation of the new creation when Christ returns; but this blessed state is anticipated now in Christ. We already have received "the earnest of our inheritance" (Ephesians 1:14). Therefore, we must expect a "new heaven and new earth" right now. The creation and fall of the family must be transformed into a new creation, a *re-creation* of the family. May God grant it to be so!

The Generation of Jesus Christ

Genesis 5 begins: "This is the book of the generations of Adam." The text then goes on to list the genealogy of Adam and his sons. It is somber parade of dying men who were created to live forever and share in the glory of God. It is a staccato recitation of the casualties list in Satan's war on the family. The only brief interruption of this morbid monotony is the life and translation of Enoch who "walked with God: and he was not; for God took him" (5:24). Otherwise, Adam's seed lived and died in predictable succession.

The generation of Adam produced a legacy of inescapable sin and death. But the New Testament begins, "The book of the generation of Jesus Christ, the son of David, the son of Abraham" (Matthew 1:1). Paul calls the Lord Jesus Christ "the second man" and "the last Adam" (I Corinthians 15:45,47). Jesus is the federal head of a new human race, a new generation. Those who are born again are born into this new humanity. This is the new creation.

The Christian family is born again. It stands in the line of the new generation of the last Adam, the Second Man. Thus, we put off "the old man" and put on "the new man" in Christ (Colossians 3:9,10). We are no longer the heirs of Adam's corruption, but now, we are the heirs of Christ's glory. We repudiate the disobedience of Adam and embrace the obedience of Christ. Thus, our family is free from the genealogy of sin and death. Of course, we still face the enemy of physical death at the last day, but Christ's resurrection has guaranteed our victory. Christ's resurrection has become ours, and He shall raise us up at the last day (John 6:40,44).

Moreover, as we have emphasized throughout this study, we are partakers of the resurrection already. We must not be content to live as if we were still Adam's seed. We have been made new in Christ, and we must live like it. We must insist that our family can be made new *now*. We must believe God that the fall of the family shall be overcome through the new creation of the family in Christ. In Christ, the creation and fall of the family has become the re-creation of the family. This is our promise and it is our prayer.

Other books by Steve Pixler:

In this small but important work Pastor Steve Pixler considers the proper procedures and guidelines established by the New Testament for church discipline. As the author states. "This paper is of necessity a simplified treatment of a vast and involved subject that holds wide-ranging implications for Christian practice and polity. But possibly a brief glance at biblical church discipline shall provoke a much closer look at the subject overall and encourage a stricter adherence to New Testament procedures."

THE BEGINNING OF JUDGMENT   *Price $7*

THE GREATER CAUSE is a unique study on the family drawn from Jesus' powerful teaching on divorce and remarriage in Matthew 19. This work carefully and deliberately avoids the thornier issues surrounding the discussion of divorce and remarriage and focuses, rather, on the broader scriptural principles that affect Christian family life and renewal. This book has a decidedly pastoral emphasis. It is written to strengthen families who seek to build up the Christian household and rear up a godly heritage for the glory of God.

THE GREATER CAUSE   *Price $12*

Available from Continuum Ministry Resources
1-866-580-9980
www.stevepixler.com.

5200 David Strickland Fort Worth, TX 76119